Sacred Estrangement

Sacred Estrangement

The Rhetoric of Conversion in Modern American Autobiography

Peter A. Dorsey

THE PENNSYLVANIA STATE UNIVERSITY PRESS
University Park, Pennsylvania

Library of Congress Cataloging-in-Publication Data

Dorsey, Peter A., 1958–
   Sacred estrangement : the rhetoric of conversion in modern
American autobiography / Peter A. Dorsey.
      p.   cm.
   Includes bibliographical references and index.
   ISBN 0-271-00902-0 (alk. paper)
   1. American prose literature—History and criticism. 2. Authors,
American—Biography—History and criticism. 3. Christianity and
literature—United States. 4. Conversion in literature.
5. Autobiography.   I. Title.
PS366.A88D67   1993
810.9′382—dc20   92-16589
                                                                CIP

Published by The Pennsylvania State University Press,
Suite C, Barbara Building, University Park, PA 16802-1003

It is the policy of The Pennsylvania State University Press to use acid-free paper for
the first printing of all clothbound books. Publications on uncoated stock satisfy the
minimum requirements of American National Standard for Information Sciences—
Permanence of Paper for Printed Library Materials, ANSI Z39.48–1984.

To my parents
David A. and Maryellen Clarke Dorsey
and to Sheila

CONTENTS

ACKNOWLEDGMENTS

This project began several years ago as a dissertation in English at the University of Pennsylvania. During the course of its composition, I received the generous assistance of many people who helped me to improve the manuscript in a variety of ways. First and foremost, I would like to thank Peter Conn, who not only contributed greatly to the formation and articulation of my argument here, but whose teaching and scholarship have influenced me in ways too numerous to mention. I would also like to thank William Craft, Robert Ducharme, William Heath, Robert Lucid, and Kevin Van Anglen for reading the entire manuscript and offering valuable suggestions. Carol Holly deserves special mention for her particularly helpful comments, which guided me in ways that strengthened the manuscript significantly, especially in the area of women's autobiography. Other friends and associates have been enormously helpful in their response to portions of this study. Among them are Bruce Boehrer, Stuart Curran, Chris Flint, Steven Goldsmith, Richard Hays, David Heddendorf, Frank Hoffman, Curt Johnson, David McWhirter, Melanie Northrop, and Joseph Torchia. I'd like to thank all of these people for respecting my own ideas, and I must confess there were times when I sought my own way and chose to disregard their advice. For this reason, all the shortcomings in this study are strictly my own.

I'm also grateful to President Wickenheiser and the Academic Council at Mount Saint Mary's for approving the two summer grants I received as I was bringing this work to completion. On the technical side, I would like to thank my colleagues Bob Karsteter, Bob Keefer, Steve Newmann, and Bill O'Toole for helping me with computer problems. I also owe much to Michael Hamson, president of Hamson-Ginn Associates, and to Edward G. Ginn, formerly of that firm, for allowing me to use their word-processing equipment during my years in Philadelphia. The exemplary service I received from the members of the library staffs at Penn, St. Joseph's, and

Mount Saint Mary's was invaluable to my research. Judy Ott worked wonders in helping me prepare this manuscript for publication. Special thanks are also due to Philip Winsor and the staff at Penn State Press for their sensitive and efficient service. Thanks also to *a/b: Autobiography Studies,* for permission to reprint portions of my essay "Women's Autobiography and the Hermeneutics of Conversion" in Chapters 1 and 5. For their advice and encouragement, I'd like to thank Joseph Feeney, S.J., and the Rev. Thomas Kilcullen. Finally—but far from least—I'm grateful to my wife, Sheila, for her patient wisdom and support; her companionship made the time spent on this project pleasant and fruitful.

Excerpt from *The Woman Within* by Ellen Glasgow. Copyright 1954 and renewed 1982 by Harcourt Brace Jovanovich, Inc. Reprinted by permission of the publisher. □ Excerpts from *Dust Tracks on a Road* by Zora Neale Hurston. Copyright 1942 by Zora Neale Hurston. Copyright renewed 1970 by John C. Hurston. Reprinted by permission of HarperCollins Publishers. □ Excerpts from *Black Boy* by Richard Wright. Copyright 1937, 1942, 1944, 1945 by Richard Wright. Reprinted by permission of HarperCollins Publishers. □ Excerpts from *American Hunger* by Richard Wright. Copyright 1944 by Richard Wright. Copyright © 1977 by Ellen Wright and Michel Fabre. Reprinted by permission of HarperCollins Publishers. □ Reprinted by permission of the publishers from *The Varieties of Religious Experience* by William James; Frederick Burkhardt, General Editor; Fredson Bowers, Textual Editor, Cambridge, Mass.: Harvard University Press, Copyright © 1985 by the President and Fellows of Harvard College. □ From *The Education of Henry Adams* by Henry Adams. Copyright, 1918, by the Massachusetts Historical Society. Copyright 1946 by Charles F. Adams. Reprinted by permission of Houghton Mifflin Company. □ Reprinted with the permission of Charles Scribner's Sons, an imprint of Macmillan Publishing Company from *A Small Boy and Others* by Henry James. Copyright 1913 Charles Scribner's Sons; copyright renewed 1941 Henry James. □ Reprinted with the permission of Charles Scribner's Sons, an imprint of Macmillan Publishing Company from *Notes of a Son and Brother* by Henry James. Copyright 1914 Charles Scribner's Sons; copyright renewed 1942 Henry James. □ Reprinted with the permission of Charles Scribner's Sons, an imprint of Macmillan Publishing Company from *The Middle Years* by Henry James. Copyright 1917 Charles Scribner's Sons; copyright renewed 1945 Charles Scribner's Sons. □ Reprinted with the permission of Charles Scribner's Sons, an imprint of Macmillan Publishing Company from *A Backward Glance* by Edith Wharton. Copyright 1933, 1934 by The Curtis Publishing Co., renewed © 1961, 1962 by William R. Tyler.

INTRODUCTION

Conversion and the Autobiographical Tradition

When I saw what had happened to me I stood rooted to
the ground with astonishment . . . my mind unable to
cope with so great and sudden a joy. I could find no words
good enough to thank the Goddess for her extraordinary
loving-kindness. (271–72)

> —Lucius Apuleius, *The Golden Ass*

In an instant my heart tendered and dissolved into a flood
of tears, abhorring my past offenses, and admiring the
mercies of God. (533)

> —*Some Account of the Fore-Part of the Life of
> Elizabeth Ashbridge*

These words of my master were like a voice from heaven
to me. In an instant all my trepidation was turned into
unutterable bliss. (102)

> —*The Life of Olaudah Equiano, or Gustavus Vassa, the
> African: Written by Himself*

The first sight of the large, three-story, brick school
building seemed to have rewarded me for all that I had
undergone in order to reach the place. . . . The sight of it

seemed to give me new life. I felt that a new kind of
existence had now begun—that life would now have a new
meaning. I felt that I had reached the promised land.
(50–51)

> —Booker T. Washington, *Up From Slavery*

I had a distinct sensation that something new and wonder-
ful had been born in my soul. A great ideal, a burning
faith, a determination to dedicate myself to the memory
of my martyred comrades, to make their cause my own.
(10)

> —Emma Goldman, *Living My Life*

Feminism spoke to our lived and our literary experience
with the fierce urgency of a revelation or a Great Awakening. (5)

> —Elaine Showalter, *Feminist Criticism*

The passages that I have chosen to stand at the head of this study—one
by a second-century pagan lawyer, one by an eighteenth-century British
ex-slave, one by an eighteenth-century American Quaker, one by a turn-
of-the century black educator, one by a twentieth-century immigrant
anarchist, and one by a contemporary feminist—all invoke the rhetoric of
conversion. The diversity of these authors and their statements themselves
suggest that conversion, in its sacred and secular manifestations, is an
almost inescapable construct in the cultures we call Western. As a trope
for self-definition, conversion was widely available at different times and
under different circumstances to conservatives and radicals, traditionalists
and innovators, and those in between. Not confined to any single theological
or ideological system, conversion experiences have been described by
feminists, communists, television-evangelists, alcoholics, psychoanalysts,
and scientists, by men, women, atheists, believers, whites, and peoples of
color. Of course, to say that conversion rhetoric is familiar is simply
another way of saying that it has carried a privileged meaning in the
Western cultures, so privileged that it was once (and, for some, still is)
called sacred, and one's worth as a human being could be dependant upon
one's adoption of it.

For all its manifold uses, however, conversion discourse displays a remarkable degree of formulaic similarity. Emma Goldman's conversion to anarchism resembles Olaudah Equiano's manumission from slavery, neither of which is far different from the language employed by Elizabeth Ashbridge. This pattern of redundancy occurs within texts as well as between them. Rather than being structured around a single decisive event, conversion narratives often contain a cyclic pattern of conversion and reconversion, as if the converted are predisposed to repeat and reinforce this fundamental experience over and over. This is true of works as different as Bunyan's *Grace Abounding*, Ashbridge's *Account*, Rousseau's *Confessions*, Mill's *Autobiography*, and *The Education of Henry Adams*.

My purpose in this study is to examine the rhetoric of conversion as it appears in the kind of life-writing often designated by the term "spiritual autobiography." This term, however, has not always been used consistently. For some, "spiritual autobiography" can be used to describe any self-portrait that examines the conditions of the "inner life." For others, a spiritual autobiography is a purely religious narrative that describes the relationship between an individual and God. In her study *Victorian Autobiography: The Tradition of Self-interpretation*, Linda Peterson employs the term to describe narratives of the self (both sacred and secular) that are based on a typological hermeneutics. I mention these various uses of the term, not to establish a "correct" definition, but merely to clarify the way I will use it in this study. I will use the term to refer to texts that employ narrative strategies centering on conversion. These need not be used in conjunction with other scriptural models, and may be found in the relatively public form of the published spiritual autobiography or in other less visible forms of discourse. In this context, I often use the terms "spiritual autobiography" and "conversion narrative" interchangeably.

With the recently expanded interest in the field, there have been two approaches to conversion in autobiographical study. One approach suggests that conversion operates in almost all autobiographies. The other approach is suspicious of conversion discourse altogether, associating it with a canonical tradition dominated by white males.

The first of these strategies—that which would equate conversion and the autobiographical act—identifies it with almost any turning point in a narrative of the self. A figure as well known in the study of autobiography as Jean Starobinski has taken such an approach:

> One would hardly have sufficient motive to write an autobiography had not some radical change occurred in his life—conversion, entry

into a new life, the operation of Grace. . . . It is the internal transformation of the individual—and the exemplary character of this transformation—that furnishes a subject for a narrative discourse in which "I" is both subject and object. (78)

In a different context, Jerome Hamilton Buckley has said something quite similar:

The major spiritual autobiographies in English are . . . records of becoming different persons, narratives of conversion, of recovering a lost identity, or discovering a new and meaningful self. (*Turning Key*, 53)

Extreme as they may initially appear to be, the points made by Starobinski and Buckley are partially operative. Most literary historians agree that the development of autobiography was made possible because of an increased valuation of an individual's life and experience. If autobiography (at least since Augustine) values the historically rooted individual, it must also privilege change, since change defines the historical process. The autobiographer becomes someone she or he was not. Conversion marks change (or difference) in a literary text, and this in part explains its frequency in autobiographical writing. Since life is a chaotic sequence of events, moments of conversion help the autobiographer plot significant changes textually. Though in many cases the changes are presented as being somehow permanent—suggesting a unified postconversion self that governs the entire narrative act—still the "saved" autobiographer located that salvation chronologically within a text. Of course, theorists have noted that any sense of a finished life story (or even of a unified self) is a fiction; but if conversion is a fiction, it has been a convenient one because it represented the dynamics of human experience in narrative form.[1]

Like Starobinski and Buckley, Geoffrey Galt Harpham finds conversion to be a fundamental pattern in autobiographical writing, though unlike these two, he examines conversion within a poststructuralist framework. In an analysis of Augustine's *Confessions*, Harpham identifies two types of conversion: the first characterized by the "epistemological certainty that heralds a sense of true self-knowledge," and the second that "actualizes

---

1. For some overviews of the recent theoretical approaches to the construction of the "self" in autobiography, see Avrom Fleishman, *Figures of Autobiography*, 1–39; G. Thomas Couser, *Altered Egos*, 15–27; and Paul John Eakin, *Fictions in Autobiography*, 191–209.

this certainty in a narrative of the self" (42). According to Harpham, these two conversions are "synchronic" in the act of writing because autobiographers inscribe their lives as "an imitation or repetition of other selves" (44). In this sense, "the autobiographical text is a kind of machine for conversion." He states, "One is 'converted' when one discovers that one's life can be made to conform to certain culturally validated narrative forms; spiritual 'conversion' might simply be a strong form of reading" (44). Though Harpham's analysis of the Christian conversion experience as a surrendering of the self is consistent with my own in many ways, his broad statement that "autobiography is a discourse of conversion" greatly extends the category of conversion rhetoric beyond its usual religious and psychological associations. For Harpham, conversion is less a language available to the autobiographer as she or he writes a life story than it is the inevitable moment that occurs when one sees one's life as text.

Of course, the approaches of Starobinski and Buckley are quite different from that of Harpham; Starobinski and Buckley imply that conversion discourse refers to something that happens "in life" that is mimetically recorded in a text, while Harpham understands conversion both as a psychological phenomenon (the realization of an "epistemological certainty") as well as a linguistic structure. Yet all three of these theorists see conversion as somehow coexisting with the autobiographical project itself.

The second critical approach to conversion in autobiographical writing appears on the surface to be antithetical to ones proposed by Starobinski, Buckley, and Harpham. This approach has been cogently argued by Philip Dodd, who recognizes that the autobiographical canon has been constructed, not according to any "objective" criteria, but according to a set of interpretive conventions. Given the current sensitivity to canon formation and its effects, few would disagree with Dodd's findings. Dodd, however, goes further by saying that a single set of interpretative conventions has narrowly defined the canon of self-writing: that set derived from literature, starting with Augustine's *Confessions* and continuing to the present, that "is organised around a 'conversion' and the discovery of a vocation" (6). According to Dodd, autobiographies that employ conversion discourse have enjoyed such a privileged status in the canon that works that cannot be interpreted according to its conventions have been excluded from consideration: "Focussed as it is on the mapping of the characteristics and history of a particular form of writing, the dominant criticism effectively neglects that writing's relationship to other writing and to non-literary practices" (7). Since Dodd believes that middle- and upper-class white males have dominated this tradition, he finds that women, minority, and working-class writers have often been victims of it.

A number of feminist critics—among them Mary Mason, Carolyn Heilbrun, Linda Peterson, Felicity Nussbaum, and Sidonie Smith—support Dodd's claim that the hermeneutics of conversion has marginalized certain writers—particularly women. Though approaches to women's autobiography have been various and occasionally contradictory, there does seem to be an evolving consensus that the spiritual autobiography form is a patriarchal form of self-writing that stifles the voices of female subjectivity. Mary Mason writes:

> The dramatic structure of conversion that we find in Augustine's *Confessions*, where the self is presented as the stage for a battle of opposing forces and where a climactic victory for one force—spirit defeating flesh—completes the drama of the self, simply does not accord with the deepest realities of women's experience and so is inappropriate as a model for women's life writing. (21–22)

Carolyn Heilbrun not only seconds Mason's point, she goes so far as to equate conversion with a male model of autobiography (75). In her study of the spiritual autobiographies of Restoration and eighteenth-century England, Felicity Nussbaum similarly writes:

> Religious women generally adopted the mode of discourse established by their (male) religious leaders—Fox, Bunyan, Wesley. . . . They inscribed themselves, or were inscribed, in the familiar patterns of awakening, conversion, and ministry, their "selves" shaped in imitation of Christ and his (male) disciples. (151)

Even those critics who examine secular versions of the spiritual autobiography draw similar conclusions. In her analysis of the *Autobiography of Harriet Martineau*, Sidonie Smith argues, "While the biblical tradition offered a template for individual conversion and spiritual growth, it could not clear a space for the figure of an empowered female selfhood" (*Poetics*, 133). If critics such as Mason, Heilbrun, Nussbaum, and Smith correctly assume that conversion discourse has (until recently) defined the canon, then inevitably women who chose to express their selves in alternate ways will be excluded from it.

I find much of value in the two orientations toward conversion discourse

I have outlined, and I don't feel they are mutually exclusive necessarily; but I do believe they need to be refined. When—as Starobinski, Buckley, and Harpham suggest—the notion of conversion is extended to cover all (or a large part) of autobiographical writing, something is lost as well as gained; and this is why I am inclined to resist the formulations of those who would make it universal. First of all, when conversion discourse and self-writing are equated, the specter of marginalization reenters: texts that conform less successfully to a conversion model may be excluded from consideration. But even if all autobiographical writing could be seen as participating in conversion rhetoric at some level of generality, it could do so only by diluting a set of interpretative conventions that continues to function in a theological framework. If one reads conversion simply as a marker of change, as Starobinski and Buckley imply, or as a strong form of reading, as Harpham argues, then one becomes less sensitive to the characteristics of the trope as it operates in an identifiable tradition of self-writing. The result would be to distance the reader from the more narrow psychological and social characteristics of the conversion narrative as described in this study and elsewhere.

I am perhaps more sympathetic to the theorists on the other side of the fence, those who react to what had been the perceived centrality of conversion discourse. Their approach is valuable to the extent that it warns against identifying a single set of interpretative conventions as being normative. Yet I resist their suspicion of the conversion narrative form in several ways. First, they overestimate the extent to which the spiritual autobiography has dominated the canon. Their case is strongest for nineteenth-century Great Britain, where the spiritual autobiography in its sacred and secular forms was the most visible mode of self-writing and where its practitioners were mainly—though not universally—white males of the middle and upper class. But in America, secular variations of the conversion narrative were never as popular as they were in nineteenth-century Britain. For example, it would be hard to imagine American autobiographies more canonical than the *Autobiography of Benjamin Franklin*, Thoreau's *Walden*, Mark Twain's *Autobiography*, and Stein's *Autobiography of Alice B. Toklas*; yet these works owe little to the structure of conversion.

Second, critics who argue that the spiritual autobiography has exercised a kind of exclusionary tyranny also fail to make sufficient allowance for the possibility that writers on the margin themselves would respond to the form. Conversion discourse, even when most imitative, is a flexible vehicle of self-expression; there are a wide variety of rhetorical stances within it. One of the assumptions of my study has been that the subversion of a literary tradition is a vastly different autobiographical act than the affirmation of it. The difference between Carlyle's politically conservative adoption of the structure of conversion in *Sartor Resartus* and Richard Wright's abhorrence of its potential tyranny in *Black Boy* is so great as not to need comment. By now, it would be a truism to say that Wright was in some way dependent on the very form he rejected, but merely to lump these two texts into a "tradition" is to dismiss the power and urgency of Wright's statement and the extent to which he freed himself from a mode of self-writing that had its locus in white male justification. The oppressed, by necessity, have to engage themselves with the oppressor on some level. I hope this study will show that black and women writers responded freely (though often irreverently) to the conventions of conversion discourse. Wright went so far as to make the restrictiveness of those conventions his rationale for employing them.

If I resist the suspicion of conversion discourse presented by some scholars, I am sensitive to their warnings. Among other things, such approaches are valuable because they illustrate how the attempt to establish the parameters of a literary genre distances us from history and the manifold uses of discourse. Any theory that attempts to define *all* autobiographical writing is bound to be false to its multiplicity. Rather than constructing a genre-defining hermeneutics, I will focus only on texts that respond to conversion rhetoric directly. Freed from the task of genre-definition, I hope that I can be more attentive to the specific biographical, social, and historical contexts under which these texts were written. The writers upon whom I focus in Chapters 3 through 6—William and Henry James, Henry Adams, Edith Wharton, Ellen Glasgow, Zora Neale Hurston, and Richard Wright—consciously invoked the spiritual autobiography tradition and shaped it to their various narrative ends. In each case, their manipulation of conversion rhetoric captures a relationship between the self and larger social and ideological systems. Ultimately, I hope to show that an analysis of conversion discourse accomplishes the very thing that Philip Dodd sees as being essential to autobiographical criticism; it plunges one into the "original conditions of production," the "ideological import of autobiographical discourse at a particular moment, and the significance of the representation of the self inscribed in a particular work" (8).

Conversion discourse provides a reliable index of the relationship between the self and larger cultures because it has traditionally served a socializing function, signifying that one had come into alignment with certain linguistic, behavioral, and cultural expectations. The communal context of the spiritual autobiography was frequently acknowledged (and sometimes celebrated) in many narratives as authors imbedded the accounts of others who have undergone similar experiences into their own texts. In many such cases "conversion" is actually triggered by reading or hearing the narratives of others. The socialization process is particularly apparent in the Christian conversion narratives of the seventeenth through the nineteenth centuries. By publicly testifying to their own conversion experiences, believers became empowered members, not only of God's elect community, but also of a local population.

As modern autobiography developed in the eighteenth and nineteenth centuries, the Christian pattern was secularized and individualized. Conversion became a model for many kinds of psychological change, yet the secular autobiographies of the period continued to respond to the socializing function implicit in conversion rhetoric: like the works in the Christian tradition, many of these narratives are centered on the acceptance of a vocation. Writers such as Rousseau, Wordsworth, Carlyle, Mill, Martineau, Stanton, and the authors of slave narratives departed from Christian models by using conversion rhetoric to affirm the dignity of their inner selves, but they nevertheless were also engaged in a process of reform—whether social, philosophical, or cognitive. They may have distrusted the kind of unquestioned submission associated with religious conversion, but they continued to affirm the value of community—even if the communities they valued became quite exclusive.

Up to the end of the nineteenth century, the remarkable degree of formulaic similarity in conversion discourse was relatively free of the "anxiety of influence." With the coming of the twentieth century, however, certain writers and thinkers began to use conversion rhetoric in a way that was radically different from the way it had been used in the past. This change cannot be located in a single author or text, and examples of it may be seen in earlier periods (in the works, for example, of DeQuincey and Melville); but it achieved a kind of visibility with the publication of William James's *Varieties of Religious Experience*. James's work gave a "scientific" validity to orthodox Protestant interpretations of conversion by merging it with a wide range of mental phenomena. But if James's Natural Supernaturalism was in that sense conservative and merely described what secular autobiographers had already done, it was in another sense baffling in that it ignored the socializing function of conversion rhetoric so central to the narrative form. The rhetoric that had typically been used to affirm a process of socialization was now being used to inscribe a sense of separateness. James's failure to account for the social consequences of conversion was not so much the result of blindness, however, but a consequence of his personal need to separate individual from corporate experience. Conversion, for him, should be a personal, private phenomenon that was true only for the individual. Any attempt to institutionalize or build dogma around such an experience opened the doors of cruelty, coercion, determinism, and insanity.

Of the major figures discussed in the second half of this book, three— Henry James, Henry Adams, and Edith Wharton—knew William James personally. Richard Wright read and admired James throughout his life. Ellen Glasgow had copies of *Pragmatism, The Will to Believe,* and Ralph Burton Perry's biography of James in her library (Tutwiler, 12). Even Hurston, whose biographical data does not show a direct link with James, may have known him indirectly through her mentor at Barnard, Franz Boas. I make these connections not to argue that James's work necessarily influenced the very different adoptions of conversion discourse by these autobiographers but to emphasize the currency of an idea that already existed in the culture of American intellectuals: the notion that the self must be separate from and resistant to a corporate identity. These twentieth-century Americans were like their eighteenth- and nineteenth-century predecessors in that they examined the cognitive, social, and aesthetic consequences of any rapturous submission. But they took the secularizing process a step further. If conversion had traditionally merged the search for illumination with the search for a defined social role, these authors increasingly used conversion as a mark of estrangement—if not exclusion—from mainstream America. They did so, of course, for different reasons, but their autobiographical acts were all acts of separation, assertions of an individualism so radical that it would have been inconceivable in earlier periods. Like Melville, whose *Typee* reveals an almost pathological fear of being submerged in a corporate whole, these writers became increasingly wary of the ways conversion had been and continued to be used as a means of merging individual values with larger ideological systems. For them, group association amounted to a loss of identity and a fall into psychological chaos. As a result, their adoption of conversion rhetoric describes, not a process of socialization, but an antisocialization. Only Wharton's *Backward Glance* seems to be an exception to this pattern. Her work, however, which appears to validate a "saved" community, reveals—even as it attempts to conceal—the same feelings of uneasiness and alienation expressed by the others.

To situate the radical revision of conversion discourse that took place in the early twentieth century into a larger body of writing, I will apply the historical theory of Hayden White to autobiographical literature. Drawing upon the work of Kenneth Burke, White identifies four "master tropes" of historical discourse: metaphor, metonymy, synecdoche, and irony. These tropes "deal in relationships that are experienced as inhering within or among phenomena, but which are in reality relationships existing between consciousness and a world of experience calling for a provision of its meaning" (72). Two of these tropes—metaphor and synecdoche—apply respectively to the traditional and to the revised versions of the conversion narrative. Because it marks a fundamental change in orientation, the traditional spiritual autobiography operates on the metaphorical level. According to White, metaphor "explicitly asserts a similarity in a difference and, at least implicitly, a difference in a similarity. We may call this the provision of a meaning in terms of equivalence or identity" (72). The "converted" authors of traditional narratives are different from the people they once were, but their "autobiographical contract" testifies to an identity also: they are the same yet different; different yet the same. Conversion thus marks a metaphorical equation. In contrast, twentieth-century auto-biographers such as Henry Adams, Henry James, Ellen Glasgow, Zora Neale Hurston, and Richard Wright employed conversion discourse to privilege not change but continuity. Their narratives are grounded on the trope of synecdoche, which White finds to operate when the "distinction between parts and the whole is made only for the purpose of identifying the whole as a totality that is qualitatively identical with the parts that appear to make it up" (74). The autobiographer remains the same in each textual act. James's autobiography, which allows him to see "the whole content of memory and affection in each enacted and recovered moment" (4), participates most overtly in the trope of synecdoche, but the other autobiographies (Wharton's again being the exception) display a similar pattern: Henry Adams saw the impossibility of education in almost every detail of his life story; Glasgow was afflicted with her particular dread of "nothing or everything" from her earliest memory; Zora Neale Hurston the autobiographer was quite similar to the girl who sat upon the gatepost in Eatonville, affirming an inner uniqueness and searching for experience; and Richard Wright was as inclined to rebel against social expectations in his rejection of Communism as he was when, as a young boy, he set fire to the white curtains in his house.

I mention these examples not to suggest that these synecdochical autobiographies are static—narrative can only exist through differentiation—but to expose the larger rhetorical stances of these writers. There is an urgent need among them to justify their orientations to the world, not just as they were at the time of writing, but as they had been and would be. Their resistance to the kind of dramatic psychological change associated with conversion became more than just the measure of their individuality, however; it became the very basis of their self-worth. On the one hand, their stances appear defensive: they needed to define the borders of their personalities quite rigidly, and their autobiographical acts were based on resistance to cultural, intellectual, and religious norms. But on the other hand, their strategies were adaptive: they sought and found a stability in themselves and in the texts they created that they found lacking in the communities around them.

What is perhaps most curious about these writers is that, despite widely different backgrounds, they all in one way or another perceived themselves to be on the margin. That writers such as Hurston, Wright, Glasgow, and Wharton would see themselves in this way might be expected; and one is more likely to be sympathetic to their feelings of alienation than to those of the two Jameses or—least of all—to Henry Adams, the grandson of an American president. Yet all of these figures felt excluded from a mainstream culture they do not take great pains to identify. The America they feel separated from is almost without a center.

Having outlined the scope of my study, I would now like to acknowledge its limitations. As I suggested earlier, conversion rhetoric has occupied a privileged position from the Bible to *Black Boy* and beyond, but it is not equally specific to all autobiographies. I have not sought a theory of autobiography that is broad enough (and therefore weak enough) to encompass all American self-writing, but rather one that situates certain works by important American writers and thinkers in the context of an identifiable discursive mode. My goal is specific readings of specific texts.

If my project cannot be said to represent all modern American autobiographies, neither can it claim to be the history of a trope; such a history would fill volumes, and even if possible, it would be woefully incomplete. In the first chapter, I do attempt to describe the Christian conversion pattern and to identify some of its major rhetorical features. Beyond that I cannot claim comprehensiveness. Conversion continues to operate for many people in ways not very different from the way Jonathan Edwards experienced it, and not all secular writers in the twentieth century use conversion discourse to express cultural estrangement. The widespread use of conversion discourse by people from all walks of life itself demonstrates that it is more than a "literary" language whose use has been co-opted by privileged groups. One need not be literary, or even literate, to experience conversion. For good or ill, its structures are woven into the fabric of American experience.

In the second chapter, I look at some of the ways autobiographers in the eighteenth and nineteenth centuries secularized the conversion process. Here I have tried to balance works from the Euro- and white-male-centered autobiographical canon with works by women and African-American writers. My purpose in this chapter is to identify some of the traditions of secular conversion narratives so as to provide a framework for their revision by twentieth-century Americans. There is, I hope, some justification for my using canonical works to provide a background for my study of American autobiography in the first half of the twentieth century. The canonical texts I discuss in this chapter were likely to have been well known in the early twentieth century, and certainly the Jameses, Adams, Glasgow, and Wright respond to them in fairly direct ways. Writers such as Rousseau, Wordsworth, DeQuincey, Carlyle, and Mill would have been perceived as being canonical to them as well as to us.

In her study of Victorian autobiography, Linda Peterson begins to explain why the British canon has been dominated by spiritual autobiographies written by male authors. She points out that while women wrote spiritual autobiographies in the seventeenth and eighteenth centuries, they did not participate widely in the sacred and secular revitalization of the genre by nineteenth-century males, which had an enormous influence on the development of the canon. Though Peterson acknowledges that nineteenth-century Quaker women continued to employ the patterns of the form and that Harriet Martineau composed a secular variation of it, she finds that women writers were forced to find alternate modes of self-expression, among them the novel and the private diary.[2] Rooted as it is in the seventeenth and eighteenth centuries, when both men and women wrote spiritual autobiographies, Peterson's work attests to the fact that the conversion narrative is not an inherently male form, though she is right to

2. See Peterson, 120–55, and 214 n. 22.

suggest that at different times and under different circumstances, women have not written spiritual autobiographies, either by choice or by constraint. This is not to say, however, that women did not use conversion discourse in the nineteenth century. Though they did not (or could not) publish many spiritual autobiographies, women on both sides of the Atlantic still participated in other modes of articulating conversion experiences, both privately—in journals, diaries, and letters—and publicly, in various forms of religious testimony. Conversion for many women, particularly in the middle class, could be a means of acquiring power.[3]

Like many British women writers of the period, American white males of the nineteenth century—unlike their British counterparts—also chose other modes of discourse to inscribe a poetics of the self. The self-conscious impulse to record a "secular self" was slow to develop in the American nineteenth century and lagged behind its manifestations in Europe. As Lawrence Buell points out, autobiographical works such as Thoreau's *Walden*, Dana's *Two Years before the Mast*, Parkman's *Oregon Trail*, Barnum's *Life*, and even Whitman's *Specimen Days* actually resist the kinds of self-disclosure expected in a conversion narrative ("Autobiography," 47–69). Emerson's "transparent eyeball" passage, Melville's pseudo-autobiography *Typee*, and certain sections of *Song of Myself* suggest that the writers of the American Renaissance invoked the rhetoric of conversion, but they rarely used it as an important organizing principle in their narratives. This is partly explained by their desire to escape from the weight of tradition in an effort to "create" a national literature.

The presence of conversion discourse is more noticeable in works by African-American men and women. The links, tensions, and rifts between evangelical Christianity and the ex-slave or free African American have been well documented, and the great variety of autobiographical works produced by them in the nineteenth century has begun to be studied. A number of critics have noted affinities between some slave narratives and the spiritual autobiography tradition, and others have observed the significant absence of Christian rhetoric in other nineteenth-century autobiographical works written by black Americans. Thanks to these studies, I have been able to examine the autobiographies of Hurston and Wright in the context of the larger tradition of African-American self-writing.

If the precise relationship between the twentieth-century authors upon whom I focus and the various traditions of the American nineteenth century

3. See, for example, Mary P. Ryan's *Cradle of the Middle Class*.

will continue to be studied, my hope is that the first two chapters still provide an important background—from a variety of perspectives—against which to examine the various responses to conversion discourse generated by the two Jameses, Henry Adams, Edith Wharton, Ellen Glasgow, Zora Neale Hurston, and Richard Wright. These writers were primarily responding to the Christian and to the nineteenth-century British (male) traditions of the spiritual autobiography as well as to its more general presence in Anglo-American culture. As the dynamic field of autobiography itself suggests, literary study does not always proceed in a chronological or even in a logical order. It is neither necessary nor desirable to wait until the vast amount of work in the nineteenth century be completed for work to proceed—as it has already done so—in the twentieth. In fact, were it not for the work of others in this period, my own study would not have been possible.

1

. . .

THE CHRISTIAN FRAMEWORK

In his influential study, *The Forms of Autobiography: Episodes in the History of a Literary Genre*, William Spengemann posits a historical theory of autobiography that recognizes both its enduring "relation to the self-biographical mode and its apparently increasing tendency to assume fictive forms in the modern era" (xiii). In tracing this development, he identifies three significant modes of autobiographical writing. From the early Middle Ages to the Enlightenment, the dominant mode was "historical," in which the writer chronologically recounted past experiences from a single, self-justified point of view. The late eighteenth and early nineteenth centuries saw the development of the "philosophical" mode, which was characterized by a reflexive self-scrutiny and a tentative search for truth. Later in the nineteenth century the "poetic" form emerged, in which self-presentation depended solely upon the "verbal action" that describes its own creation (xvi). Interestingly, however, Spengemann finds that Augustine's *Confessions* proleptically manifests all these characteristics, "accomplishing the entire course of autobiographical change in a single work" (xv–xvi). Books 1–9, which lead up to and recount Augustine's conversion, comprise the historical record of his spiritual growth. Augustine's faith becomes the source of his wisdom in books 10–12, where he launches a philosophical inquiry into the concepts of time, memory, and creation. And in book 13 Augustine's faith is "enacted imaginatively" into words as he presents a poetic reading of the first chapter of Genesis (1–33).

Spengemann's analysis, itself an extreme example of how critics have established *The Confessions* as a paradigm for autobiographical writing, accurately describes the movement in Augustine's work but fails to see how this pattern of moving outward—beyond the details of his life story and into a relationship with society—is characteristic of most of the literature focused on the experience of conversion. Augustine's tremendous influence on Western culture, no doubt, partly accounts for this tendency, but it is best explained by the theological implications of the conversion process itself. Within this framework, history, philosophy, and poetry, or—to redefine Spengemann's terms—biography, knowledge, and expression, are intimately related.

Augustine and other early Christians found a scriptural model for conversion in the life and writings of St. Paul, who regarded the receiving of the Spirit of the risen Lord as a central event in the life of the Christian. Paul viewed conversion as an entry into new life—akin to Jesus' resurrection— a turning away from sin toward faith in Christ. Paul most fully developed this Spirit theology in his Epistle to the Romans where he deconstructed the Mosaic Law, which had stood as a safeguard against transgression for the children of Israel but which for him signified the source and occasion of sin itself.[1] According to Paul, Christ wiped away the prescriptions of the Old Law in his act of personal redemption: "For all alike have sinned, and are deprived of the divine splendor, and are all justified by God's free grace alone, through his act of liberation in the person of Christ Jesus" (Rom. 3:23–25).[2] Only by turning away from a reliance on the Law to an acceptance of the gospel could the Christian achieve salvation.

Paul's conversion—a word that itself means "turning"—became a model for future spiritual autobiographers, and he refers to it directly in the first and second chapters of Galatians and in the third chapter of Philippians, where he recounts his radical departure from a life of persecuting Christians to a life devoted to spreading the gospel message:

> You have heard what my manner of life was when I was still a practicing Jew: how savagely I persecuted the church of God, and tried to destroy it. . . . But then in his good pleasure God, who had set me apart from birth and called me through his grace, chose to reveal his Son to me and through me, in order that I might proclaim him among the Gentiles. (Gal. 1:13–16)

1. For a discussion of Paul's Spirit theology and how it contrasts with the kingdom-of-God myth presented in the synoptic Gospels, see James Mackey, *Jesus the Man and the Myth*, 173–95.

2. This scriptural passage and all others in this chapter are from the *New English Bible with the Apocrypha*.

Despite Paul's emphasis on the importance of his own conversion, he makes no autobiographical reference to the startling experience on the road to Damascus, which is recounted no less than three times in the Acts of the Apostles, a book filled with conversion narratives. Luke, the supposed author of Acts, rendered Paul's conversion as a supernatural event: Paul was not only struck down and blinded by a heavenly light, he also heard Jesus speak to him directly. Vision and audition were to became common metaphors for conversion, which Paul himself described as an invisible change of the heart.

The New Testament thus presents two versions of the conversion experience: in the Epistles, Paul established the theological framework for conversion and emphasized its life-altering consequences; in the Acts of the Apostles, Luke gave it a metaphorical form. Both these writers would have found textual precedents for conversion in the ancient world, however. In his classic study of conversion in antiquity, A. D. Nock pointed out that both pagan cults and the Greek philosophical schools described the process by which they won adherents, in ways directly analogous to the Christian pattern.[3] Older and more powerful precedents for the conversion experience could be found in the divine "callings" of the Old Testament prophets; Paul himself probably interpreted his reception of grace in this manner.[4] These callings, graphically depicted at the beginning of Jeremiah, Isaiah, Ezekiel, and other prophetic books, parallel Paul's experience in many ways. In his First Letter to the Corinthians, Paul himself acknowledged that prophecy was one of the more desirable gifts of the Holy Spirit and thereby explicitly linked conversion and prophecy in a way that was already implicit in the Old Testament (I Cor. 12:4–12, 14:1–40).

3. Nock, *Conversion*, 166–74. Nock's fifty-year-old study has recently undergone a lot of revisionist scrutiny. Anne McGuire, for example, finds that his conception of Gnosticism was inaccurately generalized. McGuire also takes issue with Nock by arguing that individuals who received gnosis did experience conversion as we know it. See her "Conversion and Gnosis in the *Gospel of Truth*."

4. Paula Fredriksen argues that Paul saw his conversion as a prophetic calling, not as a dramatic reversal that overthrew the Law, in "Conversion Narratives, Orthodox Traditions, and the Retrospective Self," 16–17. Fredriksen states that Luke's late first-century description of Paul's conversion (circa A.D. 34) coincides neither with the historical data nor with the eschatological conception of salvation Paul presents in the Epistles. Fredriksen argues that theologians past and present—Augustine among them—have distorted Paul's message by evaluating his life and work according to Luke's account. Fredriksen, however, may overstate her point. Many theologians find that Paul *links* personal and eschatological redemption throughout the Epistles. This debate need not detain us. Luke may well have misread Paul; Augustine probably misread Paul through Luke. The result, however, was a vastly influential literary tradition—the focus of this study.

Like Paul's conversion, these Old Testament callings represent dramatic turning points in the lives of individual prophets. They are presented as mystical events, rooted in historical circumstances, that alter the prophet's perception of the world. Just as Paul turned away from his old life and zealously began another, the prophet too was supplied with a new center of meaning and a lifelong sense of mission. Though the prophets typically declared their unworthiness and incapacity for such an undertaking, they were nevertheless strengthened with a divine eloquence that enabled them to overcome adversity and that was sustained even when their message fell upon deaf ears. The gift of prophecy also increased awareness; prophets became powerful critics of social and political activity and discerned the motives behind the actions of individuals and nations. They read the significance of natural and supernatural events and created symbolic languages of their own.[5]

Thus, Spengemann's analysis of the juxtaposition between the historical, philosophical, and poetic sections of Augustine's narrative follows the logic of the conversion pattern as established by Luke and the prophets.[6] God's intervention in the personal history of individuals extended their knowledge and enhanced their powers of expression. Augustine's understanding of this logic was no doubt also influenced by Gnosticism, which he encountered in the Manichaeism of his early manhood. The various Gnostic sects taught that God granted certain individuals privileged knowledge about the nature of existence, which turned them from ignorance to gnosis and from rootlessness to repose (McGuire, 343–44). In the narrative structure of *The Confessions*, the reception of grace functions as gnosis because it occasions Augustine's confident speculation on the complex philosophical issues of his day in books 10–12. When Augustine encountered Christian Neoplatonism shortly before his conversion, he rejected the dualism embedded in Gnostic thought. But if he became a Neoplatonic theologian, he continued to view the world in Manichaean terms; and the radical separation between a transcendent God and the material world that characterizes Gnosticism provided a framework for his dualistic conception of conversion.

5. My discussion of the implications of the prophetic calling has been influenced by Bernhard Anderson, particularly his discussions of Isaiah and Ezekiel. See *Understanding the Old Testament*, 228–32, 303–4, 405–6.

6. Though I am emphasizing the similarities among the experiences of the prophets, Paul, and Augustine, they are by no means identical. Marilyn Harran contrasts the conversion experiences of Paul and Augustine in the historical survey of conversion that makes up a major portion of the first chapter of *Luther on Conversion*. See especially page 28.

At the moment of regeneration God bridges the otherwise uncrossable gulf between the worlds of flesh and pure spirit and infuses his wisdom (gnosis) into the mind of the believer.

Because an individual's reasoning powers are enhanced as a result of this action, Augustine's philosophical inquiry into the nature of time, memory, and creation carried a privileged meaning. This divinely inspired knowledge also gave him a heightened awareness of the beauty of God's creation and the sufficiency of His Word, which, in turn, enabled him to compose his lyrical interpretation of the first chapter of Genesis. Transcendent knowledge caused eloquent expression.

Revelation for Augustine, as for Paul and the prophets, also led to the acceptance of a specific social role. In the "historical," preconversion section of his narrative, Augustine followed his insatiable curiosity by trying out one occupation and one intellectual system after another. Christianity remained always in the background, but like the other disciplines he considered—rhetoric, astrology, Manichaeism, and the philosophy of the Academics—it failed to satisfy his probing inquiry into the nature of existence. Augustine's conversion, however, which came after he was exposed to the allegorical method of scriptural exegesis, convinced him of the justness and coherence of Christianity and excited him to pursue his study of Isaiah and the Psalms. His intellectual wandering was replaced by a steadfast longing for full comprehension of the Word that eventually led to his taking holy orders. Augustine's calling, thus, had a spiritual and a worldly side: in becoming one of God's chosen, he also accepted an ideology and a defined social role.

Though an intensely personal experience, Augustine's conversion highlights his pervasive emphasis on community and fellowship. The *Confessions* is not simply the story of how a single man became an elect member of God's invisible church, it is also the story of how he found peace in several specific communities of belief: first at Cassiciacum, then as one of the *servi Dei* at Thagaste, and finally as head of a monastery at Hippo. Augustine further emphasized the communal aspects of his conversion by recording it in the context of similar experiences by Victorinus, Antony, Nebridius, Alypius, and other friends and acquaintances. Moreover, by fulfilling Monica's lifelong desire that he become a Christian, his conversion also united mother and son in a moment of apotheosis before her death.[7]

---

7. Peter Brown emphasizes Augustine's need for fellowship throughout *Augustine of Hippo*, especially on page 161. For a discussion of the communal aspects of Augustine's conversion, see Eugene Vance, "Augustine's *Confessions* and the Grammar of Selfhood."

In book 4, Augustine makes it clear that not just his friends and family, but all Christians, are knit together by God's love: "Blessed are those who love you, O God, and love their friends in you and their enemies for your sake. They alone will never lose those who are dear to them, for they love them in one who is never lost, in God" (79). Here, Augustine reveals how the presence of grace socializes all inhabitants of the City of God.

Augustine's emphasis on community draws on the Bible's presentation of Israel as a chosen people or as a saving remnant, a sect ideal also found in Paul's letters to early Christian communities. But in addition to making use of these and other scriptural precedents to construct his redemptive history, Augustine brought together other conventions that became standard motifs in conversion rhetoric. The famous conversion scene in the garden at Milan, for instance, illustrates the close connection between conversion and the Word so characteristic of later Christian writing. Though Augustine's conversion is not the dramatic theophany found in the prophetic books or in some later narratives, it is still rendered as a supernatural event, the consequences of his opening a copy of Paul's Epistles and reading the first lines he comes upon: "Let us behave with decency as befits the day: no revelling or drunkenness, no debauchery or vice, no quarrels or jealousness" (Rom. 13:13). Augustine claims he read this passage immediately after he had heard what appeared to be a child say "*tolle lege, tolle lege*" (take up and read). In so doing, he ended his agony in the garden and gained the certainty he lacked, in spite of his own efforts to come to God. Augustine's use of the *sortes* convention in this context illustrates the way conversion accounts are frequently semimystical exercises in intertextuality. By interacting with one form of sacred literature, the successful believer was able to construct another.

Augustine further highlights the intertextuality of conversion by inserting other narratives within his own. A particularly vivid example is the story of Victorinus. Victorinus was an influential philosopher and rhetorician who converted to Christianity secretly because he was afraid his new belief would damage his public reputation. After a period of turmoil, Victorinus decided to confess his faith in front of a large gathering. Hearing of Victorinus's struggle to find Christ and to proclaim him publicly inspired Augustine to persevere in his own search. Victorinus's profession not only foreshadowed Augustine's own conversion and gave him strength, it also provided a rhetorical model for the *Confessions* itself. Augustine confesses, not only to God, "but also to the believers among men, all who share my joy and all who, like me, are doomed to die; all who are my fellows in your kingdom and all who accompany me on this pilgrimage, whether they have gone before or are still to come or are with me as I make my way through life" (210). Augustine's strategy is to make his pilgrimage—the story of his conversion and its effect upon his life—a universal Christian experience. By giving it a textual form, he too set a literary and experiential pattern later spiritual autobiographers could adapt to their own life stories. Reading or hearing the testimony of others activated the process of regeneration almost as often as did hearing the Scriptures. From fourth-century Milan to twentieth-century America, the public articulation of a faith experience prepared others for conversion and established textual models for subsequent accounts.

Despite the extent to which Augustine developed the rhetoric of conversion into a coherent mode of self-presentation, the *Confessions* was not widely imitated in the late-classical and medieval periods. Autobiography as we know it was not a popular genre, and most of the autobiographies that were written were of the *res gestae* variety. Augustine's conversion failed to be a useful model for medieval autobiographers because the Catholic church was perceived as being a universal institution and because the sacraments marked the various stages of spirituality that Augustine went through less formally as described in the *Confessions*.[8] Infant baptism and confirmation, in particular, replaced the Pauline experience as initiation rituals. In the Middle Ages, "conversion" most often meant the acceptance of a monastic way of life—a renouncing of the things of this world for the seclusion of the cloister—and consequently a hagiographic tradition based on the life of the ideal monk became the most visible biographical genre.[9] Some Christian mystics, most notably Teresa of Avila, were influenced by the *Confessions*, and the sequence of self-discipline followed by a rapturous submission that characterized their spiritual exercises borrows from conversion discourse.[10] Such autobiographies were relatively rare, however, and failed to employ fully the narrative framework Augustine developed.

8. Ironically, it was Augustine himself, in his writings against the Donatists, who solidified the position of the sacraments in the Catholic Church. See Gerald Bonner, *St. Augustine of Hippo*, 237–311.

9. Harran outlines the medieval use of "conversion" as an initiation into the monastic life, 34. Carl Weintraub uses the same approach in placing Peter Abelard's *Story of My Misfortunes* in the context of the ideal monk tradition. See his *Value of the Individual*, 72–92.

10. Louis Martz compares the spiritual exercises of the Catholic mystics and the conversion narratives of Protestants. Both employ methods of achieving self-knowledge; both move the individual from feelings of fear to feelings of assurance and from distrust of the self to confidence in God. See *The Poetry of Meditation*, 121–27, 153–75. Weintraub also compares the two forms, 211–18.

In contrast, the Reformation saw a flowering of conversion narratives, most of which follow—with important variations—the narrative pattern established by Augustine. Like the early Christians, many Protestants perceived conversion to be the primary means of initiation into the life of faith. Those who adhered to the doctrine of predestination interpreted the conversion sequence as the most obvious sign of their election, and they consequently examined their lives for evidence of its occurrence. Augustine's works were often cited by Puritan divines and, as Perry Miller points out, Augustinian piety became a Puritan preoccupation:

> The same subjective insight, the same turning of consciousness back upon itself, the same obsession with individuality, the same test of conclusions not so much by evidence or utility as by the soul's immediate approbation or revulsion—these qualities which appear in Augustine almost for the first time in Western thought and give him his amazing "modernity," reappear in force among the early Puritans. (22)

Augustine proved to be a model for Puritan writers because his theology was consistent in many ways with that of the Reformers, who consciously desired to return the Christian church to the purity of the patristic period and who often used the past ahistorically.

The same impulse toward public confession found in early Christian writings like the *Confessions*, that led to the formalization of the Catholic sacrament of penance, also seems to have caused the standardization of the conversion narrative among Calvinist writers.[11] Paul Delany accounts for this standardization by suggesting that the lack of a developed sacramental system among Reformed sects contributed to the tremendous amount of religious autobiographical writing in the seventeenth and eighteenth centuries (63). Since believers could not receive penance by making regular visits to the confessional, self-writing in itself became a ritualistic process by which the guilt associated with temptation and transgression could be overcome. By participating in accepted modes of discourse, believers were assured of the presence of grace in their souls. The struggle for an "experientially tested" religion thus led to the establishment of autobiographical conventions (Fleishman, 76).

11. For a brief history of the origins of the sacrament of confession, see Mary Flowers Braswell, *The Medieval Sinner*, 18–21.

A typological hermeneutics was especially important in the development of auto-interpretative strategies because it was a central means by which the Reformers interpreted language and experience. Protestants—in diaries, journals, slave narratives, autobiographies, conversion narratives, histories, and captivity narratives—used the methods of scriptural exegesis and sermon rhetoric to discover God's saving action in their individual lives and in the community as a whole. Typology produced a high degree of conformity in language and structure because Reformed writers tried to emulate the styles and themes of the great literary figures of the past, among them the prophets and evangelists. They sought and found correspondences between themselves and those who had produced texts before them.

Of course, Anglo-American Puritanism was by no means an integrated movement. As the American Antinomian Crisis made clear, the concept of predestination could lead to an aggressive individualism that threatened the social order; and cultural historians such as Christopher Hill and Philip Gura have emphasized that disparate elements within Protestantism had much to do with the theological and political actions of the orthodoxy.[12] Even the relatively conservative nonseparating Congregationalism of the Massachusetts Bay Colony fostered a diversity of beliefs, many of them radical. Orthodox ministers and theologians were continually called upon to qualify the individualism and potential anarchy implicit in Calvinist theology (Ziff, 68). Yet despite a diversity of beliefs, most Puritans shared a set of interpretative conventions that could be used to qualify the revolutionary challenges of the more radical elements in the population. According to Sacvan Bercovitch, typology was the "staple of Protestant writings" because it was seen by the orthodox as "an ideal method for regulating spiritualization" (36–37).

One of the more cogent responses to the potentially subversive elements in American Puritanism was the development of admission requirements for church members. These took the form of short conversion narratives that were delivered either orally or in writing in the churches of New England. This use of conversion narratives was developed in America around 1634, probably at the instigation of John Cotton, and was conceived as a test of genuine conversion in response to the Reformed impulse to merge God's invisible church with His worldly congregations. All but

12. See Christopher Hill's *The World Turned Upside Down* and Philip Gura's *Glimpse of Sion's Glory*.

universal in New England by 1640, this practice was exported back to England where it was employed by some Congregational and dissenting churches. Such narratives grew out of the personal "confession," a preestablished prayer that was a part of the covenant-making "profession of faith" orally delivered to the whole congregation in early Reformed churches. Originally designed to show that prospective members had a basic understanding of church doctrine, these confessions gradually evolved into personal accounts of spiritual conversion.[13] According to Gura, such a practice enabled ministers "to keep from their churches those whose religious experience seemed erroneous or extravagant [and] . . . also to encourage and preserve in their population the heightened piety that resulted from an acknowledgment that the spirit of God had worked upon their souls" (163). After the relation was delivered, church members voted upon whether or not to accept the candidate for full admission. If approved, the believer was allowed to take part in the Lord's Supper. Full membership not only provided spiritual rewards; there were political benefits for male members as well. Only they were qualified to vote in colonial elections.

These Anglo-American "relations" contributed greatly to the development of the spiritual autobiography tradition. Because the process of conversion described in these accounts is highly conventional, Edmund Morgan has called the pattern they follow "the morphology of conversion." He describes the narratives as a series of well-defined steps that follow an established sequence of "knowledge, conviction, faith, combat, and true, imperfect assurance" (72). According to Morgan, the narratives presented to Puritan congregations "demonstrate clearly the familiarity of the narrators with the morphology of conversion, a familiarity produced, no doubt, by a great many sermons on the subject. The pattern is so plain as to give the experiences the appearance of a stereotype" (90–91).

Though these relations do follow a number of easily identifiable conventions, it would be inaccurate to interpret them with the rigidity that Morgan's morphology implies. Morgan describes a five-stage process, but he derives his formulation from William Perkins, who formulated a ten-stage sequence. William Ames preached an eleven-step process much like that of Perkins, but Thomas Shepard spoke of only four stages. John Cotton distrusted the idea of stages altogether. Martin Luther (who may have started the formalization of the hermeneutics of conversion) spoke of only

13. The development of the Anglo-American conversion narrative is discussed by Patricia Caldwell in *The Puritan Conversion Narrative*, 51–56, and by Philip Gura in *A Glimpse of Sion's Glory*, 161–68.

two stages. As this diversity itself suggests, the sequences these Protestant divines described tended to reflect their own experiences of receiving grace. Apparently, theoretical writings on the subject of conversion show the same diversity that might be expected from autobiographical narratives.[14]

The variety of theological approaches to conversion reveals that Puritans did more than force-fit their experiences into predetermined formulas. Though they presented the conversion experience in similar ways, modern readers of their narratives would be hard-pressed to match a specific passage with a particular stage in any of the various sequences. Noticing this, Patricia Caldwell has qualified the rigidity of Morgan's morphology in her study of American conversion narratives:"If there is an American morphology," she states, "it emerges from an angle of vision and not from an arrangement of steps. It is a literary morphology, a total way of perceiving and talking about experiences rather than a particular, predetermined mold" (178). In an analysis of the British tradition of spiritual autobiography, Patricia Meyer Spacks sees similar variations in the conversion pattern. Individuals deviate from the anticipated unfolding of events because "the imagination that fills in the pattern's details simultaneously reminds the reader of the reality of possibilities rejected by the engaged human will" (*Imagining*, 28–29, 54). For Spacks, the spiritual autobiography form limits meaning but also creates it. Though highly conventional, Anglo-American conversion rhetoric is best described not as a series of steps, but as a language of spiritual examination available to writers as they recorded their lives and times.

Conversion discourse remained a flexible vehicle because it not only had to conform to a variety of personal experiences, it also had to cross generic, denominational, racial, and sexual boundaries. Accounts of conversion can be found in diaries, sermons, biographies, autobiographies, saints' lives, slave narratives, novels, poems, as well as other forms of religious literature. The pattern of conversion recorded in a diary is apt to be less decisive than that described in a relatively short narrative presented to a church congregation, and neither of these forms would present a unified overview of the lifelong effects of conversion the way an extended spiritual autobiography would. Fictional or poetic versions of the spiritual autobiography like Defoe's *Robinson Crusoe* and Cowper's *Task* would similarly have

---

14. I am indebted to Caldwell, 57; J. O. King, *The Iron of Melancholy*, 30; and Edmund Morgan, *Visible Saints*, 68–70, for pointing out the variety of sequences these divines presented.

to adapt the discourse to fulfill linguistic expectations associated with their respective genres.[15] Various theological viewpoints would affect conversion accounts as well. A Quaker, for instance, would be apt to record the reception of the "inner light" differently than a Congregationalist would describe his or her reception of grace. And though most seventeenth- and eighteenth-century Anglo-American spiritual autobiographies were written by members of the various sects loosely defined as Puritan, there were also Anglican and even Catholic variations on the form (Delany, 40–54).

If the experience of receiving grace was conveyed in similar terms by both men and women, other details in the narratives varied by gender. In seventeenth-century New England, women were more likely to deliver their relations privately rather than before an assembled congregation. This difference in audience and performing context affected the language and structure of conversion narratives articulated by women. Puritan women also tended to mention their spouses and children in their narratives more frequently than did men, and they were likely to have been preoccupied by different sins (Cohen, 143–44, 222–23). Furthermore, as Carol Edkins has shown, social differences generated by a patriarchal culture and by a valorization of certain female roles (such as midwifing and aiding the sick) are clearly evident in the literature of Puritan and Quaker women (39–52).

With the exception of the Quakers, most major sects prohibited women from pursuing a ministerial vocation, a practice that resulted in other expressions of sexual difference in the literature. One of the more fascinating tensions in the tradition occurs when women who are powerfully called to speak publicly about their faith are opposed by their husbands. (Needless, perhaps, to say, a similar conflict between male spiritual autobiographers and their spouses is totally absent from the literature.) An interesting example of this tension occurs in the autobiography of Elizabeth Ashbridge, an eighteenth-century American Quaker. After being converted, Ashbridge initially believed that union with God required that she always be in accord with her husband. She wrote, "To love the Divine Being, and not to love

15. My purpose is to illustrate the pervasiveness of conversion rhetoric in a variety of genres and periods. I do not, however, mean to belittle the importance of Defoe's radical adaptation of the conversion pattern to fictive discourse. Because Defoe's purpose in *Robinson Crusoe* was not *simply* to spread the Word, his act was potentially blasphemous. Defoe's novel and others like it began the process of secularization that transformed autobiographical writing in the Romantic and Victorian periods, even as he maintained an essentially Calvinistic worldview. According to Jay Fliegelman, *Crusoe* adheres to the conventions of the spiritual autobiography while it redefines seventeenth-century notions of the family, *Prodigals and Pilgrims*, 67–83.

my husband, I saw was an inconfidency, and seemed impossible; therefore I requested, with tears, that my affections might increase towards my husband" (530). Later in her narrative, however, Ashbridge defies her husband and says she will not obey him when his commands "imposed on my conscience" (540–41).

The interpretative battle over St. Paul's injunctions against women preaching is not confined to the autobiographies of women Quakers. Three nineteenth-century spiritual autobiographies written by African-American women also address this issue: *The Life and Religious Experiences of Jarena Lee*, the *Memoirs* of Zilpha Elaw, and Julia Foote's *Brand Plucked from the Fire*.[16] After establishing their conversions textually, these women go on to describe how they rebelled against social and religious norms by assuming roles as preachers and exhorters. Even more so than Ashbridge, they address the constraints of patriarchal culture directly and assemble scriptural arguments that counter St. Paul's injunctions against women preachers. According to Elaw, St. Paul's words were "not intended to limit the extraordinary directions of the Holy Ghost, in reference to female Evangelists, or oracular sisters" (124). Later, she proclaims "it is the high privilege of those who are begotten by the Word of truth to read the Scriptures, not as the word of man, but as they are indeed, the Word of God" (132). Foote similarly instructs her "Dear Sisters" not to be "kept in bondage" by those who misinterpret Paul's words and also not to "let what man may say or do, keep you from doing the will of the Lord" (227). Though Elaw and Foote do not question whether Paul's words are divinely inspired, they do reinterpret his references to women preaching according to their own evangelical interests. As these texts suggest, there is a place for the figure of an empowered female in the spiritual autobiography—not just among Quaker women who had a limited access to the ministry—but among other groups as well.

Daniel Shea, who disparages the literary merit of the short conversion narratives delivered before New England congregations because of their supposed reliance on the "morphology of conversion," values only those American spiritual autobiographies that deviate from the conventional pattern (91). Shea, however, fails to see how each author of a conversion account was in a position to respond to specific personal, cultural, and theological pressures. In addition to the differences of gender and genre,

16. These three works can be found in *Sisters of the Spirit*, ed. William Andrews. Lee's strategy of empowerment has been studied by Nellie Y. McKay, "Nineteenth-Century Black Women's Spiritual Autobiographies."

other cultural tensions are contained by the form. For example, many first-generation American Puritans adapted the conversion pattern to the experience of emigration.[17] In his autobiography, Thomas Shepard noticed that many of the godly were "awakened" to go to New England, and his voyage to the New World becomes the antitype of God's deliverance of his people from Egypt and of Christ's own resurrection (McGiffert, 55, 71–75). His sea crossing takes the place of conversion as a decisive life-ordering principle. Another characteristic of the narratives written by first-generation Americans is a "sense of strain" in their works caused by their failure to find an appropriate language to express their disillusionment with America. Their accounts of conversion are apt to be more subdued and tentative than those delivered by their English contemporaries (Caldwell, 121–29). A well-known example of this disillusionment can be found in Anne Bradstreet's brief spiritual autobiography:[18] "After a short time I changed my condition and was married, and came into this country, where I found a new world and new manners, at which my heart rose. But after I was convinced it was the way of God, I submitted to it and joined to the church at Boston" (241). Other variations of the pattern occurred during the Great Awakening, which stressed the affective power of conversion. Jonathan Edwards, the Awakening's leading theologian, was a zealous student of conversion who was stripped of his pulpit in Northampton because he tried to restore the practice of making the delivery of a personal relation a requirement for church membership. Based on his observation of his own congregation and his knowledge of Lockean psychology, Edwards published his own morphology of conversion that soon "became firmly fixed in the popular mind" and that persists to a large extent among evangelicals to this day (Goen, 27). Although Edwards was fascinated by the most ecstatic experiences, his morphology in its broad outline is similar to those that Morgan and others have described. Because he saw much variety in the accounts he recorded, however, Edwards distrusted the idea

17. Bercovitch, *The Puritan Origins of the American Self*, 106. Thomas Couser analyzes Shepard's autobiography as a displaced conversion narrative, where emigration takes the place of conversion, in *American Autobiography*, 13–14.

18. Bradstreet's "To My Dear Children" was written many years after she became a member of the Boston church, which may explain why she does not dwell on her conversion. Though Mary Mason suggests that Bradstreet's failure to do so is consistent with the whole tradition of women's autobiography, Patricia Caldwell argues that her subdued account of conversion is characteristic of the narratives of many first-generation American Puritans, male and female, who where disillusioned with America. See Mary Mason, "The Other Voice," 21–24, 36–44, and Patricia Caldwell, *The Puritan Conversion Narrative*, 119–20.

of predetermined stages: "The goodness of [a] person's state is not chiefly to be judged by any exactness of steps, and method of experiences."[19] As his *Personal Narrative* makes clear, Edwards had failed to find stages in his own life, and he wrote it in part so that readers would be able to distinguish between genuine manifestations of grace and those merely fabricated in the general fervor of the Awakening.

Conversion in its various manifestations continued to occupy a central place in the theology of American Protestantism throughout the nineteenth century, especially in the context of the numerous waves of evangelical revivals. Though the Puritan practice of giving an account of one's conversion in order to become a full member of a congregation was never to be as widely practiced as it was in seventeenth-century New England, public testimony remained an important, if often voluntary, practice. The great popularity of religious revivals brought the act of relating a conversion experience further into the public sphere. For the American Puritans, conversion was a relatively private phenomenon, shared orally or in writing with family members or a local congregation. Many nineteenth-century religious groups tried to reach a much wider, less homogeneous audience (Sizer, 51, 66). This tendency for conversion to be seen as an emotional, mass event was helped by the decline of the Calvinistic doctrine of predestination. The Methodists, of course, had always believed that sinners could freely repent and choose Jesus as their savior, but even some denominations still nominally Calvinistic, such as the Baptists and the Presbyterians, all but abandoned the doctrine of predestination after 1800 and claimed that salvation was open to all (McLoughlin, 114, 135). Such practices moved conversion even closer to the center of American culture.

Despite historical, generic, theological, cultural, racial, sexual, and personal variations within the discourse, the experience of receiving grace and its life-altering consequences were conveyed in remarkably similar terms. Spiritual conversion cannot be reduced to a list of stages or even a theological system, but accounts of conversion, various as they are, do share certain rhetorical features, features that go beyond even the confines

19. Letter to the Reverend Thomas Prince of Boston, *The Great Awakening*, ed. C. C. Goen, 556. For Edwards's distrust of stages and his tendency to use the *Personal Narrative* as a means of instructing others to search for genuine conversion, I am indebted to Goen's "Morphology of Conversion" in the same volume, 25–32; Shea's *Spiritual Autobiography in Early America*, 190–91; King's *Iron of Melancholy*, 65–82; and Couser's *American Autobiography*, 23. Jerald C. Brauer compares conversion in the Puritans and the revivalists in "Conversion: From Puritanism to Revivalism."

of the Western literary traditions. As a means of signifying new awareness, recording divine inspiration, and lending cogency to a narrative perspective, the conversion experience was perceived as being all but universal.

One of the outstanding features of conversion rhetoric in the West is its recurring use of extended metaphors that symbolize various spiritual states. William Haller finds that two of these dominate Puritan writings: "The Puritan imagination," he says, "saw the life of the spirit as pilgrimage and battle" (142). The use of these two metaphors, of course, is at least as old as Christianity itself. St. Paul found them particularly appropriate for discussing the life of faith, and Protestant spiritual autobiographers employed Paul's language to construct the stories of their own paths to conversion and its consequences.

Wandering, the first of these, signified anxiety, indecision, and meaninglessness in the rhetoric of conversion. Before receiving grace, the wayfaring pilgrim is typically presented as an ineffective searcher for the truth, who tries to take refuge in false or sinful activities, but who finds no rest until he or she receives the light of God's Word. Once they are assured of the presence of grace, pilgrims still suffer frequent trials on the road to salvation, but they remain steadfast because they can be sure of a final resting place. Conversion, in this sense, may be presented both as the beginning of a lifelong journey as well as the end of one.

Since temptation was a central experience for Christians, the authors of conversion accounts also described themselves as soldiers in the service of God, waging never-ending battles against the powers of evil. This duel between the forces of good and evil is akin to the *psychomachia* of the medieval hagiographic tradition. Adapting such a notion to their own theologies, Puritans and other Protestants saw themselves as active participants in an internal struggle between the dictates of right reason, whose source was God's grace, and their own fallen nature. The conflict was frequently recapitulated as a battle against Satan or popery or another manifestation of evil, but the spiritual autobiographer knew that the final proving ground was the self. After receiving grace, the struggle continued, but the believer had the comfort of knowing that God lends a hand and that He will vanquish all evil forces in the final battle. For example, after her conversion but before her "sanctification," Jarena Lee, a member of the A.M.E. church, recalls a new struggle commencing in my soul, not accompanied with fear, guilt, and bitter distress, as while under my first conviction for sin; but a labouring of the mind to know more of the right way of the Lord."[20]

Sickness and calamity were also powerful metaphors in the conversion tradition. Because affliction was regarded as the natural consequence of sin, these metaphors were often associated with the aimless wandering of the unregenerate; but their inclusion in a spiritual autobiography was often viewed positively. Although physical discomfort and calamity were typically received as punishments, they were also the means by which God brought about repentance—considered to be essential for conversion. Of course, the analogy between bodily disease and spiritual infirmity is a commonplace in religious writing, but Protestant autobiographers saw sickness as a "particularly opportune occasion for setting repentance in motion" (Starr, 103). Similarly, calamity—whether a shipwreck, the loss of a loved one, a natural disaster, or a sudden outbreak of witchcraft—could be interpreted both as a punishment for an individual's or a community's refusal to accept God's call as well as a preparation for conversion. For spiritual autobiographers, God's wrath as well as His blessing could signal the operation of grace. In her spiritual autobiography, for instance, Anne Bradstreet tells her children, "If at any time you are chastened of God, take it as thankfully and joyfully as in greatest mercies, for if ye be His, ye shall reap the greatest benefit by it" (242).

In the conversion tradition, a consciousness of the suffering associated with wayfaring, warfare, calamity, and sickness became in effect a sign of divine favor because the physical and mental pain associated with affliction indicated that the individual was actively engaged in the struggle against sin and was therefore already singled out by God. Trapped in a discourse where the believer was at pains to discover the evidence of God's grace but at the same time afraid to rest on false hope, autobiographers like John Bunyan and Thomas Shepard filled their autobiographies with the agony of sinners in constant fear for their spiritual condition. Since spiritual struggle and the physical symptoms that often accompanied it themselves indicated God's interest in their lives, such authors grounded assurance on anxiety itself. For some, a pathological condition was actually desirable because Satan was believed to send his worst horrors to the most sanctified.[21]

20. Andrews, *Sisters of the Spirit*, 33. For a discussion of the Methodist doctrine of earthly "sanctification," see Andrews's introduction to the volume, 4, 14–15.

21. Noticing this tendency to celebrate the sickness of the soul, J. O. King has shown how Puritans often interpreted their lives in the context of the Renaissance discourse on melancholy, 13–36, 54–65.

Moreover, the anxiety associated with this struggle increased the closer the individual was to receiving grace, because Satan was believed to operate most fiercely when he was about to lose a soul. Typically, conversion occurred out of the depths of the greatest despair and after periods of greatest affliction. Robinson Crusoe, the best known example of a fictional spiritual autobiographer, experienced his most profound vision when he had reached the "nadir of both his physical and spiritual condition" (Hunter, 156). Augustine's conversion similarly came when his inner turmoil, which had been increasing throughout the narrative, became unbearable.

This tendency of the light to shine precisely at the moment of deepest darkness adds a sense of drama to conversion accounts, but it too operates in a theological framework. If conversion for Paul, Augustine, and the Reformers illustrates the sufficiency of God's grace alone, then personal efforts to achieve salvation will by necessity meet with increasing frustration. Only when hope is gone, when the believer acknowledges that grace is beyond human means, can God's full infusion take place. Though the authors of conversion accounts stress their inability to describe the actual moment of rapture, they typically present it as a process of submission. Conversion entails a losing of the self in the irresistible power of God's will. The despair that comes with the exhaustion of human effort logically precedes this submission, and the joy that accompanies conversion can in part be explained as a release from "the necessity to perform" (Weintraub, 32–34; Cohen, 71).

While the conversion accounts of some Methodists and other evangelicals follow the Augustinian pattern of focusing on a single decisive event, most spiritual autobiographies depart from this pattern. The Puritan autobiographer, particularly, operated in a discourse where an overconfident assertion of election might be interpreted as a sign of hypocrisy. Edmund Morgan states, "In order to be sure one must be unsure" (70). Because Puritans believed that the fight against temptation had to continue for a lifetime, they suspected that those who complacently believed in their own election might never have received grace in the first place. As a result, except in the most evangelical and antinomian traditions, conversion narratives record not a single moment of regeneration but a series of awakenings interspersed with periods of despair and melancholy. And since an unqualified statement of assurance may be a sign of hypocrisy, each description of a conversion experience is often subsequently undercut as the author lets the reader know that the struggle goes on.

Michael McGiffert has called this cyclic, multiple conversion pattern the "paradox of Puritan piety" (20), a sequence Caldwell calls "a seesaw of hope and despair" (121). This cycle dominates Puritan diaries and autobiographies. For instance, accounts like Bunyan's *Grace Abounding* and Edwards's *Personal Narrative* record numerous quasi-mystical experiences interspersed with periods of despondency. In *The Diary of Michael Wigglesworth* the pattern is compressed, often into single sentences. Any hint recorded by Wigglesworth of the presence of saving grace in his soul almost immediately triggers an assertion of his total sinfulness. In the following selection, from a single entry in his journal, the shift from assurance to despair and back again is dramatic:

> in the unfained desires of my soul, there is true conversion. . . . yea but my very sence of my need of him is daly decaying; ergo he will cast me off as a despizer. no but though I cannot prize christ nor redemption by him, nor maintain a good desire to him, yet he that uphold's all things by the word of his power hath undertaken to uphold me and his grace in me. (37)

A despairing awareness of sin leads to a perception of the workings of divine grace that must, in turn, be immediately qualified by a statement of Wigglesworth's corruption. Nicely captured in his echo of Mark's gospel, "Lord I do beleiv, help my unbeleif" (67), this potentially endless narrative cycle illustrates the extent to which Puritans incorporated the conversion process into their perception of the world. Since the reception of grace was essential to their sense of well-being, they saw their lives as being connected by a pattern of conversion and reconversion.

This "seesaw" process of hope and despair cultivated the anxiety that scholars have discovered in the writings of many Puritans. In the multiple-conversion pattern, conversion as a "sign" of grace is destabilized because it is usually not grounded in a single event or passage. Rather, the significance of each experience is deferred until subsequent events and experiences render it convincing. As the narratives continue, authors reinforce their interpretation of previous passages with later examples of mystical experience until they believe that they have convinced readers of the efficacy of their conversion. An unstable sense of salvation arises, but only in retrospect. For narrators, it was less important to define exactly when, where, and how they discovered their election than it was to establish that they participated in the anxiety-filled process of conversion, despair, and reconversion that cumulatively could be read as a sign of grace.

Protestant theologians have reconciled the anxiety-filled, multiple-conversion pattern with the more traditional Pauline and Augustinian framework by distinguishing between God's acts and his works. Effectual calling is a "work" of God, which can take place over an extended period and which may ultimately be a lifelong process. God's "acts," however, take place in single moments of time, and any number of them may be combined to effect a single "work" such as election (John Brown, 152). Because God's call can entail a number of repeatable "acts" of conversion, even those spiritual autobiographers limited by the "seesaw" discourse can chart a course from doubt to imperfect assurance. In *Grace Abounding*, for example, the process of sanctification is never complete and hypocrisy is always a danger, but the linguistic cycles of hope and despair have a cumulative effect. Initially they express true legal terror and small intimations of grace, but as the autobiography continues, they convey a more hopeful examination of God's conflicting messages and finally suggest fulfillment. The seesaw discourse itself is purgative.

An awareness of the operation of divine grace, whether occasioned by reflecting on a series of experiences or as the result of one specific awakening, colored the entire rhetoric of the conversion narrative and was enhanced and completed by the autobiographical act itself. Once the believer felt justified, he or she viewed conversion as an empowering life principle, an act that transformed and energized the self. Written from the perspective of grace, the author's past actions, whether good or evil, all became part of the overall life pilgrimage that led to conversion. Similarly, all events subsequent to conversion took their meaning from the enlightening process of justification. According to G. A. Starr, each section of a spiritual autobiography "not only precedes or follows conversion in point of time, but takes on significance wholly as a preparation or obstacle to it beforehand, or as a result or retrogression from it once achieved" (40). Thus conversion becomes the structural center of these narratives, makes "life a meaningful story," and introduces "an ordering principle that makes coherent relation possible" (Minter, 69–77). In either the single- or the multiple-conversion pattern, the overall figuration of self is based on this "before and after" logic. The subject is fundamentally altered, but still rooted in his or her "sinful" history. In this sense, identity in the traditional conversion narrative is presented in what Hayden White would call a "metaphorical" equation. The new self is linked to the old self—it is reborn but not re-created.

Another typical consequence of conversion was that it altered the believer's perception of the world. A sense of newness and beauty ener-vated objects, and the believer, at least temporarily, felt that he or she was viewing nature for the first time. This phenomenon is particularly charac-teristic of evangelical accounts. For example, after Jonathan Edwards received grace, he recorded a change in perception almost Wordsworthian in its intensity:

> After this my sense of divine things gradually increased, and became more and more lively, and had more of that inward sweet-ness. The appearance of every thing was altered; there seemed to be, as it were, a calm, sweet cast, or appearance of divine glory, in almost every thing. God's excellency, his wisdom, his purity and love, seemed to appear in every thing; in the sun, moon, and stars; in the clouds, and blue sky; in the grass, flowers, trees; in the water, and all nature; which used greatly to fix my mind. (60–61)

In 1903, E. D. Starbuck, a student of William James, noticed the same phenomenon in his empirical study of conversion entitled *The Psychology of Religion.* Analyzing the personal accounts of almost two hundred believers, Starbuck found a *"sense of newness"* to be one of the most common consequences of conversion (118–20).

The authors of conversion literature justified their autobiographical endeavors because they assumed that all of the faithful could benefit from the knowledge of one person's life: a single life was significant because it manifested universal patterns of experience. Though the Reformation spurred an increasing fragmentation of religious authority, when minor doctrinal conflicts caused major schisms and when religious groups gath-ered around political and national issues, conversion was nevertheless viewed as a universal human phenomenon in part because the self as a cultural and literary construct from the classical age to the Renaissance rested on the belief in a common human nature (Misch, 45). Differences between sects were often so great that they considered each other to represent the Antichrist, but all Protestant groups shared a veneration for the scriptural tradition that presented revelation in a highly conventional discourse. Spiritual autobiographers, regardless of their religious affiliation, justified their narratives by reference to it. In her autobiography of 1846, for example, Zilpha Elaw anticipates the work of William James by going so far as to argue that the commonality of the conversion experience establishes its validity:

> The vast variety of mental exercises and religious experiences of all true and lively Christians, in every grade of society, in all ages, and in all denominations and sections of the Christian Church, are of too uniform and definite a character to be ascribed to the wild and fluctuating uncertainties of fanaticism: so widely spread an uniformity as that which exists in the genuine pilgrim's progress of Christian experience, can never be philosophically shewn to be an attribute of fanaticism; an uniformity, like that of the human constitution, admitting of the greatest variety of individual features, yet all governed by the same laws. (Andrews, *Sisters*, 73)

Even after cultural notions of a common human nature had been challenged by post-Enlightenment thought, authors like Elaw still assumed that conversion was a "natural" human phenomenon.

Though ground-breaking historians such as William Haller and Perry Miller have linked the intense self-examination found in seventeenth- and eighteenth-century autobiographical writing with increased individualism, the high degree of formulaic similarity in Protestant writing indicates that the presentation of a unique self was not a high priority among spiritual autobiographers.[22] Puritan individualism, in a sense, was based on a paradox: believers examined themselves for evidence of their election to the extent that they became obsessively concerned with even the most minute particulars of their daily lives, but they also believed that insofar as God chose whom he wished for election, the worldly characteristics that distinguished one person from another were completely irrelevant. No personal experience was insignificant as a sign of the individual's spiritual condition, but all hoped to find the same *microchristus* at the source of their identities. The goal of every Puritan was, therefore, not to discover his or her own uniqueness but to deny the self in the face of God's irresistible will (Bercovitch, 8–11).

22. Haller argues that Protestants stressed individualism based primarily on individual interpretation of the Scriptures, *Rise of Puritanism*, 239, 247–49, 299. Paul Delany, however, maintains that individual interpretation functioned in theory only. Religious leaders actually controlled the interpretation of the Word to such a degree that Protestant self-writing was highly conventional. In fact, Delany argues that the more radical the sect, the more its autobiographers conformed to approved models. See *British Autobiography in the Seventeenth Century*, 66, 160.

Because spiritual autobiographies presupposed the universality of the conversion experience and because they used highly conventional language to render that experience, the protagonists of these narratives took on mythic dimensions. Haller writes that Puritan preachers "hit upon a way to exemplify the working of the [conversion] formula by individualizing the soul to which it applied; that is, they transposed the theory into spiritual biography or a sort of spiritual case history" (141–42). By charting the progress of an individual's soul, ministers created a symbolic narrative that applied to all believers. In interpreting their lives according to the conventions of this rhetoric, spiritual autobiographers similarly adhered to a highly structured worldview and became members of a community of visible saints. If the individual was thought to manifest the experience and values of all Christians, then, conversely, a single believer could represent the entire community. Bercovitch has maintained that this tendency to depict the life of an individual, to make that individual representative, and then to fuse the individual into a national or communal whole is distinctively American, but this transference is, potentially at least, built into the flexible structure of the conversion process itself.

In interrelating the life of the individual and the life of the community, conversion accounts—from Augustine to Bunyan and beyond—have traditionally served a socializing function. Because conversion often takes place in the context of a specific worshiping community, in many cases the rendering of a conversion account amounted to an initiation ritual. The New England practice of delivering an account of conversion as a test of church membership is only a particularly visible example of a larger pattern. Since many Protestant groups in theory strove to admit only the elect, and since conversion was the paramount evidence of election, the act of testifying to a conversion experience—whether in the form of a private conference with a church elder, an oral narrative, a full-length spiritual autobiography, a diary, or even in a private conversation among friends—signified one's inclusion in the body of the elect. On a universal level, of course, the converted became citizens of the City of God, bound together by their love for him; on the local level, they ratified their position in the community. In this sense, using conversion discourse in a narrative of the self marks a "will to power."

A good example of this socializing movement can be found in Bunyan's *Grace Abounding*. Scholars believe that this text, like many extant American conversion narratives, was a reworking of the account Bunyan delivered at his Bedford church in order to become a full member of the congregation

(Sharrock, 35). Bunyan celebrated his inclusion in God's community near the end of his autobiography by shifting the narrative perspective from the first person singular to the first person plural. After saying Christ's "Righteousness was mine, his Merits mine, his Victory also mine," Bunyan fuses his faith experience with that of all the regenerate:

> Now I saw Christ Jesus was looked on of God, and should also be looked on by us as that common or publick person, in whom all the whole Body of his Elect are always to be considered and reckoned, that we fulfilled the Law by him, rose from the dead by him, got the Victory over sin, death, the devil, and hell, by him: when he died we died; and so of his Resurrection. (73)

Through the "publick" nature of Christ's redemption, Bunyan's story becomes the story of all Christians. For the authors of conversion accounts, then, the autobiographical impulse was more than a means of "self"-justification. In conforming to certain linguistic, theological, and behavioral expectations, they not only empowered their autobiographical acts, they also bound themselves to a community of believers who stood in a privileged position to those outside it.

The socializing function of conversion literature can be seen particularly in its emphasis on vocation. For orthodox Protestants, a divine calling, in effect, was a command and had two aspects. God proclaimed not only a "general calling" to all who must labor in the building of His church, but also a "particular calling," which individual Christians heeded by assiduously performing their daily work (Perkins 1:753). Working industriously and successfully became associated with the moral rigor of the sanctified. Thus in many journals, biographies, and autobiographies, the sinner, in working out a relationship with God, also found a social role. In secular terms, this new spiritual direction was often accompanied by the acceptance of a trade or profession. Defoe's *Robinson Crusoe* stands as a particularly vivid example of the way conversion rhetoric could be used to outline the specific relationship between the individual's general calling and his or her daily work. Max Weber has most famously made the connection between the role of work and the individual's pursuit of salvation (79–128), a connection so strong that scholars such as Michael Walzer see it as building the legal and sociological foundation for radical politics (212–19, 259).

Given the importance of the Word in Reformed thought, it is not surprising that the ministry became the occupation chosen by a majority of male spiritual autobiographers (Delany, 17). Because Protestants—like Augustine—believed that the infusion of grace brought with it an understanding of experience as well as the gift of expression, the acceptance of a role of preacher for males (and for some women) was an appropriate conclusion to a conversion account. Bunyan again provides a fitting example:

> For after I had been about five or six years awakened, and helped my self to see both the want and worth of Jesus Christ . . . some of the most able among the Saints with us . . . did perceive that God had counted me worthy to understand something of his Will in his holy and blessed word, and had given me utterance in some measure to express, what I saw, to others for edification. (83)

Even the nineteenth-century autobiography of Jarena Lee encodes the same relationship between grace, expression, and vocation central to the dynamics of Bunyan's narrative:

> That day was the first when my heart had believed, and my tongue had made confession unto salvation—the first words uttered, a part of that song, which shall fill eternity with its sound, was *glory to God*. For a few moments I had power to exhort sinners, and to tell of the wonders and of the goodness of him who had clothed me with *his* salvation. (Andrews, *Sisters*, 29)

In describing their own conversion and the call to public testimony that accompanied it, Protestants validated their social roles by placing themselves in the company of such religious leaders as the Old Testament prophets, Paul, Augustine, and numerous other bearers of the Word. Despite the great differences between Augustine's *Confessions* and the conversion narratives of Bunyan and Lee, each stresses the connection between biography, knowledge, and expression that Spengemann finds to be descriptive of the whole history of autobiographical writing.

A number of theorists of autobiography have followed Roy Pascal in dismissing (if not excluding) from the genre those works that focus on the experience of conversion. Pascal argues that autobiography represents the self in and through its relation with the outer world: "Autobiographies that are so engrossed with the inner life that the outer world becomes blurred

. . . fail to realise the potentialities of the genre" (9). Daniel Shea similarly states that the American spiritual relations delivered by prospective church members "hardly deserve to be considered as autobiography," because the "autobiographical act is reduced to testifying that one's experience has conformed with allowable variations, to a certain pattern of feeling and behavior" (91). These critics and others like them find that many conversion narratives fail to establish a viable dialectic between the self and the world, primarily because of their tendency to conform "sometimes slavishly" to models. But the high degree of formulaic similarity displayed by conversion literature in itself reveals an intimate relationship between the self and the world. Narratives based on conversion recount an inner struggle, but that struggle when brought to a satisfactory conclusion had profound implications for the external life of the spiritual autobiographer. Part of this moving outward, captured so well in the conversion framework, was the mastery of the rhetorical tropes and structures that themselves signified one's privileged position, not only in a divine community but in an earthly one as well. The very conformity found in spiritual autobiographies illustrates the way conversion rhetoric was a means by which Christians recorded their particular relationship to a larger culture.

2

. . .

DIVIDING THE WORD

Jean-Jacques Rousseau and the Consequences of Secularization

The practice of requiring the delivery of a conversion narrative in order to qualify for full church membership in seventeenth-century New England represents a dramatic moment in the history of autobiography. Because these narratives were developed and widely used in Puritan America, some critics claim that they contributed to the beginnings of our national literature.[1] But if literary historians attach much importance to this temporary practice in New England, there is irony too in that the spiritual autobiography achieved a higher visibility in the British literary canon than it did in America. America's eighteenth- and nineteenth-century secular writers were likely to have been more familiar with books like Bunyan's *Grace Abounding* and Defoe's *Robinson Crusoe* than they were with the spiritual autobiographies of American Puritans.[2] Much of this can be explained by the fact that the seventeenth-century American conversion narratives, unlike some of their British counterparts, were not published until the twentieth century (Cohen, 214 n. 47). Given the greater visibility of the

1. J. O. King, *The Iron of Melancholy*, 43. See also Patricia Caldwell, *The Puritan Conversion Narrative*, 121. Sacvan Bercovitch has argued that the whole tradition of self-writing by New England Puritans displays a conflation of individual and national ideals not found among the writings of their English counterparts, *Puritan Origins of the American Self*, 136 and elsewhere. Drawing upon Bercovitch's findings, G. Thomas Couser finds that this merging of individual and communal values in New England Puritan culture gave rise to a "prophetic mode," which he sees as dominating American autobiographical writing to the present, *American Autobiography*, 1–9.

2. On the popularity of Bunyan's works in America, see David E. Smith, "Publication of John Bunyan's Works in America"; and on the popularity of *Robinson Crusoe*, see Jay Fliegelman, *Prodigals and Pilgrims*, 39, 67–79.

spiritual autobiography in Great Britain, it is not surprising that secular variations of the form, which appeared in the eighteenth and nineteenth centuries, were more widespread there then they were in America. The use of the form was particularly common among nineteenth-century male autobiographers.

Since the spiritual autobiography occupied such a visible position in the European tradition of self-writing, I believe that any analysis of the form by twentieth-century Americans needs to be grounded on its secularization both here and abroad. The appropriation of conversion discourse to the construction of a secular self made possible an inexhaustible number of rhetorical possibilities, and such appropriations were widespread in the Romantic and Victorian periods. My purpose in this chapter is not to map all of these possibilities but to chronicle some of the major ways writers adapted the conversion framework to self-writing; in so doing I hope to provide a literary context for the radical revision of its use by the authors I study in subsequent chapters.

ROUSSEAU AND THE METONYMIC SELF

A number of scholars have followed Wayne Shumaker in asserting that by the end of the eighteenth century autobiographies began increasingly to stress the uniqueness of the individual. According to Shumaker, this tendency was brought about by the gradual substitution of inductive for deductive modes of thought and by the development of the scientific method. Such changes in cultural perceptions gave rise to a "historical" consciousness that drew concepts of the self away from universal values and that saw individual actions as being significant. Belief in the efficacy of the human will, which led to the *res gestae* autobiographies of classical and medieval times, was replaced by a deterministic worldview central to the modern developmental autobiography (52–55, 90). This Enlightenment shift in modes of thinking contributed to the secularization of religious values and literary conventions, a process that accelerated in the Romantic and Victorian periods.

The conversion pattern was one such motif that was adapted to the changing forms and interests in autobiography. To be sure, traditional spiritual autobiographies continued to be written in the late eighteenth and nineteenth centuries, yet the increased interest in the individual began to dominate secular autobiographies of the period. While the authors of Christian narratives resolved the paradox between self-scrutiny and self-abandonment by adhering to the widely accepted conventions of receiving grace, secular autobiographers began to revise conversion discourse to emphasize their individuality.[3]

As some scholars have noted, the post-Enlightenment focus on individuality was actually fostered in part by the Protestant emphasis on self-inspection. Textual evidence of such values can be found in the period of turmoil preceding conversion in the typical spiritual autobiography. If conversion traditionally entailed a losing of the self to the power of God's will, then the act of complete submission imperiled the "prior" self as it had existed. John Morris finds that those Methodist autobiographers who dwell on the period of melancholy that precedes conversion proclaim their integrity by refusing to submit "to the sanctions of a religion that in its inclusiveness promises—or, as it appears to the self, threatens—salvation at the price of identity." The Methodists Morris describes finally accepted grace, of course, but the personal conflict that preceded this submission constituted a "last-ditch stand of the ego" (139). Later secular autobiographers who believed their personal identity to be of supreme value would subvert conversion discourse altogether.

Another response to the conflict between religious acculturation and personal uniqueness was to individualize the conversion process itself. Revelation became, not a universal human experience that bound all the elect into a common body, but a particular manifestation of spiritual energy that applied to a single individual only. Thomas Paine took this approach near the end of the eighteenth century: "Admitting, for the sake of a case, that something has been revealed to a certain person, and not revealed to any other person, it is revelation to that person only . . . and *hearsay* to every other, and consequently they are not obliged to believe it" (23–24). Though Paine distrusted the notion of divine communication altogether, he argued that even if it purportedly affected the behavior of certain individuals, it contained no universal significance. Less of a skeptic, William Blake—an admirer and acquaintance of Paine's—made personal revelation a major construct in his poetry. Different as they are, the approaches of writers such as Paine and Blake signal a major restructuring of the

---

3. Linda Peterson suggests that the secularization of the spiritual autobiography form may be understood in the terms of Harold Bloom's theory of the "anxiety of influence," *Victorian Autobiography*, 17–18. This "anxiety" increased dramatically with the secularization of conversion discourse.

discourse: far from entailing a loss of identity, conversion discourse was being used to reinforce the autobiographer's sense of uniqueness.

These individualized variations of the conversion pattern in secular writing led to a loss of precision in the figurative language once used in an entirely religious context (Fleishman, 113–18). Tropes and motifs that functioned very specifically in a well-defined theological framework were now employed to express modes of thought and patterns of behavior widely divergent. While conversion continued to be viewed as an experiential reality by Christians, others began to see its utility as a metaphor for any radical change or new insight. Many nineteenth-century autobiographers used conversion to represent the acceptance of a belief system and to outline the cognitive, expressive, and social consequences of that act. In this sense, the degree to which an autobiographer followed the conversion pattern illustrates the extent to which he or she was willing to embrace a specific set of values. Since conversion discourse had traditionally inscribed a process of socialization, it can be "read" as a particularly appropriate index of the relationship between an individual and a larger culture: those who wished to define themselves in the context of an intellectual, social, or ideological system—however personal—could employ the conventions of the successful spiritual autobiography; those who wished to define themselves in opposition to such a system could subvert those conventions.

Jean-Jacques Rousseau startlingly adapted conversion rhetoric both ways in his *Confessions,* an early secular version of the spiritual autobiography. Huntington Williams notes that in a draft of the book's introduction, Rousseau paradoxically asserts that his work will be both "unique et utile" (122–26). Though Rousseau altered his phrasing in the final version, this paradox still informs the opening section. On the one hand, Rousseau asserts the uniqueness of both his autobiographical project and of himself:

> I have resolved on an enterprise which has no precedent, and which, once complete, will have no imitator. . . . I am made unlike anyone I have ever met; I will even venture to say that I am like no one in the whole world. I may be no better, but at least I am different. (17)

But on the other hand, in inviting others to compare themselves to him, he deliberately sets himself up as a useful model of sincerity and goodness. Addressing God, he states:

> Let the numberless legion of my fellow men gather round me, and hear my confessions. Let them groan at my depravities, and blush for my misdeeds. But let each one of them reveal his heart at the foot of Thy throne with equal sincerity, and may any man who dares, say "I was a better man than he." (17)

This paradox of uniqueness and utility, which dominates the structure of the *Confessions,* parallels the paradox between individuality and universality that lies at the heart of the spiritual autobiography tradition. Unable to reconcile his roles as unique individual and exemplary human, Rousseau uses conversion rhetoric to define both parts of his psyche.

Rousseau described his entry into public life as being the direct result of a dramatic Pauline experience on the road to Vincennes. This "conversion" occurred after he read in the *Mercure de France* about an essay contest, sponsored by the Dijon Academy. Once he grasped the implication of the academy's question, "Has the progress of the sciences and arts done more to corrupt morals or improve them?" Rousseau suddenly beheld "another universe" and became "another man." He states, "My feelings rose with the most inconceivable rapidity to the level of my ideas. All my little passions were stifled by an enthusiasm for truth, liberty, and virtue" (327–28). Transformed, Rousseau claimed he gained "a self assurance which owed its fullness to its simplicity and which dwelt in my soul rather than in my outward being" (388). This awakening completely altered his life and fostered a sudden eloquence, a "celestial fire," which spread to his early books and made him bold where he had once been meek.

Rousseau's occasion of reading about the essay contest and his subsequent conversion may in part be a parody of Augustine's dramatic use of the *sortes* convention, but his experience, like Paul's and Augustine's before him, was traditional in the sense that it led to increased knowledge, heightened powers of expression, and a specific social role. Rousseau insists, however, that this awakening, which established him as a Parisian *philosophe,* was temporary. Lasting only five or six years and drawing him away from his "natural" self, it caused all his subsequent misfortune: "No state of being could be found on earth," he proclaims, "more contrary to my true nature than this one" (388). While Protestant autobiographers used conversion rhetoric to inscribe their inclusion in an earthly and divine community, Rousseau employed it to describe how he was falsely socialized into a community bent on betraying him. Yet he also knew that this public, iconoclastic role, as champion of the rights of truth, liberty, and virtue, was the source of his fame; despite his social paranoia, he affirms these values and believes them to be worth imitating.

At the same time, however, Rousseau employed conversion rhetoric to construct his version of a solitary, "true" self, which was most fully realized when he wandered alone in Nature, his Enlightenment version of a transcendent deity. The language he employed to describe his repeated quasi-mystical reveries, in which he throws himself "into the vastness of things" (158), resembles that used by Christians to describe conversion. These reveries, which gave him his greatest—though temporary—feelings of happiness and self-worth, provided insight into the beauty of a natural existence and inspired his literary and musical undertakings. Rather than leading to a sense of community, however, they reinforced his sense of uniqueness and isolation. If the converted Christian became a member of a community of believers, Rousseau's reveries in Nature caused him to discover that the true self can only be found away from other human beings.

By juxtaposing two different versions of the conversion experience, Rousseau presented a "divided self" that in part explained (and justified) his often contradictory actions. In so doing, he also identified two ways of responding to the conventions of the spiritual autobiography. The first of these—that associated with his becoming a *philosophe*—is consistent with the socializing function of the traditional conversion narrative. The second of these—that associated with his solitary communing in Nature—amounts to an antisocialization. Since Rousseau says that this second self is the "true" self, one may infer that he was more interested in subverting the conventions of the tradition than in embracing them. But he undercut the authority of conversion rhetoric in both senses. Today, it is easy to overlook the blasphemy—indeed the violence—of Rousseau's subversion, which paved the way for a purely secular use of the spiritual autobiography form. For Augustine, God was the only source of grace, who in a radical act of transformation gave meaning and value to an individual's life. For Rousseau, conversion, though an experiential reality, had variable consequences. It could change one's ideas, define one's personality, merge one with a community, or draw one into isolation. Less than an absolute good, conversion simply became a means by which one perceived the world.

Huntington Williams finds that the privileging of personal identity that informs Rousseau's *Confessions* and that "underlies virtually all modern autobiographies" shifts attention away from transcendent sources of inspiration to the "interaction between men and their secular fictions." He states, "If God underwrites individual existence for the Christian autobiographer, personal identity in modern autobiography is thought to be 'natural' " (3). This loss of autobiographical sanction profoundly affected the act of authorship. Augustine, who addressed his narrative to God, needed to look no further than his dramatic experience at Milan to justify both his life and his autobiographical enterprise; Rousseau, however, who addressed his fellow humans, had only his rhetorical skills on which to ground his self-justification. To assert his personal sense of worth, he was forced to individualize the conversion pattern.

This internalization of transcendent values, a process already rooted in Christian theology, occurred widely in the Romantic period, "a time," Geoffrey Hartman writes, "when art frees itself from its subordination to religion or religiously inspired myth" (52). With the shift from a supernatural to a natural frame of reference, joined by the widespread disillusionment in political reform brought about by the violence of the French Revolution, Romantic writers increasingly based their hopes for a new heaven and earth on the transforming powers of consciousness itself (Abrams, 180–82). Redemption for them was conceived as a transformation of epistemological and cognitive processes. What they found in many ways recapitulated Christian redemption in philosophical terms, but because these writers could refer their autobiographical projects to no universally accepted authority, they presented individual variations of their respective pilgrimages. Taking the responsibility for their own narratives stimulated autobiographers to see their work aesthetically. "Justification" in a self-portrait depended not on the external imposition of grace but on the ability to fashion a text. This transformation could be both liberating and anxiety producing because secular autobiographers were confronted, as Paul Jay states, "with the freedom of poetic creation" but also "the abyss of endless figuration" (57).

Rousseau's use of conversion discourse to define opposing sides of his personality signals a dramatic shift in the way the self was constructed in the spiritual autobiography. Rather than the metaphorical equation of the traditional conversion narrative between the "sinful" and "saved" self, Rousseau presents a shifting sense of identity. If analyzed according to Hayden White's categories of historical discourse, Rousseau's autobiographical subject can be said to be grounded on the trope of metonymy, which White defines as

> the reduction of the whole to the part [which] presupposes the possibility of distinguishing between the whole and the parts com-

prising it, but in such a way as to assign priority to parts. . . . [It] is characterized by an apprehension of the historical field as a complex of part-part relationships and by the effort to comprehend that field in terms of the laws that bind one phenomenon to another as a cause to an effect. (72–73)

From the standpoint of this study, then, Rousseau's splitting of the subject through the use of conversion rhetoric may stand for the multiplicity of selves (and the parts of selves) now possible for those who defined themselves through the rhetoric of conversion.

THE COLLAPSING CIRCLE

If Rousseau inscribed a shifting sense of identity in the *Confessions*, other Romantic writers conceived of the self in what M. H. Abrams has called a "circuitous journey" of innocence, loss, and then recovery on a higher level (113–14, 179–87). One of Abrams's best examples of this circuitous journey in autobiographical form is Wordsworth's *Prelude*. Like the *Confessions* of Rousseau, the *Prelude* traces its subject's development through a series of conversion-like experiences. The depiction of these "conversions," however, changes markedly over the course of the narrative. When Wordsworth captures the transcendent awareness of Nature he experienced as a youth, he uses a language derived in part from evangelical Christianity:

> Oft in those moments such a holy calm
> Would overspread my soul, that bodily eyes
> Were utterly forgotten, and what I saw
> Appeared like something in myself, a dream
> A prospect in the mind . . . (2:349–53)

He experienced these moments of union less frequently when, as a young man, he became separated from Nature, particularly as a result of his spiritual crisis, "the soul's last and lowest ebb" (11:307), associated with the French Revolution.[4] As the poem progresses, however, the process of

---

4. I quote from the 1850 edition of *The Fourteen-Book Prelude* as it appears in the Cornell University Press edition, ed. W.J.B. Owen.

self-recovery enabled him to redefine his former experiences as "spots of time." These passages are vividly rich, concrete memories that he distinguished from the vast and vague imaginings he had known "too forcibly, too early" in his youth. While he conveyed his early visitations as if they arose from an external source, Wordsworth makes it clear that the power that informs the spots of time comes "from thyself" (12:275). The salvation he records originates in his own consciousness and amounts to a reintegration of his present and former selves, made possible by his remembering the intimations of poetic greatness he felt as a child. Like the assurance of the spiritual autobiographer, Wordsworth's recovery in the *Prelude* was fully realized only in the composing process itself.

But if the text presupposes a controlling presence able to integrate the various stages in the life of a poet, the text's subject still reflects a metonymic construction: the "natural" youth able to intuit the power and wholeness beyond the world of appearance, the "fallen" young man seduced by analytic thinking, and the mature "poet" who has returned to, yet risen beyond, his childhood vision. The focus is on different "parts" of the self and the relationships between them.

Like other Romantic writers, Wordsworth revised conversion discourse to emphasize his uniqueness, but his adoption was conventional in the sense that the narrative moves from a personal crisis toward the value of community. The *Prelude* thus conforms to the socializing function of the traditional spiritual autobiography by illustrating the relationship between the protagonist and his world. The poem not only validates Wordsworth's vocation as a poet/prophet, it also details his increasing appreciation of other human beings. While Rousseau defines his "true" self in the context of his solitary rambles in Nature, Wordsworth, who began his narrative with reveries similar to those found in the *Confessions*, describes how his love for Nature led to a love for humankind, a love movingly communicated by his tribute to Dorothy, whose companionship helped him out of his crisis.

When other Romantic writers turned toward autobiography, they grounded themselves on the same "circular" trope as found in the *Prelude*. But since many of them did not share Wordsworth's vision of wholeness, their "circles" of identity were not conceived as ascending spirals that transported the subject to different levels of consciousness. Rather, they presented circular journeys that explored the possibilities of redemption but returned their subjects to the same shores of self. One such writer was Thomas DeQuincey. If Wordsworth preserved the sacred tone and the successful outcome of the Protestant spiritual autobiography, Thomas DeQuincey subverted those conventions, even as he employed Words-worthian categories.[5] In the *Confessions of an English Opium Eater*, opium—"the true hero of the tale"—takes the place of God in a purely secular history of drug addiction. As this substitution suggests, the *Confessions* parodied the enthusiasm of the evangelical autobiographies still being written in the nineteenth century, but in so doing, of course, it necessarily relied on their motifs and structures.

In the beginning of the narrative, DeQuincey presents an autobiographical persona encountering the hardships of his early life. Though these events do not deal directly with his addiction, they set up the pattern of wandering, physical affliction, and melancholy frequently found in conversion rhetoric. Out of the depths of this despair, DeQuincey discovered opium, an event conveyed with the exaggerated rapture of an evangelical conversion. Feeling a "mystic importance" attached to his first purchase of the drug, DeQuincey called the apothecary who sold it to him "an unconscious minister of celestial pleasures . . . sent down to earth on a special mission to myself." Once he took the laudanum, his life and spirit, like those of the reborn Christian, were radically transformed:

> oh! heavens! what a revulsion! what an upheaving, from its lowest depths, of the inner spirit! what an apocalypse of the world within me! That my pains had vanished, was now a trifle in my eyes:—this negative effect was swallowed up in the immensity of those positive effects which had opened up before me—in the abyss of divine enjoyment thus suddenly revealed. (70–71)

In achieving its spiritual upheaval, opium introduced among DeQuincey's mental faculties "the most exquisite order, legislation, and harmony," which invigorated the self and gave rise to the impulses of a heart "originally just and good" (73–74). His presentation of the doctrines "of the true church on the subject of opium" almost exactly parallels the cognitive benefits of a spiritual revelation. Just as conversion for Christians led to increased knowledge and a renewed sense of life's meaning, opium enhanced DeQuincey's mind and ordered his wayward existence.

Initially DeQuincey's opium experience kindled the same socializing

5. The *Prelude*, of course, was not published until 1850, so DeQuincey could not have been responding to it directly when he wrote the *Confessions*. For a summary of Wordsworth's general influence on DeQuincey, see Jerome Hamilton Buckley, *The Turning Key*, 63.

impulse that Wordsworth described in the *Prelude*. In a drug-induced yearning for companionship, DeQuincey liked to mingle with the London poor with whom he felt a benevolent, though somewhat distanced, affinity. Yet he quickly admitted that in the "divinest states of enjoyment" the opium eater shuns crowds and naturally seeks solitude and silence. As "The Pleasures of Opium" closes, DeQuincey stands aloof and alone, transforming the sorrows of a congested, industrialized Liverpool into a vision of "halcyon calm." Opium, finally, caused a sense not of fellowship and community but of isolation and apathy. Thus, DeQuincey's chemical awakenings are more akin to Rousseau's solitary reveries with Nature than to Wordsworth's spots of time. He too undercut the socializing function of the conversion process to distance himself from communal values.

DeQuincey further subverted the conventions of the spiritual autobiography in "The Pains of Opium" by making opium—initially the means of his achieving harmony—the cause of his subsequent collapse. Here the *Confessions* returns to the pattern of affliction and indecision with which it began. While opium had once ordered DeQuincey's thought, now massive doses of the drug prevent him from coherently shaping his narrative. He becomes unable to pursue his "vocation" of exercising the "analytic understanding" and fears that his great philosophical work will stand as a memorial to defeated hopes (99). Obsessed by fantastic dreams, the product of a disordered and guilt-ridden intellect, he falls into a "suicidal despondency" and experiences a confused apocalyptic nightmare. After this crisis, the text ends with a calm discussion of the narrator's partial victory over opium; however, this sequence is not expressed in the terms of religious conversion. He achieved a physical regeneration of sorts, but he acknowledged that it was no apocalypse of the self but a gradual, pain-filled process. His anxieties, however, were far from over: still taking twelve grains of opium a day and still haunted by dreams, he continued to fear the drug's wrath.

By substituting opium for divine authority, DeQuincey did more than parody evangelical conversion accounts and highlight their textuality. The subdued ending of the *Confessions* also reveals his belief that any encompassing revelation, regardless of its origin, is more to be feared than embraced. For him, all modes of perceiving reality that depend on a sudden and radical change in thinking are suspect. Though—like the *Prelude*—a study of consciousness, the *Confessions* is as much a response to Wordsworth as to Bunyan, critiquing not only the rigid assurance of the elect but any transcendent notion of the perceptual process.

Like the narrator of Wordsworth's *Prelude*, DeQuincey's autobiographical subject can be divided into parts that are assembled in a circular pattern: the unhappy but sober youth, the young man who falls for an artificial notion of redemption, and the recovering addict who regains a degree of sobriety. Readers are confronted with a wiser and more reflective man at the end. Yet his "recovery," unlike Wordsworth's, is neither complete nor transcendent. While there is progress, there is no unifying vision, and the idea of salvation—whether physical, spiritual, or cognitive— is dramatically subverted. Other Romantic autobiographies take a similar approach; some collapse the circle even further. Instead of a progressive spiral, they inscribe a closed circuit, and present selves trapped by their own patterns of thought.

One such text is Melville's *Typee*. Though more fiction than fact, *Typee* was written and marketed as an autobiography, and it represents a rare secular use of the full conversion framework in the period of "classic" American literature. The book's protagonist, who calls himself "Tommo," resembles several of Melville's seafaring *isolatoes*. At the onset of the narrative, readers learn very little about his background, save that he is a wanderer in search of experience, who wishes to escape from the severe discipline on the *Dolly*. When he and a friend jump ship in the South Seas onto the beautiful island of Nukuheva, however, their troubles are far from over. After fleeing into a thick "wilderness," Tommo mysteriously injures his leg and encounters a series of calamities while lost in the island jungle. His aimless, pain-filled wandering evokes a whole set of typological meanings. According to the conventions of the spiritual autobiography, his predicament could be interpreted as being both a punishment for sin and a sign of God's interest, a preparation for conversion.

Tommo's physical and mental suffering reaches a crisis after he loses contact with his friend and is captured by the cannibalistic Typees. "Consumed by the most dismal forebodings" and "a prey to the profoundest melancholy" (118), he feels trapped by the natives, a problem worsened by the fact that his leg hurts him so much he is all but crippled. Immobile in an alien environment, he loses any hope of escape or recovery. In the midst of his physical and mental suffering, however, Tommo inexplicably undergoes a period of apathy that coincides with a deliverance from his physical affliction:

> Gradually I lost all knowledge of the regular recurrence of the days
> of the week, and sunk insensibly into that kind of apathy which

ensues after some violent outbreak of despair. My limb suddenly healed, the swelling went down, the pain subsided, and I had every reason to suppose I should soon completely recover from the affliction that had so long tormented me. (123)

Immediately after describing this "cure," Tommo goes on to state that his spirits have suddenly, almost miraculously, revived:

I began to experience an elasticity of mind which placed me beyond the reach of those dismal forebodings to which I had so lately been a prey. Received wherever I went with the most deferential kindness . . . I thought that for a sojourn among cannibals, no man could have well made a more agreeable one. (123)

Suddenly reconciled to life in Typee valley, Tommo declares, "Returning health and peace of mind gave a new interest to everything around me" (131). Like a Christian conversion, Tommo's experience gives rise to a radical change in perspective—a more accepting attitude toward his place in the world.

After his "conversion" Tommo starts to roam the valley. He becomes fascinated by the customs of the islanders and begins to participate in their activities. He relates in detail how they prepare food, build shelters, and produce clothing. He describes their religious rituals, saying, "I loved to yield myself up to the fanciful superstition of the islanders" (173). To the natives' great pleasure, he even adopts their style of dress. He also becomes somewhat familiar with their language and conforms to a Crusoe-like daily schedule patterned on the life-style of the valley. In short, Tommo becomes socialized: "In Typee," he proclaims, "I made a point of doing as the Typees did" (209). Tommo's socialization follows the logic of the traditional conversion narrative. As a convert to the Typee way of life, he not only becomes partly integrated into their society, he also expounds its virtues. By attacking the social disruption caused by Christian missionaries, he accepts a South Seas "calling" and preaches the benefits of a natural existence. Tommo, who began his account by saying that he was a born wanderer, has undergone a radical personality change: once unable to accept the constrictions of seaboard society, he now adopts an evangelical fervor on behalf of Typee culture. Once again, there is a clear relationship between biography, knowledge, and expression.

Tommo's fervid defense of the Typee community is based on a newfound awareness that all people share fundamental human characteristics. During the course of his ramblings, he comes to believe that family life, sexual roles, religious customs, and social practices on the island are remarkably similar to those in the West. Once "converted," he states that the Typees live by

> an inherent principle of honesty and charity towards each other. They seemed to be governed by that sort of tacit common-sense law which, say what they will of the inborn lawlessness of the human race, has its precepts graven on every breast. The grand principles of virtue and honor, however they may be distorted by arbitrary codes, are the same all the world over. (201)

By experiencing a culture completely alien, yet somehow remarkably similar, to his own, Tommo appears to have discovered the basis of a "natural" egalitarianism.

Tommo's spiritual "gift" in the valley had been an ability to transcend his own cultural perspective and to see value in all cultures. His discovery of a common humanity, however, is closely followed by a perception that all societies use coercion. Socialization carries a price, a price Tommo—despite his temporary conversion—finds to be too great. Sensing the danger of assimilation, he begins not only to distance himself from the natives but also to subvert the autobiographical conventions he once employed. When Tommo sees that Typee culture not only mirrors the benefits of Western civilization but also reflects its rigidity and incomprehensibility, his humanistic fervor is replaced by distrust and anxiety. Once reveling in the role of egalitarian ethnologist, he begins to find the Typees' language impossible to master, their religion mysterious, and their nature deceptive.

Tommo "falls away" from his vision of social union because, as an outsider, he at first failed to realize the restrictions all societies impose. The more he becomes acculturated, the more he sees that even the seemingly undemanding Typee society is subject to arbitrary rules and social distinctions. Nowhere are these restrictions more evident than in the islanders' use of the taboo. Though he had initially praised the Typees for their lack of positive law, he now comes to see that the "strange and complex" taboo system is simply the Polynesian form of legality. Ignorant of its rules, Tommo constantly transgresses its unwritten codes.

The most visible sign of Tommo's refusal to be completely integrated into Typee society is his overriding fear of being tattooed, a sacramental practice "connected with their religion" (220). The islanders who had zealously encouraged Tommo to adopt their ways no doubt saw his tattooing as a logical, but imperative, step in the socialization process. For them, becoming a Typee meant accepting their religion. "It was evident," he states, "they were resolved to make a convert of me" (220). To Tommo, however, the "circular bands" of their distinctive tattoo patterns symbolize physical and mental incarceration.

By depicting the islander's tattooing as a religious ritual, Melville reinforces the connection between religious conversion and cultural assimilation. *Typee* is fundamentally about the way religion is used to establish social control. Just as missionaries impose Western ways on the Polynesians in the name of Christianity, the Typees measure Tommo's loyalty to their community by observing his attitude toward their religious practices. Religion, Melville is saying, is used primarily to control behavior and to provide a means of social identification. By vociferously refusing to be tattooed, Tommo rebels against such restraints. His behavior recalls his reaction to life aboard the *Dolly* and triggers the familiar pattern of despair, physical affliction, and wandering that dominates the early stages of the narrative. His existence becomes "one of absolute wretchedness"; he "bitterly feel[s] the state" of his captivity; and his painful leg injury returns with renewed force.

When Tommo senses that his identity is threatened, he no longer feels a common bond with the natives. The best example of this "backsliding" is his observation of their religious chanting. Though he once found universal significance in their rituals, he now suspects that their chantings are heathenish incantations:

> Sometimes when, after falling into a kind of doze, and awaking suddenly in the midst of these doleful chantings, my eye would fall upon the wild-looking group engaged in their strange occupation, with their naked tattooed limbs, and shaven heads disposed in a circle, I was almost tempted to believe that I gazed upon a set of evil beings in the act of working a frightful incantation. (226–27)

This "awakening" is similar in structure to his earlier conversion experience, but it clearly indicates that Tommo no longer surrenders to a universal community. He moves away from his egalitarian fervor because he realizes that Typee society, like all societies, restricts personal freedom. Afraid of losing his identity in the anonymity of a corporate whole, he is fated to be one of the unregenerate. His penchant for rebelling against social systems will lead to a life of suffering and endless wandering, a pattern Melville continued in *Omoo*, the sequel to *Typee*.

Melville's ironic adaptation of conversion rhetoric to the cause of demonstrating the evils of religious and social assimilation was rooted in his own physical and spiritual wayfaring. By incorporating the conversion pattern into his first narrative of sea life and then subverting it, he captured the cyclic pattern of hope and despair, isolation and community, assimilation and escape that he found to be part of the human condition. Wordsworth had charted a circular course, but his version of self returned to its starting point on a higher plane of consciousness; DeQuincey was less confident of escaping from the confines of one's personality but nevertheless saw the possibility of self reformation. Melville's autobiographical persona is closer to that of Rousseau: it is a shifting self attracted to, yet repelled by, the redemptive possibilities of community. Like Tommo, Rousseau found that his conversion to egalitarianism introduced him to a society that threatened his identity. But if Rousseau denounced Western civilization and longed for an Edenic world peopled by noble savages, Melville tested those waters and found them equally treacherous. His fear of communal values resulted in a metonymic self doomed to a circular path of unregenerate wandering.

THE EMPIRICAL REFORMATION

When secular authors adapted conversion rhetoric to self-writing in the Romantic period, they freed it from its theological underpinnings, but, as the narratives of Wordsworth, DeQuincey, and Melville demonstrate, the narrative framework continued to illustrate one's relationship to a larger culture. The various ways Rousseau adapted the rhetoric of conversion remained available to secular autobiographers. Self-portraits such as Wordsworth's *Prelude* strike the affirmative note, transmuting the Christian form but not questioning its efficacy as an epistemological model that relates the self to a larger community. Other authors critique the form even as they adopt it. DeQuincey undercut the Wordsworthian notion of cognitive redemption, and Melville subverted the socialization process of the spiritual autobiography form. Many Victorian autobiographers, however, embraced both of these constructs, even as they distrusted the intense self-reflection so characteristic of Christian and Romantic accounts.[6] Generally, they viewed self-scrutiny as an unacceptable substitute for the active life and subscribed to an "anti-self-consciousness" position, not unlike the Christian insistence that in order to save the self one must first lose it (Hartman, 48–49). For many of them, true happiness could only come by throwing off the self's tyranny and by engaging in responsible social action. Because the conversion framework readily illustrates the relationship between self and society, autobiographical works of the period are filled with accounts of conversion, deconversion, and reconversion. Carlyle's *Sartor Resartus*, Grosse's *Father and Son*, Ruskin's *Praeterita*, Newman's *Apologia*, White's *Autobiography of Mark Rutherford*, Eliot's *Mill on the Floss*, and the poetry of Tennyson and Browning are just a few of the texts and writers that draw on conversion discourse.[7] In an increasingly secular age, Victorian authors continued to base their narratives on a personal vision; but like the Puritans, they rested easily on the paradox between uniqueness and universality that so troubled Rousseau. Their lives and principles could at once be both extremely personal and universally applicable.

Though the Natural Supernaturalism of the Romantic period has been called a secularized revision of Christian motifs and categories, its explicit transcendentalism retained many of the mystical elements of the earlier tradition. Many Victorian reformers sought to distance themselves from a metaphysics of transcendence by drawing upon the discourse of scientific rationalism—a discourse that on its surface appears to be antithetical to the sacred tradition. Conversion rhetoric, however, proved to be readily demystified and made to conform to an empirical worldview. Such adaptations were popular in the Victorian era because they communicated the sacredness and the selflessness of the Christian tradition while emphasizing its socializing function. In many respects, such narratives are actually closer to the sacred form than some of its manifestations in the Romantic period.

John Stuart Mill, whose autobiography was published in 1873, disliked

6. David DeLaura outlines the way Wordsworth helped shape Victorian autobiographical writing, in "The Allegory of Life," 334. The Victorian distrust of self-inspection is discussed in Geoffrey Hartman, "Romanticism and 'Anti-Self-Consciousness,' " 48–50, and Howard Helsinger, "Credence and Credibility," 40–41.

7. Jerome Hamilton Buckley demonstrates the importance of conversion for the Victorians in *The Victorian Temper*, 87–108.

"transcendental and mystical phraseology" and made his *Autobiography* a purely secular "record of an education" (172, 1). Because he believed that spiritual assurance could be used to impose an intellectual, moral, or legal system on a group of people, he explicitly denied the validity of any philosophical or religious system based on transcendence. Progress was Mill's religion, and institutions that traced their principles back to a divine source frequently impeded the rational process of solving social problems.

Yet, paradoxically, Mill deliberately employed conversion rhetoric to describe at least two of his life's major turning points, both of which are tied to his vocation as a reformer: the first when, as a young man, he discovered and became socialized by the utilitarianism of Jeremy Bentham, and the second when he constructed his own "affective" utilitarianism. This second "conversion" took place after he had unhappily realized that Bentham's principles had turned him into a "reasoning machine." His feelings of despair were brought to a crisis after he read a passage from Marmontel's *Memories* in which the young protagonist is inspired to take the place of his dead father: "A vivid conception of the scene and its feeling came over me, and I was moved to tears. From this moment my burthen grew lighter. The oppression of the thought that all feeling was dead within me, was gone. I was no longer hopeless" (99). This passage inscribes Mill's discovery of the value of emotion. Enhanced and completed in many ways by his appreciation of the "inward joy" of Wordsworth's poetry, his awakening gave rise to a radical change in his opinions and character. Far from being a "reasoning machine," he now stated that "the cultivation of the feelings became one of the cardinal points in my ethical and philosophical creed" (101).

Mill's adaptation of conversion discourse, which at first seems so inconsistent with his attitude toward revelation, actually lends credibility to his narrative perspective. If a major change in his personal and professional life was the acceptance of the utilitarian values of feeling and imagination, then his presentation of this event—as well as others—in the terms of an evangelical conversion reinforces his discovery of the role emotion plays in bringing about cognitive and social progress. The means by which he experienced personal change validated his philosophy.

Though Mill continued to stress the illegitimacy of basing laws on transcendent categories, he nevertheless acknowledged the reality of certain perceptual modes, among them the need for "some faith, whether religious or merely human" (167–68). Faith energizes the subject and spurs growth. Merging his life story with the philosophical creed that was the basis for his program of reform, Mill demonstrated the flexibility of conversion discourse. Effective even in the act of denying transcendent categories, conversion continued to be a powerful literary device because it had come to shape the epistemological expectations of Victorian culture: it was a virtually ineradicable structure.

The themes and issues in Mill's autobiography in some ways parallel those in *The Autobiography of Harriet Martineau*, though her approach to conversion discourse was quite different from that of Mill. Martineau wrote her autobiography in 1855, thinking that she was on the verge of death, but she lived on for another twenty years, and the book was not published until 1877, four years after Mill's autobiography appeared. Recently, both Linda Peterson and Sidonie Smith have published significant readings of the work in the context of the women's autobiographical tradition. Though the approaches of these two scholars is different in numerous ways, both read Martineau's self-portrait as being unusual in that it overtly participates in (and to a limited degree transforms) the dominant male tradition of the spiritual autobiography. For these scholars, women rarely employed the conventions of the form and generally inscribed themselves in alternate discourses.

Both Peterson and Smith agree that most nineteenth-century women were denied access to the spiritual autobiography because they were largely excluded from public ministry and thus also excluded from being formally educated in the hermeneutical modes central to the narrative form (Peterson, 130–32; Smith, *Poetics*, 133). Martineau as an independent, educated woman presents herself as being "exceptional," and her narrative stance explains why she wrote in an autobiographical mode that deviated from the norm of nineteenth-century women's writing. Only by seeing herself and writing herself as a "representative man" could Martineau participate in the dominant tradition of British autobiography (Smith, *Poetics*, 126, 141). As I have suggested earlier, the assertion that the nineteenth-century spiritual autobiography is a narrowly "male" form of self-writing seems suspect given the importance of conversion discourse in the culture generally. Despite the fact that they were largely excluded from the pulpit and from higher education, many women were abundantly familiar with the hermeneutical practices of the various protestant sects, and if spiritual autobiographies (both sacred and secular) written by women are underrepresented in the lists of published autobiographies, I don't believe, as do Peterson and Smith, that St. Paul's injunctions against women preaching and the institutional and cultural barriers based upon this doctrine sufficiently explain their relative rarity.

Rather than label the spiritual autobiography an exclusively phallocentric genre, it would be truer to say that most women have had a strained relationship with it. For example, Anne Bradstreet's "To My Dear Children" and Martineau's *Autobiography* can be seen as both adoptions of and reactions to the spiritual autobiography form that still manage to communicate each author's gendered experience. Certainly, women spiritual autobiographers have had to negotiate their versions of self within the discourses of patriarchal culture, but these kinds of negotiations are present in all autobiographies written by women and do not necessarily restrict those who appropriate conversion discourse any more or less than women using other forms.

In any case, given the vast amount of women's writing, both published and unpublished, that has been brought to light recently, I think it is premature at this time to make any definitive claims about the extent to which women did or did not employ the spiritual autobiography form in the nineteenth century. Certainly, some women of varying educational backgrounds read, wrote, and published spiritual autobiographies of one kind or another in the period, and a number of American works such as Julia Foote's *Brand Plucked from the Fire* and Elizabeth Cady Stanton's *Eighty Years and More* are versions of the form that are decidedly feminist in their orientation. If nothing else, the relationship between women writers and the spiritual autobiography seems to be rich and complex, and if Martineau's use of the form is unusual, I do not believe that later literary historians will find it to be "exceptional."

Even the assertion that Martineau's self-portrait is a spiritual autobiography is more complex than it initially appears to be. As Smith and Peterson have both pointed out, Martineau's *Autobiography* substitutes a scientific, evolutionary hermeneutic for a biblical and typological one, but she still seeks and attains the kind of narrative coherence sought by authors of traditional spiritual autobiographies, and she still focuses on attaining and describing her vocation as a woman of letters (Peterson, 137; Mitzi Myers, 66). Smith has in fact called Martineau's *Autobiography* a "series of awakenings and conversions" (131), and Peterson has persuasively shown how the book is organized by Martineau's various "conversions" to the three major stages of Auguste Comte's positivism: theological, metaphysical, and scientific (137–43). What is unexpected, however, given the conventions of the Victorian spiritual autobiography, is the extent to which Martineau distances herself from using conversion discourse to describe these changes. To be sure, her "conversion" to necessarianism (that all events proceed from an antecedent cause) has a striking resemblance to a religious conversion, and it is appropriate that she so described it, because at the time she was still a fervid Unitarian. Martineau locates the origin of this change in a conversation she had with her brother during which she "seized upon some intimation" he made about the "doctrine of Necessity":

> I uttered the difficulty which had lain in my mind for so many years; and he just informed me that there was, or was held to be, a solution in that direction, and advised me to make it out for myself. I did so. From that time the question possessed me. Now that I had got leave, as it were, to apply the Necessarian solution, I did it incessantly. I fairly laid hold of the conception of general laws, while still far from being prepared to let go the notion of a special Providence. Though at times almost overwhelmed by the vastness of the view opened to me, and by the prodigious change requisite in my moral views and self-management, the revolution was safely gone through. My labouring brain and beating heart grew quiet, and something more like peace than I had ever yet known settled down upon my anxious mind. . . . From the time when I became convinced of the certainty . . . of the ground I was treading, and of the security of the results which I should take the right means to attain, a new vigor pervaded my whole life, a new light spread through my mind, and I began to experience a steady growth in self-command, courage, and consequent integrity and disinterestedness. I was feeble and selfish enough at best; but yet, I was like a new creature in the strength of a sound conviction. (1:84)

Unquestionably, this passage corresponds to a profound psychological "conversion" of the kind I have been examining in this chapter, and to the extent that Martineau invokes conversion discourse, she participates in one of the dominant traditions of British Victorian autobiography. But it is interesting to compare this conversion with those of Rousseau, Wordsworth, DeQuincey, and even Mill. Martineau carefully maintains that this transformation was rational and gradual, the product of an intellectual "solution" rather than an emotional upheaval that had its source outside her conscious self. Mill was as much of a positivist as Martineau, but he chose to couch his "conversions" in an emotional framework much closer to that of evangelical Christianity. She clearly distanced herself from such displays of rapture, and her autobiography is similarly "dispassionate" throughout (Smith, *Poetics*, 135–49).

Martineau's second intellectual "revolution," when she moves from the "metaphysical" to the agnostic, "scientific" stage of Comtian analysis is not described in the terms of conversion discourse at all. Rather, she presents a long-winded, logical explanation of her systematic evolution of thought and its antecedent causes over the course of an extended illness and a trip to Egypt and the Near East. Her decision to do so is thematically appropriate, of course: her second awakening moved her significantly further away from a theological understanding of the universe than did the first one, and it is fitting that she describe this change in terms that are not theologically loaded. Given its dispassionate language and its movement away from the language of revelation, one might question whether Martineau's self-portrait is a spiritual autobiography at all. As Peterson and Smith have both noted, her positivistic worldview certainly transforms and extends the form. In a sense, it may be appropriate to call the book a kind of "limit case." As the book progresses, she writes herself out of the tradition with which she had begun.

Despite Martineau's necessarianism, it is similarly difficult to connect her "conversions" to her vocation in the simple cause-and-effect manner found in many spiritual autobiographies. Since Martineau's literary life was the evolutionary unfolding of her social philosophy, it was always connected to her personal history of ideas. In this sense, her conversions, first to necessarianism and then to positivism, were intimately tied to her career as a writer. On the other hand, however, she does not make these connections explicit in her autobiography. She presents herself as being a kind of workaholic, one who had difficulty refusing a challenging task whether it came from herself or from others. There is a consistency to her literary life that she distinguishes from the actual "stage" of her intellectual history. She does make it clear, however, that she sees her own development as being representative, not just of the development of human consciousness, but of the historical progress of Western society. Her autobiography thus fits into the "anti-self-consciousness" stance of her Victorian contemporaries and places her into the context of a larger corporate whole (Mitzi Myers, 70; Smith, *Poetics*, 126). But by "dispassionately" moving away from the conventions of the spiritual autobiography as the narrative continues, Martineau reveals a level of discomfort with the form that reflects a strained relationship with the patriarchal culture that surrounded her. An accomplished and recognized woman reformer, she was (doubly) both within and without the British mainstream.

Like Mill and Martineau, Elizabeth Cady Stanton merged the rhetoric of conversion with an empirical worldview as she composed her life story, *Eighty Years and More: Reminiscences, 1815–1895*. In contrast to these writers, however, her invocation of conversion discourse is light-handed, lighthearted, and decidedly relativistic. The second sentence of her autobiography presents an approach to conversion that recalls Thomas Paine's statement about revelation in the *Age of Reason* and that also anticipates the thought of William James: "What may prove a sudden awakening to one, giving an impulse in a certain direction that may last for years, may make no impression on another" (1). Despite this claim, however, Stanton believed in the power of religious awakenings and their secular analogues, and she often expressed psychological and ideological changes in the terms of conversion discourse. She noted, for instance, that the goal of her various lecture tours was "to convert" her listeners, and she explains how meeting Lucretia Mott "opened to me a new world of thought" (83), a meeting she described in the *History of Woman Suffrage* as a "new revelation of womanhood" (1:419). Later in the autobiography, she calls Susan B. Anthony "my convert" to the feminist movement. These are just a few of the relatively informal allusions to conversion discourse in the text.

If one were to predict events in Stanton's autobiography whose drama and lasting significance would make them likely candidates for a fully developed secular "conversion," in keeping with the conventions of the nineteenth-century spiritual autobiography, two incidents come immediately to mind. One would be her attendance at the first World's Anti-slavery Convention, which took place in London in 1840. On her wedding trip, Stanton attended the convention with her husband, a well-known abolitionist, and it was there that she met Mott for the first time. Rather than being known as a landmark occasion in the history of the abolitionist movement, this convention is best known for the controversy it occasioned over whether to recognize officially its American women delegates. Surely, this controversy "awakened" Stanton's already existing interest in the cause of women's rights. She had gone to the convention presumably in support of her husband's "political abolitionist" party, which advocated the use of existing legal institutions to eradicate slavery and which saw the merging of feminist and abolitionist causes as being politically inexpedient; but shortly after arriving, Stanton sided with Mott and with William Lloyd Garrison, both of whom were more radical than Henry Stanton. Garrison not only insisted that the women be seated on the convention floor, he sat in the balcony with the excluded delegates when his plea for their inclusion was voted down.[8] Stanton remembers: "The action of this convention was the topic of discussion, in public and private, for a long time, and stung many women into new thought and action and gave rise to the movement for women's political equality both in England and the United States" (82). After this convention, Stanton remembers that she and Mott agreed to hold a public meeting on women's rights when they returned to the United States.

Though the Seneca Falls convention was not to take place for another seven years, it too might have served as an appropriate autobiographical occasion for the use of conversion discourse. Stanton links her participation at Seneca Falls to her meeting Mott at the World's Anti-slavery Convention, but most scholars believe that its most immediate cause was her growing discontent with her domestic role as a wife and as a mother of a large, growing family:[9]

> Now the real struggle was upon me. My duties were too numerous and varied, and none sufficiently exhilarating or intellectual to bring into play my higher faculties. . . .
>
> I now fully understood the practical difficulties most women had to contend with in the isolated household. . . . My experience at the World's Anti-slavery Convention, all I had read of the legal status of women, and the oppression I saw everywhere, together swept across my soul, intensified now by many personal experiences. (147–48)

In the midst of this "struggle," Stanton received an invitation to spend an afternoon with Mott, Mary Anne McClintock, Jane Hunt, and Martha C. Wright, out of which grew the convention at Seneca Falls and its "Declarations of Sentiments." I mention these two incidents, not to rehash familiar material in the history of American feminism, but to demonstrate, rather, how Stanton only faintly draws upon conversion discourse to describe them. She recognized their importance and clearly perceived them to be

8. See Lois W. Banner's *Elizabeth Cady Stanton*, 35–39; and Elisabeth Griffith's *In Her Own Right*, 23–27.

9. Banner argues that the deeper roots of Stanton's discontent, though not expressed in her autobiography, were to be found in her disillusionment with her marriage to Henry Stanton. See *Elizabeth Cady Stanton*, 31–38.

major turning points in her life history, but she treats them with barely an echo of the rapture that Rousseau, Wordsworth, or Mill had treated similar moments of insight.

These two events are typical of the rather understated way Stanton draws upon conversion rhetoric in her autobiography, and they recall the way Martineau employed conversion discourse in her *Autobiography*. But Stanton's casual use of conversion discourse on these occasions was not the result of a hesitancy to do so. What at first seems strange is that she chose to apply conversion discourse fully, not to the dramatic events surrounding the antislavery convention or Seneca Falls, but to a "real" religious awakening (in this case a false one) that took place when she was fifteen years old.

A disciplined student who had excelled at a coeducational preparatory school, Elizabeth Cady was devastated when she was told that she was unable to attend the all-male Union College in Schenectady, New York. Instead, she enrolled in Emma Willard's respected "female seminary" in Troy. Studies were all but suspended during her first year of enrollment, however, with the arrival of none other than Charles Grandison Finney, the preeminent revivalist of America's Second Great Awakening. Looking back on Finney's visit, Stanton compares it to an "epidemic, attacking in its worst form the most susceptible." She continues, "Owing to my gloomy Calvinistic training in the old Scotch Presbyterian church, and my vivid imagination, I was one of the first victims" (41). Stanton then describes Finney's dramatic technique, which was built upon achieving a high level of anxiety in his congregation:

> To state the idea of conversion and salvation as then understood, one can readily see from our present standpoint that nothing could be more puzzling and harrowing to the young mind. The revival fairly started, the most excitable were soon on the anxious seat. There we learned the total depravity of human nature and the sinner's awful danger of everlasting punishment. This was enlarged upon until the most innocent girl believed herself a monster of iniquity and felt certain of eternal damnation. (41–42)

Along with her classmates, Stanton was then swept away by Finney's revivalistic techniques:

> With the natural reaction from despair to hope many of us imagined ourselves converted, prayed and gave our experiences in the meet-

ings, and at times rejoiced in the thought that we were Christians—
chosen children of God—rather than sinners and outcasts. (42)

At first, Stanton's reaction to Finney's flamboyant style seems to have had
the "desired" effect. But soon doubt and "the depravity and deceitfulness
of the human heart" destroyed her reborn hope, and she was on the verge
of collapse. Apparently, Finney's graphic presentation of the evils of human
existence outweighed the positive message of salvation he came to expound: "Such preaching worked incalculable harm to the very souls he
sought to save. Fear of the judgment seized my soul. Visions of the lost
haunted my dreams. Mental anguish prostrated my health. Dethronement
of my reason was apprehended by friends" (43).

In the context of *Eighty Years and More*, Stanton's negative reaction to
Finney's preaching is not surprising. Her desire to debunk what she called
the "gloomy superstitions of the puritanical religion" (141) is a major theme
of the autobiography, which was written when she was also occupied by
the *Woman's Bible*, a work that exposed the patriarchal biases of the
world's religions and how they have stifled the cause of women's liberation
throughout history. Even within the autobiography, Stanton reveals how
her girlhood had been haunted by ghostly fears of the devil, by the
implicating peals of church bells, and by the extreme guilt brought about
by minor acts of disobedience. As the eighty-year-old Stanton looked back
upon the days of her girlhood, she saw a culture that held "that firm faith
in hell and the devil was the greatest help to virtue" (8), and parents (hers
among them) who ruled by fear rather than by love and understanding. In
those days, Stanton's typical response was to defy or to ignore those who
employed such tactics, in what she considered "justifiable acts of rebellion
against the tyranny of those in authority" (12). For example, when her
family's Scottish nurse Mary Dunn exhorted her to "cultivate the virtues
of obedience and humility," she asked "why it was that everything we like
to do is a sin, and that everything we dislike is commanded by God or
someone on earth. I am so tired of that everlasting no! no! no!" (10–11).

Aside from being almost certainly a tongue-in-cheek allusion to the
Sartor Resartus of Thomas Carlyle (whom she takes to task in *Eighty Years*
for mistreating his wife Jennie), Stanton's own "everlasting no" parable
here reveals her fundamentally radical attitude to those who arbitrarily
base their authority on tradition, position, religion, family roles, or gender.
It is little wonder why her short-lived "conversion" under Finney—which
was driven by fear and which counseled "humility"—disturbed the fifteen-

year-old Stanton so profoundly. For her to have accepted Jesus under those terms would have been to violate every principle of autonomy and justice that she had developed in her formative years.

But Stanton's purpose is not merely to debunk Finney's Troy revival of 1831; she goes on to show how her false and temporary awakening gave way to one that was true and lasting. Disturbed by the harmful effect of Finney's revival on Elizabeth, her otherwise Calvinistic father took her, her sister Tryphena, and her brother-in-law, Edward Bayard, on a six-week trip to Niagara. During their travels, the subject of religion was forbidden from conversation, and instead Elizabeth's brother-in-law introduced her to the rational philosophy of George Combe, the "scientific" discipline of phrenology, and "many other liberal works, all so rational and opposed to the old theologies" (43; Banner, 13). As a result, a profound scientific enlightenment took the place of her evangelical wasteland:

> I found my way out of the darkness into the clear sunlight of Truth. My religious superstitions gave place to rational ideas based on scientific facts, and in proportion, as I looked at everything from a new standpoint, I grew more and more happy, day by day. . . . my mind was restored to its normal condition.
>
> . . . An entirely new life now opened to me. The old bondage of fear of the visible and the invisible was broken and, no longer subject to absolute authority, I rejoiced in the dawn of a new day of freedom in thought and action. (44–45)

Interestingly, Stanton describes this awakening not simply as a theological or an intellectual one: she and her friends had gained a new sense of independence as well, feeling able "to go out at pleasure, to walk, to ride, to drive, with no one to say us nay or question our right to liberty" (44).[10]

Interesting, too, is that despite the adult Stanton's keen understanding of the "church machinery" upon which Finney's revival was built, she, unlike Rousseau, DeQuincey, and Melville, makes no effort to undercut the socializing function of conversion discourse. Her description of the revival itself is consciously in the first person (feminine) plural: this was an

10. It appears that Stanton's "deconversion" from evangelical Christianity and her movement toward liberal theology was actually more gradual than she makes it appear in her autobiography. She continued to wrestle with religious questions into her adulthood and was influenced in later years by Lucretia Mott and Theodore Parker. See Griffith's *In Her Own Right*, 45–46.

ordeal that was endured by her seminary classmates. Even the second
"true" awakening was something she shared communally:

> As I had become sufficiently philosophical to talk over my religious
> experiences calmly with my classmates who had been with me
> through the Finney revival meetings, we all came to the same
> conclusion—that we had passed through no remarkable change and
> that we had not been born again, as they say, for we found our
> tastes and enjoyments the same as ever. (47)

Stanton makes it clear that this experience did no permanent damage to
her corevivalists and, if anything, brought them closer together. She
reinforces this perception by saying that some of her classmates became
lifelong friends and by recounting fondly a speech she delivered at a school
reunion sixty years after her graduation. She also argues that the education
they received at the Willard Academy provided her classmates with the
intellectual ammunition to successfully challenge the supposed superiority
of the male graduates from nearby Union College. In addition to freeing
her from the chain that linked fear, patriarchal authority, and a chastising
God, Stanton suggests that her "true" awakening socialized a group of
women into varying degrees of feminist awareness.

If at first it seems surprising that Stanton employs conversion rhetoric
to describe, not public events in the history of the women's movement, but
rather her earlier religious conversion, deconversion, and subsequent
awakening to a positivistic view of the world, it seems less so in light of the
impact of Stanton's escape from what she calls the "tyranny" of her
childhood. Confused by the fear of damnation and victimized by her father's
disappointment over the loss of his only son, Stanton's liberation from the
sources of patriarchal and religious authority was a psychological precondition for her subsequent political activism. This explains why her "first"
conversion occupies so much of her narrative attention in the autobiography.

The fact that Stanton—after resisting her first conversion—should go
on to describe her acquisition of rationalist discourse in similar terms,
might cause one to argue that she was not as free from the epistemological
consequences of conversion as she might have believed: that in accepting
scientific rationalism over evangelical Christianity, she merely replaced one
oppressive patriarchal system with another. To say this, however, is to
minimize the liberating consequences signified by this turning point in her

narrative. By necessity, Stanton had to be converted to one of the discourses available to her, but her appropriation of scientific rationalism also gave her a language and a point of view that enabled her to critique the patriarchal world in which she lived. She appropriated "conversion" for a feminist cause.

Despite her awareness of the devastating effect of evangelical Christianity and its patriarchal biases, Stanton's description of the Troy revival is nevertheless filled with a significant degree of irony and good humor. She seems not to be bitter. After describing the frightening and sensational techniques of "the venerable ex-president of Oberlin College," she drops, almost as an aside, the following statement: "But he was sincere, so peace to his ashes" (43). Stanton's lack of bitterness here is probably to be expected: as an eighty-year-old woman, she was fairly comfortable with her agnosticism. But there may have been other reasons for her good nature too. Though ordained as a Presbyterian minister, Finney, like many of the itinerant preachers of the Second Great Awakening, repudiated the Calvinistic doctrine of predestination. God gave sinners the power and the will to accept Jesus, and revivals were merely a natural setting for this self-determined power to be exercised. In *Eighty Years*, Stanton, who came from a family of traditional Calvinists, remembers being initially confused by Finney's Arminianism, and she directly challenged him on this issue:

> "I cannot understand what I am to do. If you should tell me to go to the top of the church steeple and jump off, I would readily do it, if thereby I could save my soul; but I do not know how to go to Jesus."
> "Repent and believe," said he, "that is all you have to do to be happy here and hereafter." (42)

Stanton's question here is quite consistent with what many orthodox Calvinists were asking Finney. As her "deconversion" makes clear, Stanton rejected evangelical Christianity, but she must also have come to sympathize with Finney's Arminian belief in the efficacy of the human will, a belief that became a major component of her own individualistic philosophy.[11] Moreover, as numerous scholars have noted, Finney's doctrine of "perfectionism," much like the Methodist emphasis on "sanctification," stimulated many people to become actively engaged in the reform movements of the mid–nineteenth century, among them temperance, abolition, and universal

11. On Stanton's individualism, see Banner, 74–76

suffrage. Finney was also quite controversial for encouraging women to exhort sinners publicly and to testify in front of mixed audiences, thereby sanctioning their greater role in religious life and in the reform movements that grew out of nineteenth-century evangelicalism.[12] Though Stanton emphatically indicates that she came to reform by an entirely different route, it is probably not surprising that in *Eighty Years and More*, she treats Finney with a degree of humor and affection. In the end, he may have done Stanton and the women's movement more good than harm.

Like the self-portraits I have discussed earlier, the narratives of Stanton, Martineau, and Mill depict metonymic selves whose lives are presented in various "stages" of development. Instead of the various circular structures constituted by the narratives of Wordsworth, DeQuincey, and Melville, one finds a linear, evolutionary framework. These narratives make no claims of ultimate knowledge or absolute truth, but neither do they exhibit a desire to revisit and regain former states of consciousness. Rather, they outline progressive selves, whose lives are open-ended and forward-looking—like the reforms they espoused. Conversion discourse was an effective vehicle for this kind of self-representation because it suggests that cognitive change has its source outside the conscious self—in a realm of "objective" truth, capable of being universally communicated in the terms of science. Its very "otherness" and "disinterestedness" allows it to be used to challenge existing power relations. Those who encode such conversions "create" selves that do not act "for" the self, but rather for a reality that exists beyond the personal context at hand. This opens a space for actions and beliefs that go against existing cultural norms, while it conceals the "will to power" embedded in the trope's use.

DIVIDING THE SELF

If the Romantic and Victorian texts I have examined represent a strong rewriting of the poetics of self, where the tropological structure has been transformed from the "metaphorical" figure of the Christian conversion narrative to the "metonymy" of the secular self, still the overall concept of a "speaking self" who records each phase of development has remained

---

12. In this paragraph, I am relying on William G. McLoughlin's description of Finney's style, theology, and social philosophy in *Revivals, Awakenings, and Reform*, 122–31. For Finney's attitude toward the role of women in revival meetings, see *Charles G. Finney: An Autobiography*, 214.

relatively stable in these texts. Other nineteenth-century autobiographers were to destabilize this notion of personal testimony (or "presence") in narrative. In various ways they question Thoreau's assertion that "it is, after all, always the first person that is speaking" (3). Here authors self-consciously blur the distinction between fictive and autobiographical discourse and explore the notion—now a commonplace in autobiographical theory—that a stable, unified, and autonomous "self" is problematic.

One text that begins to explore this issue is Thomas Carlyle's *Sartor Resartus*. Based on a social hierarchy and on traditional moral categories, it conveys a conservative social vision. In conveying these values, it follows the sequence of a successful conversion narrative, moving from doubt and despair, wandering and affliction, to assurance and order, rectitude and sanctification. As this pattern suggests, Carlyle, though influenced by German Idealism, maintained in many respects a Puritan worldview. Not only was he familiar with the narrative structure associated with his Calvinist upbringing, he also believed that he had a genuine conversion experience.[13] Numerous critics have identified the book's sequence of "Everlasting No," "Centre of Indifference," and "Everlasting Yea" as drawing explicitly and obviously on the rhetoric of conversion, and this sequence occurs conventionally after Teufelsdröckh—the book's protagonist—undertakes a world pilgrimage through a spiritual "wilderness." Furthermore, the series of conversions in *Sartor Resartus* is not confined to the three-chapter section near the end of book 2. There are a number of other spiritual awakenings in Teufelsdröckh's biography, most of which follow the typical "paradox of Puritan piety" pattern. Periods of despair are followed by moments of illumination that in turn give way to other awakenings. The end result of this purgative process, of course, is assurance.

The pattern of conversion operates outside of Teufelsdröckh's biography as well. Critics have pointed out that both the Editor and the implied reader of *Sartor Resartus* also undergo conversions as they follow the life and opinions of Herr Teufelsdröckh.[14] Ultimately, in book 3, society, too, experiences a kind of conversion. This transference is possible because,

13. For a description of Carlyle's reading, see Hill Shine, *Carlyle's Early Reading to 1834*. Carlyle's conversion experience is discussed by Carlisle Moore in "*Sartor Resartus* and the Problem of Carlyle's 'Conversion' "; and A. Abbot Ikeler traces the impact of Scottish Calvinism on Carlyle's writing in *Puritan Temper and Transcendental Faith*.

14. A number of critics have pointed out Carlyle's expansion of the conversion pattern. See, for example, G. B. Tennyson, *Sartor Called Resartus*, 177; Walter Reed, "The Pattern of Conversion in *Sartor Resartus*," 415, 421–26; Avrom Fleishman, *Figures of Autobiography*, 124; and Linda Peterson, *Victorian Autobiography*, 49–57.

as G. B. Tennyson writes, "for Carlyle society, as an organism, was essentially like man and thus susceptible to the same kind of analysis" (320). Carlyle was able to expand the conversion pattern outside of Teufelsdröckh's life because, like his Puritan ancestors, he believed that the experience of personal revelation was similar for all individuals. Teufels-dröckh, then, as the antitype of numerous biblical figures such as Adam, David, Jacob, the Hebrew slave, and Jesus, acts as a kind of Everyman. By making him a representative figure, Carlyle suggests the universality of the conversion process.[15] In so doing, he follows the logic of many Puritan conversion narratives by linking the salvation of the individual with the redemption of the community. Out of the ashes of the atheistic world will rise the phoenix of the new (184–89). Discovering his place in a global society, Teufelsdröckh also discovers his personal vocation. Just as the typical conclusion to spiritual autobiographies written by men was a call to the ministry, Teufelsdröckh, after recognizing "a living, literal *Communion of Saints*, wide as the World itself" (197), decides to spread the message of his Clothes Philosophy. He gives up his life of aimlessness and passivity and begins his life as a writer, a modern-day preacher and prophet who spreads the "Word" in much the same way as Carlyle's Calvinist forebears (158).

Sartor Resartus attests to the continued efficacy of conversion as a metaphor for cognitive change and as a measure of the relationship between the individual and society. Carlyle's stress on the Natural Supernaturalism of conversion, his obvious linking of conversion and vocation, and his fusing of individual and social concerns indicate that he followed the Puritan pattern of conversion more closely than any of the writers I have discussed in this chapter. In another sense, however, he radically undercut the Christian tradition by splitting the autobiographical persona into a fictional "character" and an Editor. In so doing he created a level of ambiguity so rooted in the text that critics are unable to agree whether *Sartor Resartus* embraces or shatters autobiographical conventions.[16] By turning aspects of

15. Feminist scholars have noted that autobiographical constructs of "representativeness" are often based on male categories. See especially Sidonie Smith's discussion of Harriet Martineau's *Autobiography*, in *A Poetics of Women's Autobiography*, 126, 141, and Bella Brodzki and Celeste Schenck's introduction to *Life/Lines: Theorizing Women's Autobiography*, 1–7. Though I do not believe that Carlyle in this case was intent on denying women access to the conversion experience or the discourse that describes it, his language and his types are unmistakably gendered.

16. See, for example, the widely divergent views of Paul Jay, *Being in the Text*, 93–96; M. H. Abrams, *Natural Supernaturalism*, 129–34, 307, 312; Avrom Fleishman, *Figures of Autobiography*, 124–29, 134–37; and Linda Peterson, *Victorian Autobiography*, 31–59.

his own life story into fiction, Carlyle had the advantage of allegorizing certain elements of the conversion process and thereby positing a universal program for social redemption, but at the same time, he also subverted the convention of personal testimony in what many consider to be an early "modernist" text. The book's pervasive irony makes the reader doubt the genuineness of Teufelsdröckh's conversion. As a social critic, Carlyle merged his plan of reform with Christian redemptive history; as an artist, however, he created a narrative that defies generic classification and that calls into question the validity of its narrating subject.

Though writers such as Carlyle, Rousseau, Wordsworth, DeQuincey, Mill, and Martineau were read and admired widely in America, secular autobiographies in the nineteenth-century American canon (as it has been constituted) employ the conversion framework less frequently than do British works of the same period. Some glaring exceptions to this generalization, however, are the numerous African-American slave narratives, which were extremely popular in the mid-nineteenth century and which borrowed heavily from the rhetorical features of evangelical Christianity.[17] Sitting in the balance between sacred and secular modes of discourse, most slave narratives are filled with the biblical language, typological significations, sermon rhetoric, and Judeo-Christian myth structures also found in traditional spiritual autobiographies. Just as the conversion narrative, by definition a success story, traces the individual's progress from sin to grace, the slave narrative depicts the successful journey from slavery to freedom. The geographical movement from South to North itself evokes both the biblical account of the Israelites' journey to the promised land and the sea-crossing narratives of the first American settlers.

Of course not all slave narratives used conversion discourse. For example, Frederick Douglass's second autobiography, *My Bondage and My Freedom*, moves away from the tradition of the spiritual autobiography, and Harriet Jacob's *Incidents in the Life of a Slave Girl* owes very little to the form. Other slave narratives are modeled on the "trickster" tale, having unregenerate protagonists who operate outside of traditional religious and moral categories. Even those narratives that do employ conversion rhetoric often display a tension between the tropological expectations of a white Christian audience and a partially resisting black writer.[18] As Henry Louis

17. Charles Nichols discusses the popularity of the nineteenth-century slave narrative, in *Many Thousand Gone*, xiv-xv.
18. See William L. Andrews, *To Tell a Free Story*, 167–204. Andrews's overall history of early

Gates succinctly puts it, "above all else, every public spoken and written utterance of the ex-slaves was written and published for an essentially hostile auditor or interlocutor, the white abolitionist or the white slave-holder, both of whom imposed a meaning upon the discourse of the black subject" (105). But if some black abolitionists risked offending a white readership, they often did so in veiled terms; the price of alienating their audience was simply too high in antebellum America to do otherwise. For this reason, many ex-slaves relied—to varying degrees—on the rhetoric of conversion.

African Americans had been writing fairly traditional spiritual autobiographies since the mid-eighteenth century. In many such texts, racial identity and the suffering it entailed were subordinated to the typical trials of the Christian in search of salvation (Andrews, *Free Story*, 44–45). When later black autobiographers wrote to expose the evils of slavery, they continued to use conversion discourse, but they adapted it to their particular rhetorical ends. In many cases, slave narratives variously combined the stories of an individual's election and liberation. Sometimes, as in the narratives of Olaudah Equiano and James W. C. Pennington, the experiences of conversion and emancipation appear as separate events. Equiano used conversion discourse to describe both his manumission and his later reception of grace. Pennington chose not to so record his gaining freedom, though his narrative contains a conventional account of his religious conversion.[19] Other writers somehow merged the experiences of receiving grace and becoming free. John Thompson, for example, validated his effort to escape from slavery by placing it in the context of a religious awakening:

> About two rods from Uncle Harry's house I fell upon my knees . . . with hands uplifted to high heaven. . . . I received a spiritual answer of approval; a voice like thunder seeming to enter my soul, saying, I am your God and am with you; though the whole world be against you, I am more than the world; though wicked men hunt you, trust in me, for I am the Rock of your Defence. (81)

African-American self-writing has been very helpful to me throughout this section. He traces the use of the spiritual autobiography by African Americans, 44–47, 64–77, and discusses its relationship to the slave narrative form, 99.

19. Equiano describes his manumission on pages 102–3 of his *Life of Olaudah Equiano*; his conversion is recorded on 139–53. Pennington recalls his arrival in the free states on 235 of *The Fugitive Blacksmith*. The account of his conversion can be found on 242–45.

Autobiographers like Thompson, Equiano, and Pennington, who combined accounts of their election and their attaining freedom, accomplished a number of things. Their narratives identified them as being among the elect, thereby reinforcing their presentation of themselves as fully human beings, those whose efforts to gain freedom were blessed by divine sanction. Their awakenings also bound them to their white audience. Both shared a belief in God, a specific value system, a redemptive rhetoric; and both had undergone similar saving experiences.

Because grace and freedom are so clearly linked in the slave narrative tradition, many authors made certain decisive events in the slave's quest take the place of conversion as a radical turning point. The physical and psychological evils of slavery corresponded to the affliction and wandering of sinners, and the movement toward freedom, either actual or cognitive, paralleled the path to spiritual assurance. In some cases, the precise moment of liberation occupied the place traditionally held by conversion. Lunsford Lane and Elizabeth Keckley, for example, directly compare their emancipations to religious conversions:

> He who has passed from spiritual death to life, and received the witness within his soul that his sins are forgiven, may possibly form some distant idea, like the ray of the setting sun from the far off mountain top, of the emotions of an emancipated slave. That opens heaven. To break the bounds of slavery, opens up at once both earth and heaven. (Lane, 17–18)

> The twelve hundred dollars were raised, and at last my son and myself were free. Free, free! what a glorious ring to the word. Free! the bitter heart-struggle was over. Free! the soul could go out to heaven and to God with no chains to clog its flight or pull it down. Free! the earth wore a brighter look, and the very stars seemed to sing with joy. Yes, free! free by the laws of man and the smile of God—and Heaven bless them who made me so! (Keckley, 55)

By comparing emancipation to justification, Lane and Keckley connect the freedom/slavery antithesis to the dualistic framework of Christian theology. Slavery was sin and freedom grace: to escape from slavery was to follow God's redemptive plan. These two writers linked conversion with the attainment of freedom; other narrators, like Thompson, invoked conversion once they had irrevocably decided either to escape or to die trying.[20]

In still other instances, the turning point occurred when the slave first fought back, when he or she refused to be treated as a piece of property. As a number of critics have pointed out, the passage in his *Narrative* describing Frederick Douglass's ordeal with the slave-breaker Covey occupies the place traditionally held by conversion in the spiritual autobiography tradition:[21]

> This battle with Mr. Covey was the turning-point in my career as a slave. It rekindled the few expiring embers of freedom, and revived within me a sense of my own manhood. . . . It was a glorious resurrection, from the tomb of slavery, to the heaven of freedom. My long-crushed spirit rose, cowardice departed, bold defiance took its place; and I now resolved that, however long I might remain a slave in form, the day had passed forever when I could be a slave in fact. (113)

Douglass represents this moment as a radical reorientation that alters his self-perception. In deciding he would rather risk severe punishment or death than submit to the degradation Covey and his type represented, Douglass recognized his worth as a human being.

Because, as Robert Stepto emphasizes, African Americans sought literacy as well as freedom (*Behind the Veil*, ix), some slave narratives described the acquiring of reading and writing skills in the terms of spiritual revelation. Though Douglass's decision to fight Covey occupies the structural center

20. Frances Foster, *Witnessing Slavery*, 85, 90. Though Lane links emancipation and Christian redemption in the preceding passage, his discourse is potentially subversive in that he privileges the slave's experience over the Christian's. The redeemed can "only possibly form some distant idea" of an even greater experience, one that opens *both* heaven and earth, both the sacred and the secular.

William Andrews points out that Lane acknowledged that he had employed a friend to help him shape his narrative. This use of editorial assistance was fairly common in slave narratives, and it raises questions about the authenticity of the autobiographical act. See *To Tell a Free Story*, 309 n. 26. On the role of editors, see 19–22. See also James Olney, " 'I was born': Slave Narratives, Their Status as Autobiography and as Literature."

21. G. Thomas Couser compares Douglass's work to the conversion narrative, *American Autobiography*, 51–61. See also Lucinda H. MacKethan, "From Fugitive Slave to Man of Letters." Rather than focus on Douglass's fight with Covey, Henry Louis Gates, Jr., identifies Douglass's "conversion" as his decision to speak publicly for the first time at the Nantucket antislavery rally. See *Figures in Black*, 105.

of his *Narrative,* he also rendered Mr. Auld's refusal to let him learn to read as an awakening:

> [Auld's] words sank deep into my heart, stirred up sentiments within that lay slumbering, and called into existence an entirely new train of thought. It was a new and special revelation, explaining dark and mysterious things. . . . I now understood what had been to me a most perplexing difficulty—to wit, the white man's power to enslave the black man. (78)

For Douglass, as for many former slaves, reading opened the gates of knowledge and convinced him of slavery's evil. Literacy too represented freedom: self-authorship itself was a product of the ex-slaves' liberation from the bonds of ignorance slaveholders employed to keep them subjugated.[22] As in the typical conversion narrative, the narratives of ex-slaves thus encode a relationship between biography, knowledge, and self-expression.

Similarly, just as many spiritual autobiographers answered a call to preach the Word, the authors of slave narratives frequently ended their stories by showing how they had become abolitionist crusaders, dedicated to a movement in some ways indistinguishable from a religious sect. Of course, many prominent white abolitionists were religious figures, and they encouraged former slaves to speak publicly about the trials of their bondage and the rewards of their liberation. Some, like Douglass, became powerful leaders in their own right, engaged in the process of converting others to the cause.[23]

In addressing the linguistic and narrative expectations of the conversion tradition, slave narrators, like their Christian predecessors, underwent a process of socialization. Douglass himself documents his rhetorical education in his *Narrative* first by describing his acquaintance within slavery with the *Columbian Orator* (83–84) and then by describing his "conversion" to the language of Garrison's *Liberator* after he had attained his freedom:

22. For discussions of the importance of literacy to former slaves, see Houston Baker, *The Journey Back*, 31–34; Sidonie Smith, *Where I'm Bound*, 10; Robert Stepto, *From Behind the Veil*, 25; Stephen Butterfield, *Black Autobiography*, 26; and Lucinda H. MacKethan, "From Fugitive Slave to Man of Letters."

23. On the role of former slaves in the abolitionist movement, see Jane H. Pease and William H. Pease, *They Who Would Be Free*, and Benjamin Quarles, *Black Abolitionists*.

The paper became my meat and my drink. My soul was set all on
fire. Its sympathy for my brethren in bonds—its scathing denuncia-
tions of slaveholders—its faithful exposures of slavery—and its
powerful attacks upon the upholders of the institution—sent a thrill
of joy through my soul, such as I had never felt before! I had not
long been a reader of the "Liberator," before I got a pretty correct
idea of the principles, measures and spirit of the anti-slavery reform.
I took right hold of the cause. (151)

As this passage suggests, many slave narrators rhetorically and actually
joined an abolitionist church. In doing so, they constituted a "self" consistent with the expectations of a white Christian audience in ways that partly
conditioned their renderings of the African-American experience. Just as
the traditional spiritual autobiographer gave up notions of personal uniqueness in embracing a set of literary conventions, blacks who authored slave
narratives de-emphasized the uniqueness of their African-American voices
by presenting their experiences in white, Christian, abolitionist terms.[24]
Their decision to do so, of course, was politically and ideologically expedi-
ent: to write a slave narrative was perhaps the only way for many blacks to
reach white America at all. According to Houston Baker, the former slave
"had to seize whatever weapons came to hand in his struggle for self-
definition. The range of instruments was limited. Evangelical Christians
and committed abolitionists were the only discernible groups standing in
the path of America's hypocrisy and inhumanity" (*The Journey Back*, 37).
As Douglass's fight with Covey reveals, former slaves radically subverted
the Southern social order, but in adapting a familiar Christian rhetoric, they
often conveyed their revolutionary acts in a borrowed idiom, and in that
sense limited the full range of autobiographical possibility.

The use of conversion rhetoric in the early history of African-American
autobiography in some ways parallels its development in Europe; as the
tradition evolved, there was a movement toward greater secularization and
an increasingly stronger affirmation of the value of the individual. Initially,
conversion rhetoric was used to bind the black writer with God's elect—a

24. Houston Baker outlines the ideological implications of fitting into a white Christian value
system, while discussing Douglass's *Narrative* in the *Journey Back*, 36–38. For an extended
treatment of this subject, see G. Thomas Couser's *Altered Egos*, 110–55. See also Stephen
Butterfield, *Black Autobiography*, 30, 48. Baker revises his view of Douglass's narrative in *Blues,
Ideology, and Afro-American Literature*, where he emphasizes Douglass's radical use of economic
imagery, 58–73.

move that to some was radical in itself. The black spiritual autobiographer, like her or his white counterpart, sought to deny the self to demonstrate God's saving action. With its incorporation in the slave narrative, however, the Christian framework was politicized and historicized; black writers drew on a sacred discourse to link redemptive history with their struggle to be free. In most cases, the presentation of a unique self was not a high priority. As the abolitionist movement gained momentum at midcentury and beyond, some slave narrators like Douglass began to incorporate the Romantic vision of personal uniqueness into their narratives (Andrews, *Free Story*, 100–102). In this sense, they employed conversion discourse in ways similar to British Victorians. They at once affirmed the dignity of the individual as well as the value of a "redeemed" community.

As with *Sartor Resartus*, those slave narratives that draw upon conversion discourse in many respects preserve the structure and tone of narratives in the Christian tradition. The variety of imaginative ways that former slaves adapted the trope of conversion, however, suggests that they did more than fit their life stories into a general formula, as some critics have argued.[25] Moreover, such narratives "split the discourse" into religious and political categories. Regardless of how they invoked the rhetoric of conversion, the authors of slave narratives generally told two stories: their reception of grace and their achieving liberation from legal bondage. Like Carlyle, they too redefined the notion of personal testimony. In defining their "spiritual" selves, slave narrators presented an internal struggle between good and evil, as the individual through grace overcomes sin and achieves redemption. But the tendency of slave narrators to encode their election (either explicitly or implicitly) was mainly an authenticating strategy designed to enhance their larger goal of achieving social change. In defining their "political" selves, former slaves asserted that the need for "conversion" was external—targeted at governing bodies, institutions, and the reading public. "Guilt" in this context was not attached to the spiritual condition of present or former slaves but to the structure of society and to those who perpetuated it. This explains why the presentation of personal uniqueness was not an important organizing principle in many slave narratives. The need for "redemption" was transferred from self to world. If the opposite were true, and freedom depended on personal salvation, then the

25. See especially Olney, who goes so far as to say that slave narratives cannot be considered true autobiographies.

implication would be that God should only free those whom he had saved. In practice, the orthodox might construe this to mean that only those like Douglass who successfully attained freedom would "merit" the liberation they attained. Such an idea was antithetical to the goals of universal abolition. Rather, slave narrators presented those who lived in bondage as being politically "sinless"—in a kind of prelapsarian state—because freedom was the enabling construct for citizenship in the American political and social system. This is why slave narrators both "testify" to the condition of their spiritual selves and "signify" on the racism that surrounds them. The idea of conversion is thus dual.

The splitting of the notion of personal testimony in the slave narrative tradition and in *Sartor Resartus*, if carried to its logical extreme, would result in an escape from the autobiographical impulse altogether or—in what amounts to the same thing—its appropriation of a "communal" or "cultural" voice. Known as he is for his intense individualism, Emerson ironically came close to such a position in his own poetics of selfhood. In an age of biography and autobiography, Emerson—like a number of other writers of the American Renaissance—did not leave anything resembling a self-portrait. Bewailing his "retrospective" age and wishing to escape from the bondage of history, it would have been strange indeed for him to have done so. But this omission is nonetheless informative: transparent eyeballs notwithstanding, Emerson deliberately distanced himself from those (primarily British) writers who found conversion to be such a powerful model for the textual construction of self. [26]

One explanation for this avoidance can be found in the Unitarianism that was the starting point of Emerson's intellectual life. The Unitarians, of course, denied the doctrine of the fall and in so doing de-emphasized the need for spiritual conversion (Ahlstrom, 391–92). If humans were born without original sin and had the spark of the divine already within them, then the kind of radical reorientation (or dramatic personality change) associated with conversion was unnecessary. An "awareness of" or even an "awakening to" the divinity in humanity may have been needed, but not a fundamental change in the "essential" self. Under such a theology, conversion could also be construed as being socially divisive in that it

26. In an interesting study, Jeffrey Steele compares the dynamics of Emerson's representation of self to conversion. Steele, however, acknowledges that Emerson assumes that the "personal can be eliminated." Therefore his "rhetoric of regeneration" entails the construction of an audience rather than the inscription of an autobiographical conversion. See *The Representation of the Self in the American Renaissance*, 1–39.

separated the saved from the damned and thereby upset the movement toward universal well-being advocated by liberal theologians.

A second and perhaps more telling explanation for Emerson's avoidance of the kind of personal testimony found in the conversion narrative may be related to his desire to write—like Dante—"his autobiography in colossal cipher, or into universality" (238). In doing so he removed the *autos* from his *bios* and left a (primarily male) discourse of universality and representativeness that lacked the details of personal redemption. His justification for so doing was his belief that the particular inward search resulted in universal knowledge. The American Scholar, for instance, learns "that in going down into the secrets of his own mind he has descended into the secrets of all minds. . . . the deeper he dives into his privatest secretest presentiment, to his wonder he finds this is the most acceptable, most public, and universally true. . . . For a man, rightly viewed, comprehendeth the particular natures of all men" (74–76). Though linking the personal and the universal (the private and the public) might impel some writers to focus on the particulars of their life histories, Emerson used the other half of this equation to escape from autobiography altogether. If *any* observation of self can yield universal knowledge, then the study of self need not depend on self-study. The focus on ahistorical "representative men" can be equally as rich.

Emerson's "Me" and "Not Me" were connected because he believed that the world of Spirit flows through all creation. This metaphysics enabled him to construct a synecdochical self, in which the universal was contained by the particular. By "shuttling" (to use a word Whitman would use to evoke the synecdochical self) back and forth between the world of phenomena and the world of Spirit, Emerson created a fluid notion of identity at odds with the "life stages" approach contained by the texts described elsewhere in this chapter. In so doing, he resisted the generic constraints of autobiography altogether. As philosophy, Emerson's representation of self is consistent with his desire to escape from history and the determinism it entailed, but, psychologically, it reveals anxiety also: a fear of personal change and an avoidance of self-disclosure. Despite its fluid nature, Emerson's notion of identity was based on *resistance* to history and all that makes it: language, culture, and thought. In this sense, he anticipates the twentieth-century writers whom I discuss in subsequent chapters.

The intellectual and political life of the eighteenth and nineteenth centuries was permeated by the ideas of revolution, freedom, and reform; and these concepts, when applied to the self, presuppose the necessity of personal change, which, when universalized, becomes the basis for social transformation. It is not surprising, then, that those who applied conversion rhetoric to their secular selves during this time continued to use it to inscribe personal reorientation and continued to define themselves in relationship to society. If the authors of religious autobiographies moved in one direction—toward God and his people—secular autobiographers, insofar as they embraced or subverted the socializing process implicit in conversion rhetoric, could affirm the value of community or resist a communal definition of the self. The American slave narrators, who were less concerned (at least in the beginning) with demonstrating individual uniqueness, took the first course; they inscribed their position as human Christian beings—members of a universal American Church. Writers such as Wordsworth, Carlyle, Mill, Martineau, and Stanton were more interested in describing the uniqueness of their respective visions, but those visions too were socially minded, and bound them to a communal ideal.[27] Rousseau, DeQuincey, and Melville took another course: though their narratives initially appear to move toward cultural assimilation, they ultimately rejected the social consequences of conversion. Salvation, if it came at all, could only come in isolation.

The autobiographers whom I discuss in the chapters to come are decidedly in the camp of these three writers. They took a discourse that in large part still signified that one had come into alignment with linguistic, behavioral, and social expectations, and they used it to represent their refusal to do so. Like Rousseau, Melville, and DeQuincey, these authors were wary of the ways conversion had been and continued to be used as a means of merging individual values with larger ideological systems; they clung to their self-constructed identities and distrusted absolute commitments to linguistic and social formulas. But these twentieth-century Americans took the secularizing process a step further. If conversion had traditionally linked the search for illumination with the search for a defined social role, they increasingly used conversion as an index of estrangement—if not exclusion—from mainstream America. Though Rousseau,

27. Lawrence Buell makes a similar point about what he calls the "more conservative forms of visionary Romanticism," which, as he states, "transmuted the eighteenth-century notion of poetry as a repository of communal wisdom into the idea of the poet as keeper of the collective conscience and prophet of a better society," *New England Literary Culture*, 69–70.

DeQuincey and Melville subverted the socializing function of conversion discourse, their narratives are nevertheless marked by an anxiety—an attraction to and a repulsion from—a communal identity. One might say there is a sense of guilt about their social and linguistic acts of subversion. The works of William and Henry James, Henry Adams, Ellen Glasgow, Zora Neale Hurston, and Richard Wright do not share this anxiety. Their resistance to the dramatic social and psychological changes signified by conversion became more than just an assertion of their individuality; it became the very measure of their self-worth. Their narratives do not describe a process of assimilation and then withdrawal as found in *Typee* and the *Confessions* of Rousseau and DeQuincey; rather their self-portraits present subjects who seek to "justify" themselves in each narrative act, individuals who resist the kinds of changes associated with conversion. Like Emerson, they inscribed synecdochical selves, but unlike him, they lacked confidence in a spiritual world that unites the universal and the particular. Like Mill, Martineau, and Stanton, they perceived a world dominated by the terms of scientific rationalism, but they lacked the optimism of these writers as well. Without the certainty of a unifying cosmology or the comfort of an evolutionary faith, they found stability in the autobiographical act itself.

3

. . .

CONVERSION TO PRAGMATISM

The Varieties of Religious Experience and *The Education of Henry Adams*

In *Righteous Empire: The Protestant Experience in America,* Martin Marty argues that a theological and cultural split occurred within Protestantism near the end of the nineteenth century. This split was a result of post–Civil War sectionalism, the increased separation of the African- and Euro-centered churches, the influence of social Darwinism, and the growth of immigrant, urban, non-Protestant populations (133–209). Using the words of Josiah Strong, Marty notes that the "divisions were 'not to be distinguished by any of the old lines of doctrinal or denominational cleavage. Their difference is one of spirit, aim, point of view, comprehensiveness. The one is individualistic; the other is social' " (177). The first, most popular, of these groups emphasized personal redemption and a private relationship between the self and God. This individualism contributed to the demise of the Protestant "empire" by driving a wedge between the religious and socio-political dimensions of American life. According to Marty, "Colonial Protestantism involved believers in custodianship of the covenant for the whole community," and "early nineteenth-century evangelicalism called people to trusteeship of a religious-political empire" (168). But in the late nineteenth century such communal goals largely dissolved into what Marty calls "Private" Protestantism, which "accented individual salvation" and otherworldly concerns. As I hope the previous chapter makes clear, this privatization of the religious life is quite consistent with the way the spiritual autobiography was secularized in the eighteenth and nineteenth centuries.

On the other hand, Marty also describes a smaller, less popular faction that challenged this "Private" Protestantism: one that reemphasized and reconstructed older theologies of social consciousness, that focused on the regeneration of the present world, and that saw redemption in terms of society as a whole. This second movement, which Marty calls "Public" Protestantism, moved away from the techniques of evangelicalism and pursued a "Social Gospel," "Social Service," and "Social Realism," without totally giving up ideas of otherworldly salvation (179).

If one were to look for a mid-nineteenth-century figure who embodies the dialectic between public and private religion that Marty describes, one could do worse than to examine the writings of Henry James senior, a somewhat idiosyncratic disciple of the eighteenth-century Swedish mystic Emanuel Swedenborg. Unfortunately, other than his being the patriarch of a distinguished American family, what many are likely to remember about the elder James are things that were said of him at his own expense: the phrase, for instance, of William Dean Howells, who reportedly said James "wrote the Secret of Swedenborg and kept it"; or E. L. Godkin's remark that "one of his most amusing experiences was that the other Swedenborgians repudiated all religious connection with him, so that the sect to which he belonged, and of which he was the head, may be said to have consisted of himself alone" (Perry, 33, 23). As funny and as apt as these quips may be, had the elder James heard them, he would justifiably have been saddened, not only because they poke fun at his very earnest theology, but because they suggest that James's views were extremely individualistic and personal, so personal that only he knew where he stood.

The irony of course is that for all of James's individualism, his theology was socially minded, so much so that it anticipates the progressive "social" theology that Marty identifies. Salvation, for James, could come only with the renunciation of individualism and the general reformation of society. As Ralph Burton Perry famously put it, "According to Calvinism, men fall collectively, and are saved individually. . . . for James men fall individually, and are saved collectively!" (7). Interestingly, however, despite James's progressivism, his view of redemption coincided with older, orthodox explanations of conversion. For him, as well as for his Calvinist ancestors, regeneration occurred only when one had overthrown the "evils of selfhood" and embraced the divine principle. James's recollection of his Swedenborgian "vastation" reveals this principle nicely. This event took place in 1844, when James and his young family were in Windsor, England, where, after eating a "comfortable" dinner at home, he was suddenly struck by an "insane and abject terror," seemingly caused by "some damned shape squatting invisible to me within the precincts of the room, and raying out from his fetid personality influences fatal to life" (55–56). According to James, this emotional crisis lasted for two years, until he was introduced to the ideas of Swedenborg. He interpreted this terrifying experience as a destruction of the self that was a necessary precondition of his subsequent awakening:

> It was impossible for me . . . to hold this audacious faith in selfhood any longer. When I sat down to dinner on that memorable chilly afternoon in Windsor, I held it serene and unweakened by the faintest breath of doubt. Before I rose from table it had inwardly shrivelled to a cinder. One moment I devoutly thanked God for the inappreciable boon of selfhood; the next that inappreciable boon seemed to me the one thing damnable on earth, seemed a literal nest of hell within my own entrails. (67)

Though James believed that orthodox "Private" religion was in large part responsible for the privileging of selfhood that held society back (50), his view of conversion as an emptying of self is nevertheless orthodox. Though a friend and confidant of Emerson's, James distrusted the personal egotism and unperturbed "self-reliance" of the transcendentalists; in this and in other respects his theology is consistent with Calvinism. Giles Gunn argues that he did not want to "overthrow Calvinism, but rather to *humanize* it" (11). This statement captures the tensions within James, who was at once private, individualistic, innovative, and heterodox, while at the same time being outgoing, affable, conservative, and orthodox.

If the elder James manifests an internal tension between a "Public" and "Private" religious sensibility, his eldest son William was solidly and squarely an advocate of private religion, as his *Varieties of Religious Experience* makes clear. Insisting that he was "intensely an individualist" in a letter written to Grace Norton the same year the book was published, James argued that a believer's religion "must be the one which he finds best for *him,* even though there were better individuals, and their religion better for them."[1] In the *Varieties,* James not only identified a chasm between an individual's religious experience and the religion promulgated by institutions, he did not want to have anything to do with the latter. He

---

1. This letter, dated 12 September 1902, appears in Ralph Barton Perry's *Thought and Character of William James*, 262.

argued that the religion of the "conventional" believer, whether Christian or pagan, "has been made for him by others, communicated to him by tradition, determined to fixed forms by imitation, and retained by habit. It would profit us little to study this second-hand religious life" (15). The founders of the world's great religions were inspired by "firsthand" experiences, but by the time their belief becomes an orthodoxy "its day of inwardness is over: the spring is dry; the faithful live at second-hand exclusively and stone the prophets in their turn" (270). Clearly, James believed that "firsthand" (private) religion was the only religion worth studying.

Certainly father and son were very different. Henry senior was an antinomian monist, who went so far as to equate personal morality with egotism. William, on the other hand, was a pluralist who insisted on the efficacy of ethical behavior. For all of his distrust of the elder James's brand of social religion, however, he and his father were temperamentally very similar. Among other things, both wanted to transform religious rhetoric and religious consciousness in ways acceptable to the modern world—and both had dramatic, life-altering conversion experiences.[2] Indeed, religious experience played such an important part in William's life and background that he was personally disposed toward accepting its reality. From his father's vastation he knew of the powerful intellectual and behavioral effects of a spiritual rebirth, and he had undergone a similar turning point as a young man in 1870, when, unsure about his own career, he was afflicted with nervous symptoms and sickness. Triggered perhaps by the recent death of Minny Temple and reinforced by his being temporarily convinced that the universe could only be explained by a deterministic materialism, he succumbed to a deep depression (Allen, 164–65).

According to William's son Henry, James surreptitiously inserted a description of this emotional crisis in that section of the *Varieties* entitled the "Sick Soul," claiming that it had been anonymously sent to him by a "French correspondent":

> Whilst in this state of philosophic pessimism and general depression
> of spirits about my prospects, I went one evening into a dressing
> room in the twilight to procure some article that was there; when

2. For descriptions of the striking similarities between these two men, who had fundamental differences in their respective philosophies, see Perry, 8, and Gerald E. Myers, *William James*, 17–18.

suddenly there fell upon me without any warning, just as if it came out of the darkness, a horrible fear of my own existence.

James goes on to describe how he imaginatively associated himself with an "entirely idiotic" epileptic patient who looked "absolutely non-human": [3]

> There was such a horror of him, and such a perception of my own merely momentary discrepancy from him, that it was as if something hitherto solid within my breast gave way entirely, and I became a mass of quivering fear. After this the universe was changed for me altogether. . . . It was like a revelation.

What is striking about this passage is its similarity to the vastation account of Henry senior, which took place thirty-six years earlier. Curiously, both Henry senior and William personified the evil influence they perceived, the father, as an invisible "damned shape," and the son, as an epileptic patient. Both men were also relieved by reading: Henry senior, by the works of Swedenborg, and William, by the second of Charles Renouvier's *Essais*. After reading Renouvier, James recorded his sense of liberation in an 1870 notebook entry: [4]

> I think that yesterday was a crisis in my life. I finished the first part of Renouvier's second "Essais" and see no reason why his definition of Free Will—"the sustaining of a thought *because I choose to* when I might have other thoughts"—need be the definition of an illusion. At any rate, I will assume for the present—until next year—that it is no illusion. My first act of free will shall be to believe in free will. For the remainder of the year, I will abstain from mere . . . speculation . . . and voluntarily cultivate the feeling of moral freedom, by reading books favorable to it, as well as by acting. . . . For the present then remember: care little for speculation; much for the *form* of my action; recollect that only when habits of order are formed can we advance to really interesting fields of action— and consequently accumulate grain on grain of willful choice.

3. James's account of this episode, ostensibly written by an anonymous French correspondent, appears in the *Varieties*, 134–35. See also *The Letters of William James* 1:145–47.

4. This notebook entry, dated 30 April 1870, appears in *The Letters of William James* 1:147–48.

James was able to assuage his severe melancholy by making his first act of free will to believe in its existence. This belief justified his cultivation of positive thoughts and actions—a rationale that permanently relieved him from the worst of his suicidal despondency and ill health, though he was never wholly free from depression and sickness.

Howard Feinstein has argued that James's crisis of 1870 was more a literary posture than a genuine turning point in his life and that Ralph Barton Perry and subsequent critics have erroneously claimed that this crisis amounted to a spiritual and intellectual rebirth similar to both his father's vastation and to a typical Christian conversion (306–12). Feinstein points out that James was already familiar with Renouvier's thought in 1870 and that the "crisis" was merely one of several such events he records in his notebook. Regardless of the extent to which the actual events of 1870 conform to James's diary entry, however, the fact that he inscribed his "discovery" of free will as a significant crisis and a liberating reversal reveals his grasp of the cognitive reality of the conversion process. Like his father, he best understood what happened to him in 1870 in the terms of conversion discourse.

If James's life changed dramatically after he read Renouvier, his rebirth did not lead directly to a vocation, though he admitted that his appointment at Harvard three years later and his subsequent immersion in the social and intellectual life there became his salvation. Like many of his nineteenth-century contemporaries, including Henry Adams, James found the process of deciding on a vocation to be a trying ordeal. For him, relief came not by acquiring a specific occupation but by embracing the Protestant work ethic generally (King, 164). Even after he had become established at Harvard, he found it difficult to occupy an academic niche. He was at once physician, philosopher, literary figure, public speaker, theologian, psychologist, and not quite any of these.

Still, James's entry into the academic life at Harvard resembles the call to the ministry experienced by many spiritual autobiographers. As a faculty member, he embraced oratorical roles such as those generated by the Lyceum and Chautauqua movements. According to Bruce Kuklick, James, like other members of Harvard's philosophy department, became a secular minister by addressing large, educated audiences who believed that what they heard had an impact on their daily lives. These philosophers were particularly anxious about the validity of religious beliefs. Kuklick states, "Religious skepticism troubled them, as it troubled society's leadership, and the outcome of their thinking was predictable. They defended conventional spiritual values, if in chastened form" (xviii). Acting as philosophical pastors, intellectuals like James ultimately reassured their audiences about the basic worth of human existence and of traditional institutions.

Darwinism was responsible for much of the anxiety experienced by the cultural elite, principally because it forced individuals to decide between the apparently irreconcilable positions of empiricism or rationalism. To many, the universe was either a single system governed by a transcendent power or a destructive blend of impersonal forces, but it could not be both (Kuklick, 21–27). James responded to this problem throughout his career and believed his pragmatism mediated between the tenets of monism and pluralism.[5] He agreed that the universe was diverse, yet he stressed the mind's ability to unify the chaos of objects and ideas. In a footnote to the *Varieties* he wrote:

> Order and disorder, as we now recognize them, are purely human inventions. We are interested in certain types of arrangement, useful, aesthetic, or moral—so interested that whenever we find them realized, the fact emphatically rivets our attention. The result is that we work over the contents of the world selectively. It is overflowing with disorderly arrangements from our point of view, but order is the only thing we care for and look at, and by choosing, one can always find some sort of orderly arrangement in the midst of any chaos. (346)

It is in passages like these that James sounds most like Henry Adams.

Thirty-seven years after his crisis in 1870, William wrote to Adams and asked for a privately printed copy of the *Education*. In that letter he justified his request by arguing that "autobiographies are my particular line of literature, the only books I let myself buy outside of metaphysical treatises."[6] James's claim to be interested in autobiography is amply supported by the *Varieties*, a text filled with excerpts from autobiographies both sacred and secular. He mentioned many of the writers I have discussed, among them Augustine, Bunyan, Edwards, Wordsworth, Carlyle, and Mill: "If the inquiry be psychological, not religious institutions, but rather religious feelings and religious impulses must be its subject, and

---

5. See *Pragmatism*, 9–26, and Henry Levinson, *The Religious Investigations of William James*, 166, 243–47.

6. James's letter and Adams's reply both appear in *Letters of Henry Adams (1892–1918)*, 485–86.

I must confine myself to those more developed subjective phenomena recorded in literature produced by articulate and fully self-conscious men, in works of piety and autobiography" (12). Though he probably would not have seen it that way, his work was as much a study of autobiography as it was an examination of religious experience. Published in 1902, the *Varieties* can thus stand as the first "modern" study of self-writing.

Though James differentiated between narratives that record genuine religious experience and those based on "suggestion" and "imitation," he failed to explain his procedure for doing so, other than by stating that the works he studied had widely acknowledged literary merit. Yet for all his reliance on autobiographical documentation, he paid little attention to textual conventions themselves. When he noticed patterns among religious experiences, he assumed that they were caused by the congruity of certain psychological phenomena, rather than by the existence of a literary tradition. Critics have explained that James overlooked autobiographical conventions because, throughout his work, he emphasized that discourse itself constitutes experience and is a means by which individuals fashion reality, but nowhere in the *Varieties* does he explicitly separate textual experience from "firsthand" phenomena.[7] For James, literary conventions had little to do with the testimony of religious geniuses "best able to give an intelligible account of their ideas and motives" (12). He presented their narratives as "objective" representations of their subjective experience.

James's almost antinomian privileging of personal religious experience at the expense of established creeds and institutions reflects the post-Enlightenment emphasis on the uniqueness of the individual, a conception that informs much of his philosophical thought. Even if James admitted that some religious autobiographies were the products of imitation and suggestion, he nevertheless considered the works he chose as empirical data. Seeking to steer a middle course between rationalism, which grounded its assumptions on unverifiable categories, and traditional empiricism, which confined its investigations to sense impressions, he believed that scientific judgments could be made about extrasensory experience. The best sources for such data were the personal accounts of exemplary religious figures because, for James, beliefs spring primarily from the emotions and are somehow divorced from the conscious operations of the reasoning mind. "I do believe," he wrote, "that feeling is the deeper source of

---

7. J. O. King argues that James saw discourse as reality, in *The Iron of Melancholy*, 93, 150.

religion, and that philosophic and theological formulas are secondary prod-ucts, like translations of a text into another tongue" (341). Empiricists who disregarded emotional, intuitive, and other extrasensory experiences se-verely limited their study of reality.

Applying his brand of empiricism to religion, James called his Gifford Lectures—which later became the *Varieties*—a "laborious attempt to ex-tract from the privacies of religious experience some general facts which can be defined in formulas upon which everybody may agree" (342). In the conclusion to the book, James did just that, drawing the diversity of religious experience into a single system, observing that "there is probably no autobiographic document, among all those which I have quoted, to which the description will not well apply":

> The warring gods and formulas of the various religions do indeed cancel each other, but there is a certain uniform deliverance in which religions all appear to meet. It consists of two parts:
> 1. An uneasiness; and
> 2. Its solution.
> 1. The uneasiness, reduced to its simplest terms, is a sense that there is *something wrong about us* as we naturally stand.
> 2. The solution is a sense that *we are saved from the wrongness* by making proper connection with the higher powers. . . .
> It seems to me that all the phenomena are accurately describable in these very simple general terms. (400–401)

James's ability to extract a single formula from his mass of autobiographical data, which has caused critics to complain of a lack of variety in the *Varieties*, illustrates his tendency to choose examples that conform to some stage of the Christian conversion pattern. More than anything else, James's synthesis attests to the pervasiveness (and to the privileging) of conversion discourse in autobiographical literature.

Conversion, for James, was the quintessential religious experience be-cause he saw it as the mechanism by which the divided self struggles toward a new center of meaning and activity. Following his former student E. D. Starbuck, James located the site of conversion in the subliminal or subconscious portion of the mind: "To say that a man is 'converted' means, in these terms, that religious ideas, previously peripheral in his conscious-ness, now take a central place, and that religious aims form the habitual centre of his energy" (162). James explained that the pain and anxiety that precede conversion correspond to a period of "order-making and struggle" resulting from the subconscious incubation of new ideas or beliefs. These ideas become the center of conscious activity during conversion, which James defines as the "process, gradual or sudden, by which a self hitherto divided, and consciously wrong inferior and unhappy, becomes unified and consciously right superior and happy, in consequence of its firmer hold upon religious realities" (157). Using the "hackneyed symbolism of a mechanical equilibrium," James explains how this event takes place: "A new perception, a sudden emotional shock, or an occasion which lays bare the organic alteration, will make the whole fabric fall together; and then the centre of gravity sinks into an attitude more stable, for the new ideas that reach the centre in the rearrangement seem now to be locked there" (163). Possessed by a new center of conscious activity, the believer feels reborn, perceives the world with rejuvenated faculties, and does things he or she was never able to do before.

The essential feature of the conversion process, for James, was the moment of self-surrender. Though he admitted that some forms of regeneration appear to be willed, in the final analysis volitional conversion is indistinguishable from the conversion of submission:

> Even in the most voluntarily built-up sort of regeneration there are passages of partial self-surrender interposed; and in the great majority of all cases, when the will has done its uttermost towards bringing one close to the complete unification aspired after, it seems that the very last step must be left to other forces and performed without the help of its activity. In other words, self-surrender becomes then indispensable. (171)

According to James, conversion, at bottom, always entails a surrender because only then can the conscious preoccupation with the inadequacy of the self be replaced by a new field of subconsciously incubated mental activity:

> Since, in any terms, the crisis described is the throwing of our conscious selves upon the mercy of powers which, whatever they may be, are more ideal than we are actually, and make for our redemption, you see why self-surrender has been and always must be regarded as the vital turning-point of the religious life, so far as

the religious life is spiritual, and no affair of outer works and ritual and sacraments. (173)

The subconscious origin of conversion thus explains why the regenerate feel that grace is imposed from without and why they are unable to activate their own faith.

James's psychological account of conversion coincides with its theological explanation to such an extent that even he admired the "congruity of Protestant theology with the structure of the mind as shown in such experiences" (198–99). He went so far as to leave open the possibility that conversion was caused by a divine agency that works on the subconscious: "It is logically conceivable that *if there be* higher spiritual agencies that can directly touch us, the psychological condition of their doing so *might be* our possession of a subconscious region which alone should yield access to them. The hubbub of the waking life might close a door which in the dreamy Subliminal might remain ajar or open" (197). Statements such as these, of course, must have drawn a sigh of relief from the believers in James's audience. In an age increasingly wary of the scientific challenge to traditional faith, James gave an empirical validity to the most fundamental Christian process.

Despite James's intricate merging of Christian and psychological explanations for conversion, he nevertheless claimed that it was a "natural" human phenomenon, a type of personality change not confined to the Christian life. Throughout the *Varieties*, he maintained that religious states are psychologically identical to other subjective events. For those whose conscious fields have a "hard rind of a margin," for instance, conversion resembles "any simple growth into new habits" (197); and an individual can be converted to a wide range of attitudes and beliefs:

> To find religion is only one out of many ways of reaching unity; and the process of remedying inner incompleteness and reducing inner discord is a general psychological process, which may take place with any sort of mental material, and need not necessarily assume the religious form. . . . For example, the new birth may be away from religion into incredulity; or it may be from moral scrupulosity into freedom and license; or it may be produced by the irruption into the individual's life of some new stimulus or passion, such as love, ambition, cupidity, revenge, or patriotic devotion. In all these

instances we have precisely the same psychological form of event. (146–47)

The conversion process thus became a model for many types of cognitive activity and could be used to explain how individuals embraced any belief system or achieved a personal reorientation. In this respect, James viewed conversion in much the same way as many of the Romantic and Victorian autobiographers I have examined. This congruity is hardly surprising, of course, since his text-based study was largely dependent upon their formulations. To the degree, however, that James incorporated conversion into the individualistic pragmatism that he was beginning to formulate in the *Varieties*, his interpretation moved well beyond theirs and amounted to a radical redefinition of the conversion experience.

Placing his thinking in the context of his psychobiography, J. O. King has said that the *Varieties* represents a synecdoche of James's own life: his physical and intellectual wandering, his despair, his crisis and regeneration, and his acquiring of a vocation.[8] James's personal familiarity with spiritual rebirth, as well as his obvious fascination with the tradition of spiritual autobiography, was so much a part of his conception of religious experience that, except for the opening and closing chapters, he structured his *Varieties* along the lines of a typical conversion narrative (King, 165, 192). Piecing together bits of autobiographies, James moved an ideal religious figure through periods of healthy-mindedness, spiritual sickness, the divided self, conversion, sanctification, and mystical union.

If one views the *Varieties*, however, as a synecdoche of James's own life, there is an interesting tension between his willingness to see his experience with Renouvier in the terms of a conventional "metaphorical" conversion and his practice of assembling bits and pieces of spiritual autobiographies in the construction of a universal religious self. As "scientific" as he believed this approach to be, it is not very different from Emerson's escape from autobiography on the grounds that the particular always informs the universal. That James anonymously inserted his own autobiographical fragment into the narrative reveals that he believed his recorded experience illustrated the general structure of the human mind. In the *Varieties*, his crisis of 1870 was a small piece of evidence used to illustrate a universal psychological pattern; in the discourse of his notebook, however, it marked

8. King, 195. For other psychobiographical studies of James's *Varieties*, see Cushing Strout's two articles "The Pluralistic Identity of William James" and "William James and the Twice-Born Sick Soul."

a fundamental change in his personal history. In the *Varieties*, he insisted that conversion always entails "self-surrender," while in the notebook he indicated that he was able to "voluntarily cultivate" his liberating belief in free will. Here he is caught in a contradiction so profound that he appears to have been completely unaware of it. On the one hand, his scientific impulse was to merge data into a single all-encompassing paradigm; on the other hand, he needed to establish a unique, "personal" history that enabled him to escape from the universalizing determinism of empirical rhetoric. It was out of such a contradiction that his pragmatism was born.

Though James left open the possibility that conversion was the result of divine intervention, he pragmatically assessed religious awakenings, not by appealing to a transcendent authority, but "by their effects." Using Jonathan Edwards as an example, James showed how even the orthodox ultimately gauge the genuineness of a reported conversion by its consequences. For James, "beliefs are rules for action," and he judged specific awakenings according to the utilitarian value they had for individuals. Though he acknowledged that these judgments were based on "prejudices, instincts and common sense," he defended his means of evaluation by arguing that "common-sense prejudices and instincts are themselves the fruit of an empirical evolution" (263–64).

James's awareness of the wide variety of conversion experiences and their manifold consequences, both constructive and destructive, made him skeptical of the veracity of any single belief system. "No one organism," James states, "can possibly yield to its owner the whole body of truth" (28). Sectarians have traditionally grounded their various social, political, or religious creeds on personal revelation, but James—like Thomas Paine one hundred years before him—insisted that, though revelation may be authoritative for individuals, it had no authority over others. He denounced emphatically the process by which religious belief became a source of coercion, finding that "intolerance and persecution have come to be vices associated by some of us inseparably with the saintly mind" (274). When religion becomes a corporate endeavor, overzealousness, fanaticism, cruelty, and even murder can result. This shift from the religious certitude of individuals to the tyranny of institutional belief skirts possibilities themselves suggested by James about the extramental (and perhaps divine) origin of conversion: finally only a psychological pattern remains. James's individualism thus covers a hole in his argument; he comes close to saying that the individual is always justified in acting upon her or his belief; but spreading that belief—by persuasion or other means—is always wrong.

This underlying contradiction can only be explained in terms of James's own personality. His fear of group dominion was psychologically linked to his fear of determinism: both limited the freedom that he had willed himself to believe after reading Renouvier.

James distrusted the rigid assurance of those who believed themselves to be elect, because he realized that despite "common sense," diverse judgments about religious phenomena are unavoidable and that the "theorizing mind tends always to the over-simplification of its materials." This inevitable consequence of discovering unity in multiplicity was "the root of all that absolutism and one-sided dogmatism by which both philosophy and religion have been infested" (30). Admitting that absolute conceptions of truth comfort many, he nevertheless insisted that truth is made, not experienced or intuited:

> Since it is impossible to deny secular alterations in our sentiments and needs, it would be absurd to affirm that one's own age of the world can be beyond correction by the next age. . . . He who acknowledges the imperfectness of his instrument, and makes allowance for it in discussing his observations, is in a much better position for gaining truth than if he claimed his instrument to be infallible. . . .
> . . . The wisest of critics is an altering being, subject to the better insight of the morrow. (266–67)

Without excluding the possibility of the absolute, he argued that "pragmatism has to postpone dogmatic answer" (*Pragmatism*, 144).

Though James renounced the possibility of achieving certitude, he, in a sense, still tried to have it both ways: individuals should conduct inquiry as if absolute truth were attainable, yet at the same time they should recognize that their search is relative. He states, "To admit one's liability to correction is one thing, and to embark upon a sea of wanton doubt is another" (*Varieties*, 267). For James, "*the true opposites of belief*, psychologically considered, *are doubt and inquiry, not disbelief*" (*Principles* 2:284). Rather than despair over their inability to merge with the absolute, individuals should enthusiastically participate in the creation of reality. For him, idea formation was an endless process: the truths obtained from empirically derived facts are always being tested by their ability to immerse the subject in the continual flow of existence: " 'Facts' themselves . . . are not *true*. They simply *are*. Truth is the function of the beliefs that start and terminate among them" (*Pragmatism*, 108). According to James, absolute truth was static and therefore dead; it limited inquiry and artificially fixed ideas in an ever-changing world.

James was psychologically predisposed to reject absolutist claims because the inexhaustible process of cognitive transformation gave his life value. To James, determinism was an inevitable consequence of absolutist or materialist positions, both of which signified moral inertia, intellectual confinement, and despair. His pragmatism, "a mediator between tough-mindedness and tendermindedness," steered a course between these two positions and justified the belief in free will that he considered to be essential to his well-being. Pragmatism, for James, was finally a form of therapy, a realization that human beings meaningfully contribute to the creation of a pluralistic universe. He revealed his emotional attachment to his philosophy by calling it "happy-go-lucky," "melioristic," "forward," "friendly," and "democratic."

If James focused, not on the intellectual contents of conversion experiences, but on their effects, he strangely failed to examine conversion as a social or a linguistic event. Insisting that religious experience was personal and private, he demonstrated that it often led to positive mental change and to a life of productivity, but he paid little attention to conversion as an initiation into a community of believers or as a prelude to the acceptance of a vocation. Conversion, for him, was not so much the result of social and linguistic structures as it was a psychological event fostered by an individual's subconsciousness. James's failure to discuss the socializing function of conversion discourse is a product of his deeply felt need to separate individual from corporate identity, a need that is manifested by the dual treatment of his own conversion. Because he feared the tyranny of group dogmatism and the external imposition of fixed beliefs, he overlooked the social and linguistic implications of conversion and distrusted the rigid self-definition associated with traditional notions of a "vocation." His own rebirth may have led to the cultivation of beneficial cognitive and behavioral habits, but he took comfort in knowing that his thoughts and activities were always subject to change. To the pragmatist, boundaries are man-made and arbitrary, and for James to have limited himself to a single discipline or professional role would have been to embrace fixity and to flirt with his greatest fear—madness. To combat this fear, he constructed an identity based on resistance to social and linguistic imperatives—a sacred estrangement.

Toward the end of the *Varieties*, in his critique of the value of philosophical speculation, James concluded that the "attempt to demonstrate by purely intellectual processes the truth of the deliverances of direct religious experience is absolutely hopeless." Instead he called for philosophers to "abandon metaphysics and deduction for criticism and induction" and to embrace a science of religion that could "eventually command as general a public adhesion as is commanded by a physical science" (359–60). James modestly offered his own Gifford Lectures as a "crumb-like contribution to such a science" (342). By denouncing age-old philosophical methods, however, he revealed that his study was far from unambitious. The definitive religious experience, conversion, for James, was so vast in its scope and so integral to the way the mind functions that it provided an all but universal epistemological model. In this sense the *Varieties* was more than a study of a religion; it was a systematic attempt to arrive at an empirically grounded worldview that acknowledged the reality and utility of subjective states. By studying conversion, James was able to test his pragmatic method and to illustrate the mind's ability to run order through chaos.

In positing this synthesis, James also radically revised conversion discourse. By treating conversion "scientifically," he shifted the focus away from communities of belief toward the psychology of the individual. Instead of binding one to the world, or trying to persuade others to transform the world, conversion became an inner transformation that, if anything, drew one's attention to the "essential" isolation of human existence. His approach to conversion provides a revealing introduction to how later Americans would adopt the rhetoric of conversion to their own autobiographical acts. Earlier in this chapter, I argued that James was the first "modern" theorist of autobiography; in the sense that his *Varieties* seeks to define the self in generic terms, he may also have been the most influential. Though today's theorists of autobiography would find his failure to investigate the social and linguistic dimensions of conversion to be naive, his focus on the psychology of the individual is the starting point for the current obsession with the problematics of "self" in narrative.

In the same letter to Henry Adams previously referred to, William James playfully upbraided his friend for failing to send him a copy of the *Education*, suggesting that the two should fight a duel because in the book Adams had accused him of "having made of Cambridge a conversational desert." Two days later, Adams responded by sending the book, saying that his correspondent certainly had a "right to the volume" but adding that he would be "rather inclined to weep and wail in advance" if James got hold of it because, he states, "I knew your views better than my own" (485). This exchange reveals an intellectual and literary intimacy between two former Harvard colleagues whose philosophies are normally considered to be very different. Though Adams called James his "oldest teacher" (*Letters*, 543), he found him overly optimistic, disagreeing especially with his belief in free will. Adams found little justification for the meliorism implicit in James's pragmatism, while James, on his part, found Adams's scientific determinism narrow and needlessly pessimistic. If James perceived the usefulness of existing institutions and practices, Adams blasted the moral and political values of his generation for being hopelessly out of touch with the complexity of twentieth-century life. James particularly disliked Adams's attempt to turn history into a predictive science. He admitted that past events were irrevocably fixed but felt that the future could be influenced by the free actions of human beings. As Adams's biographer, Ernest Samuels, states, James "offered a kind of scientific Arminianism to combat the scientific Calvinism of his friend" (*Middle Years*, 233).

For all of his fire and brimstone, however, Adams had ambivalent feelings about his own pessimism and, according to Samuels, maintained a Jamesian "practical optimism" that "lingered on in spite of his carefully cultivated cynicism" (233). Samuels's observation illustrates an underlying similarity between these two men that is frequently overshadowed by their disagreement over free will and determinism. Despite their differences, Adams and James both saw the limitations of reason, and both were fascinated by the role of religion in an increasingly secular world.

In the *Education*'s two prefaces, Henry Adams immediately invoked the subject of conversion by announcing—grandly, yet modestly—that his "great ambition was to complete St. Augustine's 'Confessions,' but that St. Augustine, like a great artist, had worked from multiplicity to unity, while he, like a small one, had to reverse the method and work back from unity to multiplicity."[9] By borrowing Carlyle's tailor-and-clothes metaphor and alluding to Franklin and Rousseau, he further set his work in the context of the existing canon of self-writing. Saying that no modern writer "has discussed what part of education has, in his personal experience, turned out to be useful, and what not," Adams ironically belittled the efforts of autobiographers such as Franklin, Rousseau, Carlyle, and Mill; but in so

9. The *Education*, vii-viii. Though the first or "Editor's" preface to the *Education* is signed by Henry Cabot Lodge, both prefaces were written by Adams. See Ernest Samuels, *The Major Phase*, 559–60.

doing he also invited readers to interpret his work according to the conventions of the spiritual autobiography. [10]

Adams claimed that he was the first writer to examine the usefulness of education. Just as James focused on the practical consequences of religious experience, Adams pragmatically proposed to "fit young men, in universities or elsewhere, to be men of the world, equipped for any emergency" (x). Though Adams could not have been influenced by *Pragmatism*, because most of the *Education* had been written before it was published, enough of James's philosophy appeared in his *Principles of Psychology* (which Adams read carefully in 1902), as well as in the *Varieties*, to suggest that he had been profoundly influenced by his friend's thought. [11] Despite their differences, their epistemologies mirror each other to such an extent that the *Education* echoes words, phrases, and categories found in the *Varieties*. Both men tried to establish a scientific basis for a faith they needed psychologically but in which they could not possibly believe. In this respect, the *Education* is much like the *Varieties*; both works offer evaluations and interpretations of the literature based on conversion. While Adams and James placed conversion into a "natural" cognitive framework, however, they did so to make vastly different statements. James merged the process of conversion with a wide variety of other personality changes, but he presented a psychological framework that coincided with orthodox interpretations of religious conversion. Adams, however, inverted the spiritual autobiography form and in so doing "reverses the method" of Augustine's *Confessions*. Finally a story of failed conversion, the *Education* nevertheless depends upon the narrative structure of the traditional spiritual autobiography.

If James claimed that conversion was an experiential reality for many individuals and left open the possibility that its source was divine, Adams, like John Stuart Mill before him, completely demystified the conversion pattern: moments of illumination became simply occasions of education. Yet throughout the *Education* the process of acquiring knowledge is most often couched in religious language. Education is a matter of personal faith

10. Gene Koretz compares Adams's autobiography to Augustine's in "Augustine's *Confessions* and *The Education of Henry Adams*." For a comparison of the *Education* and *Sartor Resartus*, see R. P. Blackmur, *Henry Adams*, 151–60. The following critics compare Adams to Franklin and place the *Education* in an American autobiographical tradition: James Cox, "Autobiography and America"; Ross Miller, "Autobiography as Fact and Fiction"; David Minter, *The Interpreted Design*, 103–36; and Robert Sayre, *The Examined Self*, 90–136.

11. Max Baym examines Adams's annotations to a copy of the *Principles of Psychology* in "William James and Henry Adams."

and social redemption. In his boyhood, for example, Adams learned that "education was divine, and man needed only a correct knowledge of facts to reach perfection" (33). Even while contemplating the dynamo at the book's end, he decided to "risk translating rays into faith" (383). Adams may have lost hope in a personal God, but his tropes were often derived from his Puritan ancestors.

If Adams demystified the conversion pattern, he, like James, nevertheless maintained an almost antinomian distrust of reason.[12] Since education is described as revelation, its lessons occurred unexpectedly and spontaneously, somehow divorced from the conscious operation of the mind. A priori thinking, for Adams, was next to useless. He comments, for instance, on the incomprehensibility of his diplomatic education: "From the facts, the conclusion was correct, yet, as usual, the conclusion was wrong" (193). Referring to his family's break with Charles Sumner, he states, "The profoundest lessons are not the lessons of reason; they are sudden strains that permanently warp the mind" (108). Elsewhere, he says, "The mind resorts to reason for want of training, and Adams had never met a perfectly trained mind" (370). To him, knowledge was faith, and humans could not reason themselves into belief. Like Augustine, Edwards, Carlyle's Teufelsdröckh, and ultimately all of James's subjects in the *Varieties*, the manikin Adams acquires the most profound knowledge from sources outside the conscious self.

Daniel Shea, who includes the *Education* in the tradition of spiritual autobiography, states that Adams found himself continually in "rhetorical situations" comparable to those of his Puritan predecessors. As an example, Shea compares the young Adams's sudden appreciation of Beethoven to a religious conversion. Though Adams loathed Beethoven at first, he underwent a dramatic reversal while drinking beer in a German music hall:

> Sitting thus at his beer-table, mentally impassive, he was one day surprised to notice that his mind followed the movement of a Sinfonie. He could not have been more astonished had he suddenly read a new language. . . . A prison-wall that barred his senses on one great side of life, suddenly fell, of its own accord, without so much as his knowing when it happened . . . a new sense burst out like a flower in his life, so superior to the old senses, so bewildering,

12. For Adams's distrust of reason, see R. P. Blackmur, *Henry Adams*, 56; J. C. Levenson, *The Mind and Art of Henry Adams*, 321–22; Melvin Lyon, *Symbol and Idea in Henry Adams*, 3–8; and Yvor Winters, "Henry Adams or the Creation of Confusion," 380–88.

so astonished at its own existence, that he could not credit it, and watched it as something apart, accidental, and not to be trusted. (80–81)

Analyzing this passage, Shea states,

In language Jonathan Edwards would have found familiar, an experience of conversion has just been set forth in its distinguishing marks: suddenness, awe, inexplicability, a rapturous "new sense," and a consequent alteration of mind. . . . But like previous appeals in the *Education* to a non-utilitarian sense of the heart . . . this one must be rejected. Education which is both accidental and aesthetic is no education at all for the twentieth century. (267)

Shea calls this experience a "mock-conversion" because, unlike the spiritual awakenings of Jonathan Edwards, it provided no center of meaning from which Adams could order his life. Without faith, Adams was capable of accidental education, but such knowledge was without any ultimate value.

Although Shea calls Adams's reaction to Beethoven a unique turning point, he fails to see the pervasiveness of the mock conversion pattern in the *Education*. Just as many traditional spiritual autobiographies record not one but a series of conversion events, Adams's musical education is merely a single instance of his typical method of perceiving reality. This passage—along with many others like it—reveals the synecdochical character of Adams's entire text. He describes similar experiences and draws similar conclusions when he meets Swinburne, when he sits for the first time on the steps of the Ara Coeli in Rome, when he lies on the grass at Wenlock Abbey, when he visits world's fairs, and elsewhere. At every turn Adams's nonconversions occur when his hopes for genuine understanding are highest. In moments of spontaneously generated awareness, however, these hopes are utterly crushed. Typically, each disillusionment is followed by another process of hopeful inquiry, which in turn is shattered by another intuitive realization of failure. The baffled self is identical in each textual moment.

An example of this inverse conversion pattern can be found in Adams's chapter on Darwin. Darwin's ideas were so attractive that Adams initially felt that he had anticipated them: "He was a Darwinist before the letter; a predestined follower of the tide" (224). As a young man Adams had "insisted on maintaining his absolute standards" (232), and Darwin's theories, along with those of Lyell, appeared to unify natural history and to justify a faith in progress:

> Natural Selection led back to Natural Evolution, and at last to Natural Uniformity. This was a vast stride. Unbroken Evolution under uniform conditions pleased every one—except curates and bishops; it was the very best substitute for religion; a safe, conservative Common-Law deity. . . . the idea was only too seductive in its perfection; it had the charm of art. (225–26)

Yet in working with Lyell, Adams was impressed not by the uniformity of his theories but by the exceptions to them, most notably *Terebratula* and *Pteraspis*, two animals that stubbornly resisted evolution for millions of years:

> He was conscious that, in geology as in theology, he could prove only Evolution that did not evolve; Uniformity that was not uniform; and Selection that did not select. To other Darwinians—except Darwin—Natural Selection seemed a dogma to be put in the place of the Athanasian creed; it was a form of religious hope; a promise of ultimate perfection. Adams wished no better; he warmly sympathized in the object; but when he came to ask himself what he truly thought, he felt that he had no Faith. (231)

Ultimately, Darwinism, like all definitive intellectual systems, was elusive and unverifiable.

A number of critics have noticed the rising and falling pattern of failure in the *Education*. Tony Tanner, for instance, states that "every new idealistic expectation is followed by a disillusioning event." Melvin Lyon likens this pattern of "repeated disillusionment" to the Fall: "The fall—the collapse of unity—comes to seem to him the basic experience of human life. . . . The form paralleling the movement is wavelike, question and answer being always the same."[13] This wavelike sequence is a mirror image of the cycles of hope and despair, the "paradox of Puritan piety" pattern found in the traditional spiritual autobiography. While the author of a conversion narrative receives grace after periods of profound despair and

---

13. Tony Tanner, "Henry Adams and Henry James," 100; Melvin Lyon, *Symbol and Idea in Henry Adams*, 115. See also George Hochfield, *Henry Adams: An Introduction and Interpretation*, 121.

an awareness of the meaninglessness of life, Adams has his "conversions" while most hopeful, when he believes he has gained genuine and useful knowledge. About to embrace a political, philosophical, or scientific system, he unexpectedly discovers it to be completely untenable. In each case, by using the rhetoric of conversion, Adams effectively communicates his sense of bewilderment and awe, his recognition of the innate intellectual depravity of humankind.

Adams illustrates the potentially destructive side of this epistemology as he remembers his sister's death. Just prior to this event he had been awakened to the beauty and healing power of Nature: "When spring came, he took to the woods which were best of all, for after the first of April . . . 'the vast maternity' of nature showed charms more voluptuous than the vast paternity of the United States Senate" (282). Soon afterward, however, this same benign Nature delivered its harshest blow, "the sum and term of education," when his sister suffered miserably from tetanus. Adams presented his reaction to her death as a horrible satanic conversion, as illuminating as it was devastating:

> Impressions like these are not reasoned or catalogued in the mind; they are felt as part of violent emotion; and the mind that feels them is a different one from that which reasons. . . . The first serious consciousness of Nature's gesture—her attitude toward life—took form then as a phantasm, a nightmare, an insanity of force. For the first time the stage-scenery of the senses collapsed; the human mind felt itself stripped naked, vibrating in a void of shapeless energies, with resistless mass, colliding, crushing, wasting, and destroying what these same energies had created and labored from eternity to perfect. (288)

Combining the language of apocalypse and revelation, Adams shattered his former assertion of Nature's restorative power. Like Cotton Mather, who fell prostrate on the floor in recognition of his total helplessness before God, Adams feels his absolute powerlessness in the face of a resistless and indifferent Nature.

Though at almost every instance of conversion, Adams claims that education is a failure, on each occasion he draws the same conclusion: "that in the last synthesis, order and anarchy were one, but that the unity was chaos" (406). Each awakening offered little or nothing in the way of usable knowledge, but like the numerous moments of revelation in a conversion narrative, together they had a cumulative effect. The cyclic process of hope and despair, insight and failure, led to Adams's basic understanding of the universe. It was an understanding based on a paradox: order is chaos. A "conservative Christian anarchist," Adams, from first to last, reveled in the verbal possibilities of this paradox. The *Education* is filled with such phrases as "The more he was educated, the less he understood" (44); "Education began at the end, or perhaps would end at the beginning" (73); "the more he knew, the less he was educated" (239); and "He knew enough to be ignorant" (300). Adams's cumulative understanding of the chaotic multiverse matches the believer's growing awareness of the effect of saving grace. Just as assurance gives a sense of form and relation to the traditional conversion narrative, Adams's paradoxical realization unites the various and often chaotic strands of experience and language in the text. In the *Varieties*, James found that mystics frequently use "self-contradictory phrases" (333) to describe their ineffable union with higher powers; in the *Education*, Adams did so to illustrate the incomprehensibility of all experience.

Even though he subverted the conventions of the traditional spiritual autobiography, Adams's discovery of the impossibility of achieving definitive knowledge corresponds to James's interpretation of conversion. If James made it clear that the process of acquiring any belief system was psychologically identical to a religious awakening, then Adams's "conversions" are the result of his acquiring a pragmatic epistemology. Adams began his life thinking that truth was fixed and absolute; unable to forget this presupposition completely, he was continually shocked into realizing that truth is a human creation, subject to change and hopelessly imprecise. His final, begrudging acceptance of this position constitutes the "saved" or enlightened perspective from which he wrote his text—though his new awareness caused dread instead of spiritual comfort.

Education was a failure, and chaos the only true revelation, because Adams finally believed that to commit oneself to a belief system was to distort reality. To expound a single worldview was to embrace falsehood. Much like James, Adams believed that intellectual attainment limits inquiry; the established "fact" kills: "Nothing in education," he states, "is so astonishing as the amount of ignorance it accumulates in the form of inert facts" (379). In the *Education*, Charles Sumner functions as the supreme example of intellectual fixity. Adams compared his mind to a pool of water that "receives and reflects images without absorbing them; it contained nothing but itself" (252). Though Adams believed that Sumner had the best political mind of his time, he destroyed it by limiting himself to a single perspective, a single purpose. Aware of such dangers, Adams thus made his autobiography "a treatise on inconclusion" (Wagner, 91, 170–80).

While the traditional conversion narrative joins the search for grace to the search for a vocation, the *Education*, as an anticonversion narrative, frustrates this pattern. Unlike the conversion narrative's male author who typically embraces the ministry, or his secular descendants who become writer/prophets, Adams is condemned to lead a life without ever establishing a permanent social position. Describing his early career as a reformer, Adams states, "He was a free-lance and no other career stood before him." In a sense, this phrase is prophetic. Adams remains a "free-lance" throughout the book. Just as the fact kills, the "office" is poison:

> In his fancy, office was poison; it killed—body and soul—physically and socially. Office was more poisonous than priestcraft or pedagogy in proportion as it held more power. . . . [Hay's] poison was that of the will—the distortion of sight—the warping of mind—the degradation of tissue—the coarsening of taste—the narrowing of sympathy to the emotions of a caged rat. (365)

Though Adams specifically refers to his friend John Hay's acceptance of a political office here, he clearly associates the evils of office with any kind of an established "career." Official positions do more than corrupt, they promote stagnation and fixity. A "stable-companion to statesman" with "no position in the world," Adams, from beginning to end, refused to define himself by a vocation, whether as a diplomat, a lawyer, a professor, a journalist, an editor, or a gentleman. Just as James would not be limited by academic boundaries, Adams believed that the only way to be intellectually active was to remain professionally undefined. Adams even downplayed his role as a historian. The manikin Adams takes to his pen, not with conviction and confidence, but because he cannot think of anything else to do: choosing to write was a process of elimination. Critics and biographers have shown that in reality Adams had high ambitions, that he saw history as a branch of literature, and that he defined himself as an artist; but his autobiographical persona submerges these conceptions.[14] His most produc-

14. One of the major concerns of Ernest Samuels's three-volume biography of Adams and of William Dusinberre's *Henry Adams: The Myth of Failure* is to show how important Adams considered his literary life to be. According to these scholars, Adams set out to be a man of letters, and he remained committed to this "vocation" until his death.

tive years as a historian, when he did in fact have a defined cultural role, have been excised from the story of his life. To have included this relatively stable period would have been to disrupt the antisocialization stance of the *Education*.

Adams emphasized this stance by depicting himself as a perpetual wanderer in search of education. His frequent travels both abroad and in America reinforce the narrative's pattern of aimlessness and identify him with the unregenerate sinner, the wayfarer who never receives grace. Even near the end of his life, he continued to search blindly for the education he never finds: "Adams could only blunder back alone, helplessly, wearily, his eyes rather dim with tears, to his vague trail across the darkening prairie of education, without a motive, big or small, except curiosity to reach, before he too should drop, some point that would give him a far look ahead" (396). In this passage, Adams, in a sense, becomes the antitype of Moses; he sees not the promised land, however, but a wasteland of confusion and disaster. Although the cumulative lesson of Adams's education is the impossibility of acquiring absolute truth, he nevertheless maintained a never-ending search. The search for knowledge was more than a habit, however; it was a necessary condition of existence. When it stopped, life stopped. Even at sixty, Adams rededicates himself to "the Pursuit of Ignorance in Silence," saying "the pilgrimage began anew" (359), knowing that such a pursuit will lead to no final destination. Ultimately, Adams's skepticism, like James's pragmatism, was therapeutic. The search itself became valuable because it made action possible. In this sense, the cycles of hope and disillusionment impelled Adams forward; they insured renewal and drove him toward further inquiry.

If Adams subverted the socializing function of conversion narratives, he nevertheless followed their logic by making the individual life representative. A solitary soul in search of an education, Adams at the same time functions as the typical citizen of the modern world, an "archetype . . . of the American mind."[15] For Adams, all are alike in their ignorance: he knew nothing, but no one else knew more; not individuals, not governing bodies, not entire nations. With the habit of seeing the universal in the particular, Adams saw his own life not only as the life of the typical American, but also that of America itself.[16] The entire nation pursued ignorance in silence. By extension, then, he sought to lead by example: his own choice of doubt

15. Tanner, 94. See also Sayre, 80; and Lyon, 124–26.
16. Sacvan Bercovitch includes the *Education* in his category "auto-American-biography," 136, 243–44.

and inquiry over dogmatism should become the choice of the modern world.

If James offers a synthesis of religious experience at the end of the *Varieties*, Adams similarly leaves his Dynamic Theory of History at the end of the *Education*. Both works move from the particular to the general and the concrete to the abstract at their close. Adams presents his Dynamic Theory after one of the book's most dramatic conversion experiences, his recognition of the power of the dynamo at the Chicago Exhibition of 1900. Unlike the mock conversions found elsewhere, this one is genuine, not because it reveals eternal truth but because it suggests how the mind processes information—by turning images into symbols:

> To Adams the dynamo became a symbol of infinity. As he grew accustomed to the great gallery of machines, he began to feel the forty-foot dynamos as a moral force, much as the early Christians felt the Cross. . . . Before the end, one began to pray to it; inherited instinct taught the natural expression of man before silent and infinite force. Among the thousands of symbols of ultimate energy, the dynamo was not so human as some, but it was the most expressive. (380)

His "historical neck broken," Adams is awakened not only to the importance of force, but to the unifying power of the mind. Realizing that he has attained a relative truth, he, like James, also knows that to formulate that truth is to impose order on chaos: "Images are not arguments, rarely even lead to proof, but the mind craves them, and, of late more than ever, the keenest experimenters find twenty images better than one, especially if contradictory; since the human mind has already learned to deal in contradictions" (489). The mind craves images because they make communication possible. "Chaos is the law of nature and order the dream of man," but it is a dream realizable because of the transforming power of human consciousness. Adams's construct of the "mind" here—which is able to find unity in multiplicity in ways analogous to the conversion process—is strikingly similar to the transhistorical view of cognition posited by William James.

Despite Adams's awareness of the limitations of knowledge, he articulated his Dynamic Theory of History because life demands a response. To give up the search was to invite paralysis, and the modern world, more than any other, needed people who would react intelligently to the prevailing lines of force. By praising Hay and his diplomatic accomplishments, Adams extolled humankind's ability to make decisions—even progress—in the face of incomprehensibility. He resolved "to shape after his own needs" (473) the Dynamic Theory, knowing that it would be "subject to correction," because he found that previous theories were dangerously out of step with the accelerating pace of modern society.[17] Aware of the limits of his historical theory, Adams nevertheless constructed it because he realized the necessity of breaking intellectual barriers. Despite his overtures to the value of silence, the relativist abhorred quietism.

Though the *Education* impresses readers by its literary naturalism, Adams's pragmatic approach, philosophically if not rhetorically, leaves room for hope. At the book's close, he cautiously reveals the "practical optimism" noticed by his biographer, Ernest Samuels, by imagining that he, Hay, and Clarence King could return to the world after their deaths:

> Perhaps some day—say 1938, their centenary—they might be allowed to return together for a holiday, to see the mistakes of their own lives made clear in the light of the mistakes of their successors; and perhaps then, for the first time since man began his education among the carnivores, they would find a world that sensitive and timid natures could regard without a shudder. (505)

Despite the apparently prescriptive nature of Adams's Dynamic Theory, the *Education* is as much a warning as a forecast. Because intelligent minds can harness blind forces and use empirical facts to do work, Adams's epistemology finally, albeit partially, undercuts his devastating picture of the twentieth-century world. By using religious language and by structuring his search for education along the lines of the conversion narrative, he preaches the urgent necessity of uncompromising inquiry. The fate of humankind depended upon it.

Despite great differences in temperament, fostered in many ways by their respective families, James and Adams shared an intellectual restlessness.

17. For a summary of the vast social and technological changes occurring in the late nineteenth and early twentieth centuries, see Peter Conn, *The Divided Mind*, 1–17. Conn uses Adams's term "Conservative Christian Anarchist" as an epigraph to the cultural history of the years covered by his book, 1898 to 1917. Adams's inversion of the Puritan rhetoric of conversion may be taken as an example of the "conflict between tradition and innovation," which Conn sees as part of the internal dialectic of the period.

Both feared being limited by a belief system or a determined social role. To them, truth was a human creation, a product of the mind's ability to impose order. If truth did not provide answers, it nevertheless paved the way for further investigation. While Adams focused on the inadequacy of truth—conditions were constantly outstripping humankind's ability to order them—James saw its efficacy and its ability to make work possible. Both, however, understood that dogmatism led to fixity and destruction. Their adoption of conversion discourse was radical: they employed the rhetoric of assurance to attack the philosophical basis of surety. But in illustrating the inconclusiveness of human knowledge, they urged the necessity of its transformation.

4

. . .

CONVERSION TO SIGNIFICATION

The Autobiography of Henry James

Critics have often called Henry James's long and difficult autobiography an act of usurpation. James ostensibly began his memoirs attempting "to place together some particulars of the early life" (3) of his brother William, but his work almost immediately became the self-portrait of "a man of imagination at the active pitch" (455), a study of Henry's aesthetic growth and development. The autobiography grew out of a discussion between Henry and William's wife, Alice Gibbens James, both of whom thought a "Family Book," written by the family's sole survivor, would be a fitting tribute to the remarkable Jameses. But according to scholars such as Leon Edel, Adeline Tintner, and Paul John Eakin, when he composed his memoirs, Henry fell victim to the latent hostility he associated with his upbringing, especially toward his father and brother.[1] The autobiographical volumes gave him the opportunity to reverse his perceived position of inferiority. By righting—or rewriting—the past, however, James at best achieved an uneasy compromise with the sources of his continuing anxiety.

Psychoanalytic critics frequently find that James's muted resentment had its source in the atmosphere of extreme freedom fostered by Henry James senior who encouraged his children to examine all of life's possibilities but who discouraged them from settling for any limiting vocation. Without any authoritative models—either for imitation or rebellion—Henry junior suf-

---

1. See Leon Edel, *The Untried Years*, 59; Carol Holly, "A Drama of Intention in Henry James's *Autobiography*," 23; and Adeline Tintner, "Autobiography as Fiction." Paul John Eakin does argue that critics have overemphasized James's hostility, especially toward William, but he still finds it operative in the autobiography. See *Fictions in Autobiography*, 76–81, 86–90.

fered from a permanent sense of detachment: "Freedom to be everything and anything," according to Daniel Schneider, "was also freedom to be nothing," and as a result the "absolute, the fixed, the established come to have an almost irresistible appeal" (25). But if James frequently longed for fixed values as a child, in looking back he saw the advantages of his "typeless" education. Far from repressing the conflicts he experienced with his father and older brother, James was remarkably candid about familial tension. His dominant tone is one of sympathy, generosity, and comprehension. The consistency of his approach—as well as the sheer weight of his material on Henry senior and William—suggests that he had resolved many of the conflicts he felt as a younger man. Even though *A Small Boy and Others, Notes of a Son and Brother,* and the uncompleted *Middle Years* are told from the perspective of a single consciousness, James in a sense did write the "Family Book" he originally intended. His autobiography marked an intellectual reconciliation with his father and brother and validated his own upbringing.

James's ability to unify his memoirs was made possible in large part by his assimilation and actualization of the respective philosophies of William and Henry senior. This unity, the "fine silver thread" (454) upon which he hangs a rich matrix of memories and associations, can best be understood in the terms of spiritual conversion, a subject that absorbed both his father and brother. In an aesthetic program that took advantage of the conversion narrative's ability to unite an often chaotic array of events, James synthesized major aspects of his father and brother's thought and applied the result to the history of his own consciousness.[2] To achieve such a synthesis, however, James had to secularize—one might say collapse—conversion rhetoric to such an extent that most critics have failed to realize how pervasively he employed it. In the autobiography, conversion became a metaphor for his own symbolic method, the process by which he became continually immersed in the flow of experience. But if James defined himself as an artist by using conversion discourse, his memoirs are not a "portrait of the artist as a young man" in the Joycean sense. He did not use conversion discourse to encode his discovery of a vocation; like Henry Adams he used it to emphasize his detachment from mainstream America.

Despite T. S. Eliot's claim that James had a mind never violated by an idea, he was deeply engaged by many ideas, among them his father's

2. Millicent Bell and Robert Sayre identify conversion as a major theme in the autobiography, though neither examine the full extent to which James drew on conversion discourse. See Bell's "Henry James and the Fiction of Autobiography" and Sayre's *Examined Self,* 140–205.

theology.[3] James reveals his familiarity with the thought of Henry senior in the autobiography itself, where he discusses his father's idiosyncratic educational theory. Clearly, James once had misgivings about his father's educational method—or lack of it—yet, as he wrote, he found that education did occur, precisely as his father would have had it, any time his "subjective passion" was stirred (17). His education was "as intense as any other and a record of as great a dignity." The educational system espoused by the elder James was based on an epistemology derived from the process of conversion. The novelist wrote,

> The authors of our being and guardians of our youth had virtually said to us but one thing, directed our course but by one word, though constantly repeated: Convert, convert, convert! . . . We were to convert and convert, success—in the sense that was in the general air—or no success; and simply everything that should happen to us, every contact, every impression and every experience we should know, were to form our soluble stuff. (123)

According to Henry senior, natural facts could be continually converted into spiritual truth. This symbolic epistemology merged with his social vision, which—according to Henry junior—saw "the imminence of a transformation-scene in human affairs" and which converted the waste of personal egotism into the selfless acceptance of a redeemed society that, paradoxically, preserved the value of the individual (362).

In *A Small Boy and Others*, James conveyed his gratitude for the intellectual warmth and receptivity of his father by describing a conversion-like experience on the banks of the Hudson, after the two of them had traveled to Rhinebeck to assist a sick aunt:

> Vivid to me still, as floating across verandahs into the hot afternoon stillness, is the wail of [my aunt's] protest and her grief; I remember being scared and hushed by it and stealing away beyond its reach. I remember not less what resources of high control the whole case imputed, for my imagination, to my father; and how, creeping off to the edge of the eminence above the Hudson, I somehow felt the great bright harmonies of air and space becoming one with my

---

3. In *The American Henry James*, Quentin Anderson states that James was the only man who ever "*used* his father's belief" and goes so far as to argue that the novels of the major phase present an allegory of the elder James's redemptive history.

rather proud assurance and confidence, that of my own connection,
for life, for interest, with such sources of light. (105–6)

Here, the young James is bathed in the warm, fostering, and finally powerful
grace, not of God, but of his father, who, like his transcendentalist
contemporaries, saw divinity in a complete humanity.[4] This awakening
functions powerfully in the narrative: it not only illustrates Henry's appreciation for the elder James's ability to convert waste into usefulness, despair
into hope; but because it is conveyed in the terms of conversion discourse,
it testifies to the efficacy of Henry senior's epistemology.

The autobiographical volumes also mark an intellectual and emotional
reconciliation with William, further supported by Henry's enthusiastic
response to William's philosophy in their late correspondence. In these
letters, Henry not only told William that he had "unconsciously pragma-
tized" all his life, he also claimed that this mode of thinking accurately
described his process of artistic creation.[5] According to Richard Hocks,
William's thought is "literally *actualized* as the literary art and idiom" of
Henry's late work (4). Hocks, however, is careful to state that Henry did
not consciously expound or apply William's pragmatism. Instead, Henry
discovered an affinity already there, due as much to the late nineteenth-
century intellectual climate as to any direct influence. Hocks supplies
further evidence of a reconciliation between the two by noting that after
Henry began to praise William's work, the philosopher stopped criticizing
his brother's fiction (3–37).

Just as Henry, in looking back, saw that his mature vision was closer to
that of his father than he had once believed, he also described a "conversion" to William's way of thinking, though he dramatized it less overtly than
he did in the Rhinebeck scene. Throughout the autobiography, Henry
consistently represented himself as being smaller, less courageous, and
less sure than William, but he also recalled how he succumbed with an
"ecstasy of resignation" to the intellectual stimulation provided by his older
brother (246). Though he doubtless remembered feeling inferior, he also
recognized that William opened worlds to him that he would not otherwise
have experienced. One of those worlds, of course, was to become the

4. James's relationship to transcendentalism and to his father's theory of conversion is
discussed by Thomas Cooley, *Educated Lives*, 115–18. See also Daniel J. Schneider's *Crystal
Cage*, 8–9, and F. W. Dupee's *Henry James*, 9–11, 29–32.
5. Excerpts from these letters can be found in *The James Family*, ed. F. O. Matthiessen, 343–
45. See also *The Letters of Henry James* 2:83 and 2:140–41.

world of pragmatism; and even if Hocks correctly asserts that Henry did not consciously expound William's philosophy, it is reasonable to suggest that in reading and responding to his brother's work, he was better able to formulate his own aesthetic creed in the memoirs. If the young James possessed a mind much differently constituted than that of his brother, late in life he found much similarity. Once believing that "life and knowledge were simply mutual opposites," Henry here suggested that "impressions might themselves *be* science" and that "neither was of the least use—use to myself—without the other" (254). In these statements and others similar to them, James argued that subjective phenomena have an empirical validity, a position William carefully expounded in the *Varieties of Religious Experience*, which Henry read in 1902.[6] Though James did not directly address William's fascination with conversion, as he did with his father, he clearly was well attuned to the pragmatic method that grew out of his brother's study of religious phenomena. Conversion, for both Jameses, became an appropriate model for the process of acquiring knowledge: it was a "natural" psychic process by which one "field of consciousness" was displaced by another one, previously peripheral.

Henry's dream of the Galerie d'Apollon serves as a particularly apt example of how both men perceived psychological change in similar ways. One of the most famous of his autobiographical passages, this dream essentially dramatizes William's mechanical model of conversion. Calling this experience the "clearest act of cognition and comparison, act indeed of life-saving energy, as well as in unutterable fear," Henry dreamt that, sleeping in a bed chamber, he was suddenly roused by an "awful agent" attempting to force his way into the room. Desperately barring the door against this forced entry, James acted upon a spontaneous inspiration and achieved a dramatic reversal:

> The lucidity, not to say the sublimity, of the crisis had consisted of the great thought that I, in my appalled state, was probably still more appalling than the awful agent. . . . The triumph of my impulse, perceived in a flash as I acted on it by myself at a bound, forcing the door outward, was the grand thing, but the great point of the whole was the wonder of my final recognition. Routed, dismayed, the tables turned upon him by my so surpassing him for

6. Robert Reilly discusses James's view of subjective phenomena in "Henry James and the Morality of Fiction," 21. Henry indicated that he had read the *Varieties* in a letter to William that can be found in Matthiessen's *James Family*, 338.

straight aggression and dire intention, my visitant was already but
a diminished spot in the long perspective, the tremendous, glorious
hall. (195–97)

Critics have variously identified the "awful agent" as Henry senior, William,
or James's alter ego, but they agree that this dream—which Leon Edel
believes occurred when Henry was depressed by the failure of the New
York Edition—psychically justified James's choice of an artistic vocation
and, as such, helped relieve the almost suicidal despondency he had been
experiencing.[7] Much like a religious conversion, the dream signals a radical
shift from despair to hope.

This passage has been a fruitful source for psychoanalytic critics, who
find that the dream dramatizes an incursion from the unconscious to the
conscious portions of the mind. Critics, however, have failed to recognize
what James must have: that the dream coincided with the interpretation of
conversion William presented in the *Varieties*, where, on at least one
occasion, he used a door to signify the site of psychological transfer (197).
If the dream were analyzed according to William's scheme, the room Henry
defends would represent his subconscious mind; his struggle to defend the
room is analogous to the mental conflict that precedes conversion; and the
breaking through into the Galerie and its accompanying feeling of liberation
would signal the breakthrough of subconscious thought into consciousness,
a shifting of cognitive fields that William said was the primary mechanism
of conversion. In this case, Henry's consciousness (represented by the
Galerie) is associated with the world of art, and his subconsciously generated "conversion" affirms his place there—with images of power and
mastery. Henry, here and elsewhere, used the word "crisis" to describe
the psychodrama, the same word William used to record his conversion-
like experience after reading Renouvier.

I don't believe that this passage overtly allegorizes William's conversion
theory as much as it indicates that Henry too was fascinated by the
psychology of sudden awakenings, an interest further documented by his
alluding in the memoirs both to William's experience with Renouvier and to
his father's vastation (340–41, 395). There is a major difference, however.
Even though William and Henry senior viewed conversion as an unfinished

7. Edel dates James's dream in *The Master*, 444–45. Interpretations of the dream can be
found in Edel's *Untried Years*, 67–80; in Saul Rosenzweig's "Ghost of Henry James"; in Cushing
Strout's "Henry James's Dream of the Louvre and Psychological Interpretation"; and in Eakin's
Fictions in Autobiography, 76–82.

process, their awakenings were conventional in the sense that they marked dramatic turning points in their respective lives. As Henry responded to the very different thought of his father and brother, he chose not to describe conversion as a decisive turning point. William Dean Howells may have suggested to him that his decision to stop studying law and to start wooing the muse represented such a point, but in the autobiography James himself does not describe this event in the terms of regeneration.[8] If he did experience such a moment—when he saw his vocation clearly before him— its manifestation occurs "off stage," as it were, much like the "conversions" of Lambert Strether and Merton Densher. James made it clear, in fact, that the kind of dramatic psychological change associated with the typical conversion would have overwhelmed him. Instead, he fills his autobiography with "assimilations small and fine," minute experiences such as those he remembers having while, as a sick boy, he was bedridden in a London hotel:

> I lay, much at my ease—for I recall in particular certain short sweet times when I could be left alone—with the thick and heavy suggestions of the London room about me, the very smell of which was ancient, strange and impressive, a new revelation altogether, and the window open to the English June and the far off hum of a thousand possibilities. I consciously took them in, these last, and must then, I think, have first tasted the very greatest pleasure perhaps I was ever to know—that of almost holding my breath in presence of certain aspects to the end of so taking in. . . . We seize our property by an avid instinct wherever we find it, and I must have kept seizing mine at the absurdest little rate, and all by this deeply dissimulative process of taking in, through the whole succession of those summer days. (158)

These minute conversions are not a series of decisive (though unfinished) moments that portend lasting change such as the awakenings experienced by his father and brother. Rather, they describe the process of perception

8. James himself considers whether he had a turning point at Harvard in an autobiographical fragment presented and analyzed by Carol Holly in "Henry James's Autobiographical Fragment." James could not remember whether he had one or not, but thought that if he were going to dramatize a life-turning, the Harvard experience would have provided good material. Yet when he wrote his autobiography several years later, he did not so dramatize his life. Edel discusses the same fragment, *Untried Years*, 199–201.

itself. Revelation involves the continuous "taking in" of possibilities. Here the multiple conversion, "paradox of Puritan piety" pattern approaches a limit: the play of a strong imagination "constitutes in itself an endless crisis" (454).

But if "taking in" was a continuous revelation, James did single out a variety of events from his life and surround them with the mystical language often employed in conversion accounts. These resonant "scenes," which emerge spectacularly out of the narrative, always trigger new ruminations and associations until they, in turn, are displaced by other equally vivid memories. James admitted that he was often able to see the significance of these events only in the process of composition itself, but he says that they nevertheless have, throughout his life, retained a "tenacity of my impression" that signaled their "truth" even if his full grasp of it had been delayed (60). If James, by necessity, selected specific acts of perception to illustrate the workings of his artistic consciousness, he was careful to let readers know that these events were not qualitatively different from the multitude of unmentioned revelations. For instance, on his first visit to London's Craven Street, James, as a young adult, had a conversionlike experience when he realized that the neighborhood revealed the "socially sinister" world of Charles Dickens (572). Though James called this experience a "hallucination," his account of it follows the conventional conversion pattern. It is described as an ineffable moment accompanied by a loss of "despair," which gave him a mystical insight and which appeared to arrive from beyond the workings of his conscious mind. James went on to admit, however, that this experience was simply one of many and merely served as an example of his typical process of converting life into art:

> Why, however, should I pick up so small a crumb from that mere brief first course at a banquet of initiation which was in the event to prolong itself through years and years?—unless indeed as a scrap of a specimen, chosen at hazard, of the prompt activity of a process by which my intelligence afterwards came to find itself more fed, I think, than from any other source at all, or, for that matter, from all other sources put together. (573)

James's overall pattern was to merge conversion discourse with the more general terms of mystical, occult, or religious experience, all of which describe his giving way to a "throbbing consciousness." Because Henry, like William, saw self-surrender as an indispensable part of the conversion process, he often used such terms as "fond surrender," "submission," "yielding," and "self-abandonment" to suggest his passivity to "impressions." James's description of his Newport years, when he studied painting with William, illustrates this "inexact" use of conversion discourse: "I recall at all events less of the agitation than of the ecstasy; the primary months, certain aspects even of the few following years, look out at me as from fine accommodations, acceptances, submissions, emotions, all melted together, that one must have taken for joys of the mind and gains of the imagination so clear as to cost one practically nothing" (296). Whether James describes his "taking in" as a "visitation," a "hallucination," a "revelation," an "initiation," or one of the many other terms he employs for a process of perception almost mystical in its intensity, all of his remembered scenes conform, with varying degrees of specificity, to conversion rhetoric.

James's tendency to "melt together" terms normally differentiated is illustrated by his using the word "fusions" to describe moments when "every feature . . . had something of the quality and interest of every other" (477). James's substitution of a multitude of terms for "conversion" coincides with a larger tendency in the autobiography to merge terms semantically different. As I have noted, he mentioned that "impressions might themselves *be* science"; he also said that "knowledge" and "life" are one, that "the house of life and the palace of art" are "mixed and interchangeable," and that the "pictorial" is also the "dramatic" (254, 198, 482). Here he followed his father's synecdochical epistemology, which located the universal in the particular and the social in the personal. As R.W.B. Lewis says of Henry senior, all symbols are "veiled and interchangeable metaphors" (*American Adam*, 57). Interchanging a wide variety of "mystical" terms with "conversion," James constructed a discourse designed to suggest an infinity of meanings and the most overarching syntheses, a vocabulary that expressed his method of signification.

In rendering his "fusions," James characteristically gave them an emblematic function (Walsh, 63). One such moment occurs near the beginning of *A Small Boy and Others*, where James pictures himself gaping at a New York barnyard scene:

> I at any rate watch the small boy dawdle and gape again, I smell the cold dusty paint and iron as the rails of the Eighteenth Street corner rub his contemplative nose, and, feeling him foredoomed, withhold from him no grain of my sympathy. He is a convenient little image

or warning of all that was to be for him, and he might well have been
even happier than he was. For there was the very pattern and
measure of all he was to demand: just to *be* somewhere—almost
anywhere would do—and somehow receive an impression or an
accession, feel a relation or vibration. (16–17)

With a mystical intensity of recognition directly analogous to the conversion
experience, James "loses" himself in the contemplation of all he was to
become: the Eighteenth Street corner represents a lifetime of "taking in."
This passage, like many others, conveys a rich matrix of meanings that
enable him to see "the whole content of memory and affection in each
enacted and recovered moment" (4). If each recollection enabled him
synecdochically to see the whole content of memory, then in a sense, all
memories are interchangeable: one is neither better nor worse than
another.

R.W.B. Lewis finds that these peaks of intensity occur rarely in James's
fiction, when "the presence of the sacred is suddenly felt in the awesome
surrounding silence" ("Histrionic Vision," 42), but they can be found so
often in the autobiography that they can be said to constitute the pleasure
of James's text. Vividly pictorial, these emblematic scenes capture complex
emotional states and unlock an inexhaustible stream of memories. As
labored readers can attest, James's autobiography thus approaches what
Paul Jay has called "the abyss of endless figuration" (57). Because they
trigger what William would call a "stream of consciousness," James's
autobiography lacks the chronology found even in so stylized a form as the
spiritual autobiography, yet his seemingly endless "scenes" impel the
narrative forward and form its dominant organizing principle.

James's iconography reveals two competing tendencies in his work. The
first is his attraction to fixity, to the concretely realized picture or type
that Daniel Schneider believes was a reaction to the atmosphere of
indeterminacy cultivated by his father. As a boy, for example, James
regretted that his father had no definite profession. Similarly believing that
"fun in the religious connection closely depended on bondage," he found it
troublesome that his open-minded family "could plead nothing less than the
whole privilege of Christendom" when it came to public worship (341–42,
133). His own family "typeless," James was attracted to the fixed figure,
evident in his otherwise unaccountable fascination with his uncle, the
inconsequential husband of his aunt Helen Wyckoff Perkins, an "excellent

and consistent . . . shade of nullity" and a complete "little old-world figure" (78–82).

This longing for the finished figure or image is opposed, however, by an even stronger attraction to indefiniteness and ambiguity, actually consistent with his father's (and brother's) distaste for the inert fact (126). Henry enjoyed his visits to Mrs. Cannon's combination of linen shop and parlor, for example, because they conveyed a charm, "the finer part of which must yet have been that it didn't, as it regularly lapsed, dispose of *all* mystifications" (55). He remembers his cousin Albert's orphaned state as vivid and romantic "for being quite indefinite" (70). James admitted elsewhere, "I like ambiguities and detest great glares," and proclaimed a "positive saving virtue of vagueness" in reference to his days at the Harvard Law School (299, 412).

Occasionally, the opposed values of fixity and vagueness appear to have caused a conflict between what James called being "monotonous" and being "literary." To be monotonous, a fixed type, was to have a definite "figurative side" that enabled the observer to form an immediate chain of signification with the observed object or image. Because being monotonous suggested a specific association, however, its meaning was therefore limited. To be "literary," on the other hand, was to be indefinite and undifferentiated, potentially rather than actually figurative.

James shed further light on this conflict by juxtaposing two of his Harvard classmates, a "certain young New Yorker"—identified by Edel as Sam D. Craig—and George Abbott James, an unrelated friend, referred to in *Notes of a Son and Brother* as G.A.J. (Edel, *Untried Years*, 196–97). Henry admired the monocled New Yorker, who was something of a dandy, for his perfectly consistent "effect of cultivated detachment," so much so that he described him as a "revelation." In a "fusion" typical of the autobiography, James states, "it was his rare privilege to cause the note of derision and the note of affection to melt together, beyond separation, in vague but virtual homage to the refreshment of felt type":

> He reappears to me as a finished fop, finished to possibilities we hadn't then dreamt of, and as taking his stand, or rather taking all his walks, on *that*, the magician's wand of his ideally tight umbrella under his arm and the magician's familiar of his bristling toy-terrier at his heels. He became thus an apparition entrancing to the mind.

This "character man," who had a ground of reference that was "for the most part hoardedly English and French," was " 'like' some type in a collection of types" (451–52). James, here and elsewhere, assigned a European quality to the fixed image, while he found vagueness to be something American. He was attracted to the dandy because, in typeless America, he revealed the world of Europe. The New Yorker's high degree of finish conveyed rich and exciting—but definite and limited—associations.

James compared this New Yorker to George Abbott James who rendered "not quite the same service." Though he precisely portrayed the dandy, he neglected to describe G.A.J. physically and said that he evoked confused connections. But G.A.J. was "brilliant to a degree that none other had by so much as a single shade the secret of." For all his vagueness, he made James

> read wonders, as it were, into whatever it might be that was, as we used to say, "back of" him. He had such a flush of life and presence as to make that reference mysteriously and inscrutably loom—and the fascinating thing about this, as we again would have said, was that it could strike me as so beguilingly American. That too was part of the glamour, that its being so could kick up a mystery which one might have pushed on to explore, whereas our New York friend only kicked up a certainty (for those properly prepared) and left not exploration, but mere assured satisfaction. (453)

James here reveals a qualified preference; both men "evoke," but he values G.A.J. for his ability to suggest an undetermined and therefore infinite suggestiveness. This quality, which he associated with the vagueness of America itself, connected a glamorous "presence" to the multitudinous possibilities of signification. Throughout his memoirs, when he could link a particular person or image to what he believed was an infinity of figuration, he conveyed his realization with the psychological power of a religious conversion. The greater the suggestiveness, the more attractive the image became.

James's use of conversion discourse satisfied his rage for both fixity and vagueness, opposite sides of the same symbolic coin. The effective symbol began with a fully realized image, scene, character, or type, but its value rested in its ability to convey a mystical indeterminacy. He states, "When once type is strong, when once it plays up from deep sources, every show of its sincerity delivers us a message and we hang, to real suspense, on its continuance of energy, on its again and yet again consistently acquitting itself" (557). James's desire to merge the fixed with pure process, the passive with the active, is illustrated by his insistence, throughout the autobiography, that the "pictorial" and the "dramatic" were one and the same. James's choice of the word "scene" to describe this "fusion" was particularly appropriate because the scene, as he described it, contained the static quality of a picture or illustration, yet histrionically suggested continuing action (Walsh, 63).

The relation between James's symbolic method and his adaptation of the conversion experience is vividly conveyed by the "fresh revelation" that occurred during a carriage trip through France when he was a boy. Suddenly, through the window of the carriage, James saw a "peasant in sabots," wearing a red petticoat and working in a field, with a ruined castle in the background:

> Supremely, in that ecstatic vision, was "Europe," sublime synthe-
> sis, expressed and guaranteed to me—as if by a mystic gage, which
> spread all through the summer air, that I should now, only now,
> never lose it, hold the whole consistency of it. . . . Europe mightn't
> have been flattered, it was true, at my finding her thus most
> signified and summarised in a sordid old woman scraping a mean
> living and an uninhabitable tower abandoned to the owls; that was
> but the momentary measure of a small sick boy, however, and the
> virtue of the impression was proportioned to my capacity. It made
> a bridge over to more things than I then knew. (161)

The words "gage" and "bridge"—used to describe a number of "scenes" in the autobiography—effectively articulate James's symbolic method. This scene in its resonant totality evoked all the class-bound mystery of Europe, not just for what it represented to the young boy, but for what it would continue to represent as James's consciousness played over it, again and again, as he became immersed in the flow of his European experience.

In this context, James's symbolic method closely parallels William's pragmatism. In the *Meaning of Truth*, William even used the word "bridge" to describe the difference between "saltatory" and "ambulatory" processes of knowing. The results of saltatory or abstract reasoning are often falsely detached from the ambulatory "bridge of intermediaries" that is an indispensable part of the cognitive process (248). According to William, "conjunctive relations" (or cognitive associations) were as much a part of the "tissue of experience" as were the objects of perception (*Pragmatism*, 72). Trying to reveal the workings of his aesthetic consciousness, Henry similarly emphasized the scene's ability to immerse him in constantly expanding acts of cognition. The pictures in the Louvre, for example, "threw off the rest of monumental Paris . . . as a vast bright gage" and the Galerie d'Apollon constituted a "bridge over to Style" (195–96). Any act of cognition could lead to a potentially infinite multitude of further acts. James states, "The relations of any gage of experience multiply and ramify from the moment the mind begins to handle it" (56). Truth, as William says— and Henry implies—is "essentially bound up with the way in which one moment in our experience may lead us towards other moments which it will be worth while to have been led to" (*Pragmatism*, 98).

James, then, used the mystical overtones of conversion discourse to illustrate how he believed his consciousness was able to read infinite possibilities into the particular image or event. Even the "obscure hurt" passage conforms to this pattern. The most lasting effect of this "crisis" was that from the beginning, it established a "queer fusion or confusion" between his own suffering and the suffering associated with the Civil War:

> The twenty minutes had sufficed, at all events, to establish a relation—a relation to everything occurring round me not only for the next four years but for long afterward—that was at once extraordinarily intimate and quite awkwardly irrelevant. I must have felt in some befooled way in presence of a crisis. . . . [T]he interest never did fail. It was naturally what is called a painful one, but it consistently declined, as an influence at play, to drop for a single instant. (415)

More than anything else, the obscure hurt established an inexhaustible relation with the "hurrying troops, the transfigured scene," a relation that somehow also justified his sedentary, artistic life. James's visit to Portsmouth Grove extended and enriched his connection to the war "even to the pitch of the last tenderness of friendship" (424). On the steamboat home from this trip, he gave way to "a strange rapture, of reflection," whereby he saw that both he and the wounded soldiers were equally engaged in "the common fact of endurance." Their pain and his pain, their experience and his experience, become one: to have, to hold, and to *use*, unceasingly, as he turned life into art:[9] "The hour seemed, by some wondrous secret, to

---

9. In the *Untried Years*, Edel shows that Henry's trip to Portsmouth Grove had to have occurred before his obscure hurt, 173–79. Henry's distortion of chronology, intentional or otherwise, demonstrates the symbolic significance of his linking these two events and the war. In

know itself marked and changed and unforgettable—hinting so in its very own terms of cool beauty at something portentous in it, an exquisite claim then and there for lasting value and high authority" (426–27). This sudden illumination (taken with the obscure hurt), which occurred at a moment of intense affliction and which defied rational explanation, is the most traditional of James's conversions because it presented "a sharp parting of the ways" (417), a radical and irreversible change in the direction of his life. But if this scene is presented as a fairly traditional conversion, James focused primarily the endless stream of associations it gave rise to. Like the numerous other "assimilations" in the text, this was a conversion to signification.

James claimed that the injury he received and the events following it constituted a turning point in his life, yet he did not directly connect these events, or any other for that matter, to his acquiring a vocation. In an influential and cogent analysis of the autobiographical volumes, Paul John Eakin suggests that James does resolve a vocational crisis in those sections of the text surrounding the war, his stay at Harvard, and his visit to Portsmouth Grove, but I am struck by how often Eakin, discussing the earlier parts of the work, illustrates how James the artist is prefigured in his boyhood activities.[10] With considerable skill and subtlety, Eakin presents a fairly convincing reading of the obscure hurt/Portsmouth Grove sequence as significant to James's search for a vocation. The very length and complexity of Eakin's psychological reading suggest two things; first, that James did in fact see special significance in these two incidents, and second, that his conscious rhetorical posture was *not* to identify these two events with his acquiring of a vocation. Comparing James's treatment of this sequence to the obvious ways the acquisition of a vocation is evoked in other spiritual autobiographies—in the *Prelude*, *Sartor Resartus*, or *Portrait of the Artist as a Young Man*, for instance—one sees that he was not modeling his artistic calling on a conventional pattern of redemption. Stephen Dedalus experiences a dramatic awakening on Sandymount Strand that leads directly, if ironically, to his acceptance of a vocation. If anything, James avoids making such a statement in his autobiography. He was less

---

"The Memoirs of Henry James," James Cox analyzes the aesthetic capital James made of the "obscure hurt" and the Portsmouth Grove experience, both of which he associated with the Civil War, 19–23.

10. See Paul John Eakin's chapter on James in *Fictions in Autobiography*, especially pages 65, 68, 75, 81, and 100.

interested in recording his artistic *development* than he was in documenting a consciousness "saved" from the beginning. He argues that even his parents recognized the gifted nature of their second child by taking him to places they did not take their other children, simply for the sake of his receiving impressions:

> What I look back to as my infant license can only have had for its ground some timely conviction on the part of my elders that the only form of riot or revel ever known to me would be that of the visiting mind. Wasn't I myself for that matter even at that time all acutely and yet resignedly, even quite fatalistically, aware of what to think of this? (16)

James did not acquire a vocation; he was born with one. Eakin himself quotes a passage from the latter part of the autobiography where James asks himself, "What was *I* thus, within and essentially, what had I ever been, and could I ever be but a man of imagination at the active pitch" (455). These and numerous other passages like them illustrate the primarily synecdochical character of James's narrative. For James (as he constructs himself in this text), life was a continual conversion, not a sequence of events that hinged on any one event or period. In this sense, James undercut the socializing function of conversion discourse more directly than did his brother in the *Varieties*. William simply neglected it; Henry overtly dramatized that it did not apply to him.

When the two brothers were young, their father held that the artist stood at the pinnacle of spiritual development. Though the elder James perversely altered this opinion when William decided to study painting, it lived on in the "religion of consciousness" of his second son.[11] In his essay "Is There Life after Death?" James reconstructed the distinction between the elect and the damned based on cognitive rather than on moral grounds. Here he somewhat snobbishly suggested that only those who have lived the fully imaginative life possess a consciousness that will exist beyond the grave. In the same essay, James linked the artist's process of perception to the conversion experience even more directly than he did in the autobiography: "If he were not constantly, in his commonest processes, carrying the field of consciousness further and further, making it lose itself

11. Henry senior's view of the artist is discussed by Howard Feinstein in *Becoming William James*, 93. The phrase "religion of consciousness" is used by F. O. Matthiessen in *Henry James: The Major Phase*, 131–51. See also Kathy Phillips, "Conversion to Text," 382.

in the ineffable, he shouldn't in the least feel himself an artist" (Matthiessen, *James Family*, 611). Artists are soldiers in the service of consciousness, who by their very nature, occupy a position of highest privilege in the kingdom of the redeemed.

If the autobiography is designed to portray James's mystical ability to transform life into art, however, it also reveals that his powers carry the price of a "foreseen and foredoomed detachment" from the everyday current of affairs (122). Being open to the "invasive floods" of signification involved suffering, isolation, and estrangement from life's active mainstream. Conversion became a resonant metaphor for aesthetic perception because it too centered on moments of self-denial. In the section of the autobiography describing Henry and William's apprenticeship in Newport under William Hunt, James revealed his preference for the sacrificial artist over the dogmatically confident one by comparing Hunt and John La Farge. His taste here parallels his admiration for G.A.J. over the New York dandy. La Farge, like the New Yorker, was a European "type," a "settled sovereign self" who maintained an imperturbable consistency:

> The artist's serenity, by this conception, was an intellectual and spiritual capital that must never brook defeat. . . . That was at any rate the case for the particular artist and the particular nature he felt himself, armour-proof as they became against the appeal of sacrifice. Sacrifice was fallibility, and one could only of course be consistent if one inveterately *had* hold of the truth. (295)

James indirectly showed the limitations of such an attitude by recalling an exhibition of La Farge's work that took place after his death. Though James hoped the exhibit would foster a positive reappraisal of the artist, he found that it "fell a little short, alas, of rounding itself off" (298). James's review of the exhibit is not surprising, given the distrust for the firmly held truth that he shared with his father and brother. The artist who held such conviction necessarily closed himself off from the multitudinous possibilities of figuration essential to the farseeing aesthetic vision. La Farge, like Adams's Sumner, was "monotonous" rather than "literary."

In contrast to La Farge, James depicted the quixotic Hunt, who became his model artist, in the following terms:

> Into the world so beautifully valid the master would occasionally walk, inquiring as to what I had done or would do, but bearing on

the question with an easy lightness, a friendliness of tact, a neglect of conclusion, which it touches me still to remember. It was impossible to me at that time not so to admire him that his just being to such an extent, as from top to toe and in every accent and motion, the living and communicating Artist, made the issue, with his presence, quite cease to be of how one got on or fell short, and become instead a mere self-sacrificing vision of the picturesque itself. (286)

The difference between La Farge and Hunt, of course, is the difference between conviction and skepticism. La Farge, like the New York dandy, was an acculturated figure, a "personality" who reveled in his artistic identity. Hunt, on the other hand, focused on the aesthetic process itself and was not concerned with a socialized self-fashioning that he presented to the world. As James's preference here suggests, he believed that in order to achieve the most profound insight the artist must sacrifice his "personality" and give in—with a negative capability—to the changing flow of "impressions." To be dogmatic was to be out of step with both life and art, which, according to the late James, were interdependent.

In addition to illustrating his approach to his own artistic method, the parallel comparisons between the New York dandy and G.A.J. and between La Farge and Hunt signal an unexpected privileging of America and things American at odds with James's well-known antipathy for the American scene, as expressed earlier in his life. In this sense, James's memoirs seem to offer an apology to his native land, just as they mark a reconciliation with his father and brother. Near the end of his career, James decided that being "literary" was most possible if one embraced the open-endedness of America. Europe offered more in the way of artistic material, but American culture—precisely because it operated in a kind of vacuum—was the best training ground for the potential artist. Here James engages in an act of self-justification: being an American artist in Europe—culturally prepared for the multitudinous possibilities of figuration—was the best possible combination.

If James's vision entailed self-abandonment and the loss of a fixed identity, it also enabled him to confer on objects a kind of redemption.[12] In the autobiography, James consciously put himself in the position of saving

12. David Kirby discusses James's realization of the interdependence of life and art in "Henry James: Art and Autobiography"; and Jane Tompkins finds redemption to be a central theme of the autobiography in "The Redemption of Time in *Notes of a Son and Brother*."

people and places from the oblivion of forgetfulness, and toward that end he actually lamented that he could not rescue many more "of these values from the dark gulf" (504). In a very literal sense, James felt that his autobiography put his belief in the immortality of consciousness into action. He appears almost desperate to load the seemingly infinite objects of his memory into a consciousness that would exist beyond the grave:

> To look back at all is to meet the apparitional and to find in its ghostly face the silent stare of an appeal. When I fix it, the hovering shade, whether of person or place, it fixes me back and seems the less lost—not to my consciousness, for that is nothing, but to its own—by my stopping however idly for it. (54)

In this passage, James came close to professing panpsychism, the view that all objects possess consciousness, a position William also approached near the end of his life. If existence is consciousness, then the artist was in a position to perpetuate it, not only for himself and for those who view art but for the art object itself. James considered his greatest act of redemption to be his portrait of Minny Temple—a Jamesian artist with a consciousness much like his own (Tompkins, 684). After *Notes of a Son and Brother* had been published, a pleased Henry wrote Alice Gibbens James, "I seem really to have . . . made her emerge and live on, endowed her with a kind dim sweet immortality that places and keeps her" (*Letters* 4:707).[13]

James's belief that, autobiographically, he could render the objects/ subjects of his art immortal represents a radical outgrowth of the conversion narrative's tendency to lose much of its theological precision during the Romantic and Victorian periods. Like a variety of nineteenth-century writers, including Henry Adams, James inverted the rhetorical stance of the spiritual autobiographer. Rather than describe the acceptance of an absolute belief system, James's memoirs illustrate the evils of dogmatism. But his work goes even further. If the protagonist of the typical spiritual autobiography achieved a kind of redemption (secular or otherwise), James as artist became the redeemer himself; the converter took the place of the converted. In collapsing conversion discourse, James came close to losing its social, psychological, and theological connotations; but by positing a new spirituality, he finely managed to preserve the sacred overtones of the

13. On James's distortion and misappropriation of Minny Temple's biography, see Alfred Habegger's *Henry James and the "Women Business,"* 126–49.

spiritual autobiography. This is why in 1911 he could tell Edith Wharton that he was working on a project "extremely special, experimental and as yet occult" (*Letters* 4:592). According to James, the process of aesthetic perception gained one admission to the only spiritual world knowable, because it opened one to constantly expanding acts of figuration.

5
. . .

CONVERSION AND SEPARATION

Edith Wharton's *Backward Glance* and
Ellen Glasgow's *Woman Within*

Henry James appears as a character in both Edith Wharton's *Backward Glance* and in Ellen Glasgow's *Woman Within*. James, of course, was Wharton's good friend, and they developed a mutually satisfying relationship that lasted for many years. Wharton made him a central character in her autobiography, where his role is at once magisterial and mischievous. In contrast, Glasgow had only a passing acquaintance with James, and she mentioned him briefly in her autobiography, where she portrayed him as being insensitive and pompous. His stuttering, long-winded manner was at odds with the limited amount of time he chose to spend with her. Among other things, James functioned as a kind of touchstone to both of these women. To Wharton, their friendship solidified her sense that she had joined an inner circle of artists; to Glasgow, his seeming indifference reinforced her perception of herself as an outsider.

Despite their very different attitudes toward James, Glasgow and Wharton had much in common. Although Glasgow was eleven years younger than Wharton, she published fiction from the turn of the century to the Second World War, roughly the same years as did Wharton. Both writers developed realistic styles that revolted against the genteel standards of late nineteenth- and early twentieth-century romantic fiction. In their many novels, they depicted the evils of a patriarchal society that saw women as ornaments, deliberately sheltered from experience. Yet they introduced strong female characters into this world, which they frequently filled with ineffectual men. In the latter part of their careers, both writers longed nostalgically for the social values against which they had rebelled as younger women, feeling that the realistic standards they had helped to create had deteriorated into a "lunch pail" sensationalism. Wharton and Glasgow also shared many personal characteristics. Despite their coming from cities as different as New York and Richmond, both women were born into aristocratic families that looked down upon their desire to write. Both were shrewd businesswomen who loved foreign travel, fashionable clothes, impeccable manners, and dogs. Though Wharton was married for almost thirty years and Glasgow remained single throughout her life, both had an important affair with a married man and a long-term relationship with a bachelor friend. Both fought a painful shyness, often taken for snobbery, yet they were known to be elaborate and successful hostesses.

Although their autobiographies reflect these similarities and display a remarkable congruity in their respective philosophies of composition, at bottom they are very different works. Wharton's *Backward Glance* illustrates her overriding sense of decorum and proportion. In the book's preface, she acknowledged that she would not reveal everything about her personal affairs. Presenting readers with a finished self-portrait, she smoothed over the rough details of her life. Glasgow, on the other hand, gave an intensely personal, sometimes savagely brutal account that she admitted was "more or less incoherent" but that was "as true to actual experience as I have been able to make the written word" (214, v). While Wharton's *Backward Glance* describes a woman apparently sure of her place in the world, Glasgow tried "to attain a clearer understanding of my own dubious identity and of the confused external world in which I have lived" (130).

The contrast between these two works is illuminating when placed alongside some of the delineations of women's autobiography and the ways in which these delineations compare to and pull away from the spiritual autobiography form. Since Estelle Jelinek first edited a collection of essays that sought to describe the characteristics of the tradition of women's autobiography, a significant amount of research has been done on the subject. Recently, the theoretical dialectic has become increasingly sophisticated and has moved well past the partial consensus achieved in Jelinek's collection, but interestingly many of the descriptions of women's life-writing return to a fairly common set of traits. Among them is the idea that women's autobiography tends to be nonlinear, diffuse, discontinuous, and exploratory—in part because of the "multidimensionality" of women's lives. Unlike the rhetorically controlled—and therefore simplified—narratives characterized by the canonical male traditions, women's self-portraits tend to be focused on the unfinished process of "dailiness" and are in many cases either diaries or somehow modeled on the diary form. Also appearing quite frequently in the criticism is the idea that women's autobiographies are often built on relationships—on defining the self in and through a definition of the Other(s). As such, women's narratives are said not to focus on the postromantic definitions of individuality so characteristic of the dominant male tradition. Where men autobiographers are inclined to separate themselves from the world around them, women most often encode an interconnectedness between the self and the world. Another recurring approach to women's life-writing recognizes a tension (and often a negotiation) between the private and the public selves. Women's autobiographies are often seen as making incursions into public (male-dominated) modes of discourse, but doing so by way of expressing and transforming their private (and often silenced) subjectivity.[1]

By summarizing some of the recurring delineations of women's autobiographical discourse, I am perhaps falsely suggesting a theoretical consensus that doesn't quite exist. Almost all of those who describe women's autobiography acknowledge that there are many exceptions to the generalizations suggested above, that not all women's self-portraits have any or all these characteristics, and that there are many autobiographies written by men that share some of them. In fact, rather than providing a dualistic definition, where women's autobiography is seen as being the antithesis of the male tradition, most of the more recent scholars talk about the "double voicedness" or "duplicity" of women's narratives. Such approaches recog-

---

1. Feminist theorists who incorporate the characteristics of discontinuity, circularity, and diffuseness into their descriptions of women's autobiography are Estelle Jelinek, "Introduction: Women's Autobiography and the Male Tradition," 17; Lynn Z. Bloom and Orlee Holder, "Anaïs Nin's *Diary* in Context," 209–13; Suzanne Juhasz, "Towards a Theory of Form in Feminist Autobiography," 221–24; Jane Marcus, "Invincible Mediocrity," 140; and Bella Brodzki and Celeste Schenck, Introduction to *Life/Lines*, 1, 6. Theorists who discuss the tradition of women's life-writing and the diary form are Juhasz, 224; Linda H. Peterson, *Victorian Autobiography*, 124–26; and Felicity A. Nussbaum, "Eighteenth-Century Women's Autobiographical Commonplaces," 156. Among those who find that women's autobiographies are often centered on relationships and an inner-connectedness are Mary G. Mason, "The Other Voice: Autobiographies of Women Writers"; Brodzki and Schenck, 9–11; and Shari Benstock, "Authorizing the Autobiographical," 16. Among those who find that women generally do not participate in the postromantic discourse of individuality are Brodzki and Schenck, 1; Benstock, 29; Marcus, 134; and Susan Stanford Friedman, "Women's Autobiographical Selves," 35. Theorists who describe a tension or a movement between the private and public selves are Juhasz, 224–25; Domna C. Stanton, "Autogynography: Is the Subject Different?" 13; and Sidonie Smith, *A Poetics of Women's Autobiography*, 51. For a contrasting view that sees some women's autobiographies as moving from the public to the private spheres, see Marcus.

nize the realities of self-writing in the context of the discourses of a patriarchal, phallocentric culture. Noticing, for example, that earlier defini- tions of women's autobiography, which seek to differentiate between male and female modes of self-writing, often break down, Sidonie Smith presents a poetics of women's autobiography where the writer "must suspend herself between paternal and maternal narratives, those fictions of male and female selfhood that permeate her historical moment. . . . Thus the autobiographer confronts personally her culture's stories of male and female desire, insinuating the lines of her story through the lines of the patriarchal story that has been autobiography" (19).[2]

As I suggested earlier, feminist critics have generally situated the spiritual autobiography tradition in the context of patriarchal discourse, despite their acknowledgment that women have written spiritual autobiog- raphies at least since the late Middle Ages. Ironically, however, certain characteristics of the traditional Christian conversion narrative are in keeping with the recurring descriptions of women's self-writing outlined above. As I hope I have demonstrated, the traditional conversion narrative is centered much more on a relationship and an interdependency (between the self and God) than it is concerned with individuality. This idea of the relational self is further emphasized by the communal nature of the autobiographical act: in the process of testifying to a conversion experi- ence, the autobiographer binds him- or herself to a community of believers. Even the secularized conversion narratives that emphasize individuality, such as those written by Wordsworth, Carlyle, and Martineau, still move from an individual to a corporate self-definition. A second way that the recurring delineations of women's autobiography are consistent with the spiritual autobiography tradition is that conversion narratives encode a bridge between personal, private experience and more public modes of discourse. Though occasionally accompanied by publicly identifiable mani- festations, conversion is most often presented as an inner transformation that can then become the subject of more public forms of testimony. This negotiation between the private and public, of course, is a primary focus in

2. Other feminist critics who have pointed out the problems of past delineations of women's autobiographies, either by exposing the dualism of such approaches or the general difficulty of identifying a normative discourse for either men or women, are Stanton, 11–15; Brodzki and Schenck, 14; Nussbaum, 153; and Germaine Brée in the foreword to *Life/Lines*, ix–xii. Like Smith, Nussbaum (149) and Stanton (15) describe women's autobiography as containing a negotiation between two competing discourses. For similar approaches, see Jane Marcus, and Patricia Meyer Spacks, "Female Rhetorics," 177.

the recent theories of women's life-writing. And, finally, though many spiritual autobiographies exhibit the kind of narrative closure associated with the canonical male tradition, many others exhibit a close relationship to the diary form, considered to be extremely important in the discourses of female subjectivity. Quite a few spiritual autobiographies were extracted from diaries, and they retain that sense of "dailiness" that is also found to be characteristic of many autobiographies written by women.

I hope these similarities between the conversion narrative form, as practiced by both sexes, and the larger tradition of women's self-writing suggest that conversion discourse is not exclusively phallocentric. From its beginnings, Christianity has remained a largely patriarchal institution, but at no point in its history did it systematically deny women access to the relationship between the self and God that the spiritual autobiography seeks to capture. In fact the social pressures of Protestant cultures were such that women were encouraged to appropriate conversion discourse, to make it their own, and to apply it to their lives. I am not suggesting that instances of conversion discourse or the spiritual autobiography form are gender neutral, far from it; rather, I am saying that the conversion framework, from its inception, was consistent enough with other modes of female expression to allow women to encode their subjectivity within it.

Conversion discourse, in fact, has some distinguishing features that make it particularly effective for appropriation within the context of a phallocentric culture. For one thing it does not presuppose an ideology of humanism, where the dynamics of personal change are rooted in a rational, autonomous self. Those who describe conversion normally locate the source of personal change outside the self. This is true even of those who employ it in a secular context. Rather than present themselves as "writing" conversion discourse, they present themselves as being "written" by it. As such, conversion discourse is not typically grounded on a phallocentric notion of agency and the rationalism it presupposes. This expectation actually makes it a powerful discourse in repressive cultures. Those who encode conversion "create" a self that does not act "for" the self, but rather for a source (divine or otherwise) whose motives transcend the worldly context at hand. This expectation opens a space for actions and beliefs that go against existing cultural norms.

Of course, the dynamics of passive self-denial associated with conversion and mysticism have frequently been labeled "feminine" in patriarchal cultures. Admittedly, such notions of the mystical reinscribe patriarchal definitions of femininity and present God, the "author" of conversion discourse, as the ultimate logo- and phallocentric authority figure. In such cases, however, the experience of conversion is not usually represented as an entry into the symbolic realm of the "Logos." Typically, authors of conversion narratives confess their inability to describe what has happened to them: one of the recurring themes of conversion discourse is the inadequacy of language to represent experience.

Wharton's *Backward Glance* and Glasgow's *Woman Within* both contain the kinds of negotiation between maternal and paternal traditions that I have been describing. Both participate in and deviate from the expectations of the traditional (male) spiritual autobiography, and both exhibit a sense of "strain" with the form that effectively communicates a perception of sexual difference. In doing so, both works inscribe each writer's relationship to a larger, primarily patriarchal culture, even as they expose her exclusion from it.[3] Wharton's narrative is consistent with many other women's self-portraits to the degree that it is centered on a set of relationships; she consciously describes her life in the context of the lives of others. Her work is also like many other women's autobiographies in that it is often nonlinear, digressive, and anecdotal. On the other hand, unlike many women's self-portraits, her narrative is smoothly finished, rhetorically controlled, and largely based on a life made possible by her literary vocation. With one significant exception, she wrote a fairly traditional spiritual autobiography.

Begun only a year after *A Backward Glance*, Glasgow's *Woman Within* fits into the prevailing definitions of women's autobiography insofar as it is a fragmentary narrative that seems akin to the diary form. Her autobiography, which took nine years to complete and which was composed in separate units, is an exercise in self-discovery. Unlike Wharton, Glasgow does not dwell on the consequences of a literary vocation. If Wharton embraced the communal values of the traditional conversion narrative, Glasgow, like Adams and the two Jameses before her, subverted the socializing function implicit in the form.

To call the rhetorical control of *A Backward Glance* a male characteristic is probably to push a generalization too far, yet Wharton clearly organized her narrative around three objectives: to describe her place in an artistic community, to preserve a vanishing way of life, and to illustrate the effects of the First World War. By adapting the spiritual autobiography form to her narrative of the self, Wharton was able to reconcile these three goals.

3. My analysis of the cultural dialectic between these two authors and mainstream American culture has been influenced by Peter Conn, *The Divided Mind*, 173–93.

Though most spiritual autobiographies recount a series of awakenings, Wharton, like Augustine, constructed her narrative around a single illuminating moment. She explicitly revealed that her "conversion" occurred in 1899, upon the publication of *The Greater Inclination*, her first volume of stories. This event, which enabled an already middle-aged author to leave her stifling aristocratic world and to become a member of an artistic and intellectual community, appears to follow the typical conversion pattern. But something is missing. As critics and biographers have noted, the pain, sickness, anxiety, and some significant personal details are excised from the story of her life. Wharton failed to mention her divorce, her affair with Morton Fullerton, her creative lapses, and the times her friends disappointed her. Even the triumph of her first published collection is presented without reference to the trying and often debilitating period of her artistic apprenticeship. The "missing half" of this success story began in 1893, after her first three stories had appeared in *Scribner's*, when Wharton's publisher, William Brownell, suggested she do a collection, a project that would take her five agonizing years to complete. In 1894, Wharton told Brownell that she had lost confidence in her work and that poor health was preventing her from proceeding. Wharton's biographer, R.W.B. Lewis, describes this period:[4] "One can only employ the phrase 'severe identity crisis' to describe the terrible and long-drawn-out period Edith Wharton was passing through: a period of paralyzing melancholy, extreme exhaustion, constant fits of nausea, and no capacity whatever to make choices or decisions" (76). Wharton recovered enough to have a productive period in 1898, but soon suffered a severe breakdown that landed her in the care of S. Weir Mitchell, a leading neurologist. Mitchell's treatment was successful, but from October of 1898 through January of 1899, she was not allowed a single visitor. *The Greater Inclination* appeared that March.

By saying that after publishing *The Greater Inclination* she "was naturally in the first fever of authorship," Wharton appears to take for granted that her experience corresponded to a literary "conversion"; yet, strangely, she silently passed over the agony that would have been a rhetorically appropriate prelude to her subsequent awakening. Wharton did refer to her suffering retrospectively: only after describing her awakening, for instance, did she mention "the chains which had held me so long in a kind of torpor" and the people who were "so indifferent to everything I really

4. Cynthia Griffin Wolff gives a convincing psychological analysis of this difficult period in Wharton's life, in *A Feast of Words*, 80–88.

cared for" (122, 124). But if Wharton mentioned her affliction in passing, the spiritual autobiography form itself causes readers to infer the missing turmoil. Even without knowing the full details of her life, reviewers and critics have read pain into Wharton's smoothly composed autobiography. In 1953, for example, Blake Nevius said it was "a book as interesting for what it leaves out as for what it includes" (6), and eleven years later Annette Baxter found that "what is not said illuminates what is so gracefully said." Sensing that tragic silences must accompany her narrative triumphs, these commentators, perhaps unconsciously, insert the suffering embedded into the structure of the conversion narrative. Awakenings, by convention, must be preceded by moments of crisis. Wharton's omission of the melancholy, sickness, and indecision that occurred before her literary success reveals an uneasiness about her choice of the spiritual autobiography form itself.

If Wharton's departure from the conventions of the spiritual autobiography suggests an anxiety about her professional initiation, however, her analysis of this event otherwise follows the logic of the typical conversion narrative. Conversion signified an initiation into a group of like-minded individuals. Before *The Greater Inclination* had been published, Wharton lived in two worlds: a conventional girlhood—of archery contests, dances, social dinners, and ornamentation—and an inner, "secret" world, composed of "making up" stories, reading in her father's library, and communing with nature. In a passage that borrows from the language of mystical experience, Wharton revealed her preference for this isolated life:

> I was a healthy little girl who loved riding, swimming and romping; yet no children of my own age, and none even among the nearest of my grown-ups, were as close to me as the great voices that spoke to me from books. Whenever I try to recall my childhood it is in my father's library that it comes to life. I am squatting again on the thick Turkey rug, pulling open one after another the glass doors of the low bookcases, and dragging out book after book in a secret ecstasy of communion. . . . There was in me a secret retreat where I wished no one to intrude, or at least no one whom I had yet encountered. (69–70)

Even as a young, recently married woman, Wharton found the "kindly set" she had grown up with to be "somewhat cramping" and preferred "the cool solitude of my studies" (92).[5]

---

5. Part of Wharton's New York set, Egerton Winthrop was the first person with whom

Wharton's "awakening" enabled her to bridge her private and public selves. Her early stories and *The Decoration of Houses* had attracted attention, but they brought her "no nearer to other workers in the same field." As a result, she "continued to live my old life" and "had as yet no real personality of my own" (112). But after publishing her first volume of stories, she remembered, "I was overmastered by the longing to meet people who shared my interests. . . . What I wanted above all was to get to know other writers, to be welcomed among people who lived for the things I had always secretly lived for" (122–23). As the rest of *A Backward Glance* makes clear, Wharton was tremendously successful in forming relationships with individuals who shared her interests. Though she had once been painfully shy of such people, the publication of her first books caused a radical personality change that made her fully aware of her literary calling:

> At last I had groped my way through to my vocation, and thereafter I never questioned that story-telling was my job. . . . I felt like some homeless waif who, after trying for years to take out natural-ization papers, and being rejected by every country, has finally acquired a nationality. The Land of Letters was henceforth to be my country, and I gloried in my new citizenship. (119)

> My long experimenting had resulted in two or three books which brought me more encouragement than I had ever dreamed of obtaining, and were the means of my making some of the happiest friendships of my life. The reception of my books gave me the self-confidence I had so long lacked, and in the company of people who shared my tastes, and treated me as their equal, I ceased to suffer from the agonizing shyness which used to rob such encounters of all pleasure. (133)

> From a childhood and youth of complete intellectual isolation—so complete that it accustomed me never to be lonely except in company—I passed, in my early thirties, into an atmosphere of the

---

Wharton shared her secret life. Though they became friends well before her "awakening," Wharton left the chronology of *A Backward Glance* vague enough so that the reader could link the beginning of their friendship and her professional initiation. In this way Wharton, without distorting facts, preserved the spiritual autobiography form. See pages 92–103.

rarest understanding, the richest and most varied mental companionship. (169)

At the time, Wharton—who had always believed herself to be inferior to her fashionable friends—was shocked by her achievement: "*I* had written short stories that were thought worthy of preservation! Was it the same insignificant *I* that I had always known? . . . The whole business seemed too unreal to be anything but a practical joke played on me by some occult humourist" (113). If the success of Wharton's first collection surprised her, however, it also helped her to become a stronger and more independent woman. Though her husband, family, and New York friends continued to be indifferent to her literary career, she wrote, "I no longer cared, for my recognition as a writer had transformed my life. I had made my own friends, and my books were beginning to serve as an introduction to my fellow-writers" (144).

As Louis Auchincloss has observed, Wharton's friends "make up the largest part of the memoirs" (Introduction, xiv), and they were indeed a distinguished company: Henry James, Paul Bourget, Howard Sturgis, Percy Lubbock, Vernon Lee, Bernard Berenson, and Henry Adams, among many others. The conversion narrative form conveniently allowed Wharton to present her artistic community as an "elect" group, an aristocracy, not of wealth or ancestry, but of sensibility and intelligence. She frequently used religious terms to describe this "spiritual kin." Walter Berry, for example, was an important part of her "life of the spirit." She even playfully echoed the gospel by saying "wherever two or three educated French people are gathered together, a *salon* immediately comes into being" (262).

The French salon, in fact, becomes a model for Wharton's elect community. She preferred the French taste for general conversation, "where social intercourse is a perpetual exchange," to that of Anglo-Saxon countries, where "two-and-two talks" predominate. She also admired the way that fashionable and sophisticated people complemented each other in France, while in provincial societies like Old New York they did not mix. Wharton not only presented an insider's view of the tastefully arranged gatherings at the house of Madame de Fitz-James, she also described her "spiritual kin" in the terms of a French salon. Several times she calls friends such as James, Walter Berry, Bay Lodge, Gaillard Lapsley, Robert Norton, and John Hugh Smith *de fondation* of the social group that met at the Mount, at Wharton's apartment in the rue de Varenne, at Howard Sturgis's "Qu'Acre," and at Mary Hunter's Hill Hall.

Explaining that her idea of society is "the daily companionship of the same five or six friends," Wharton nevertheless designated the members of her inner group "if not by the actual frequency of their visits, yet from some secret quality of participation" (192). This "secret quality," which has prompted Nevius to call Wharton's conception of society a "free masonry of intelligent, cultured individuals" (88), reinforced her notion of an elect group. She lamented that their "common stock" of allusions, cross references, and pleasantries, especially James's "huge cairns of hoarded nonsense," could not easily be shared with her readers. She underscored the exclusivity of this inner group—and offended, perhaps, the egalitarian reader—by satirizing the "simpleminded" who lay outside it. The humor of *A Backward Glance* often draws upon the foibles of the philistine.[6]

Throughout the autobiography, Henry James stands as the ideal citizen of Wharton's Land of Letters. Not simply a great writer, he is an exemplary companion and friend. All his qualities—his artistic integrity, his incisive wit, his sense of propriety, and his gaiety—combine to justify the kind of intellectual elite Wharton described. James demonstrates how Wharton's aristocracy of sensibility rose above differences in sex, nationality, and taste. For instance, citing his admiration for Whitman, she found "new proof of the way in which, above a certain level, the most divergent intelligences walk together like gods" (186).

After speaking at length about the social world in which she lived, moved, and had her being, Wharton presented a "picture" of a typical, yet ideal day at Madame de Fitz-James's prewar salon:

> I linger with a kind of piety over the picture of that pleasant gray-panelled room, with its pictures and soft lights, and arm-chairs of faded tapestry. I see Bourget and James talking together before the fire, soon to be joined by the Abbé Mugnier, Bonnard, and Walter Berry; Monsieur d'Haussonville, Hervieu and Larreta listening to Matilde Serao, and Chambrun, Berenson and Tardieu forming another group; and in and out among her guests Madame de Fitz-James weaving her quiet way, leaning on her stick, watching, prodding, interfering, re-shaping the groups, building and rebuilding her dam, yet somehow never in the way, because, in spite of her incomprehension of the talk, she always manages to bring the right people together and diffuses about her such an atmosphere of kindly

6. For examples, see *A Backward Glance*, 183, 244, 209–12, 303, 310.

hospitality that her very blunders add to the general ease and good
humour. (281–82)

This vision merges two of Wharton's major rhetorical goals in *A Backward
Glance*: by describing her ideal social organization, she both ratified her
inclusion in a spiritual aristocracy and recorded for posterity how such a
group functioned. This desire to preserve a vanishing way of life is
consistent with the book's extended archaeological metaphor, a metaphor
she applied to the autobiographical act: "The compact world of my youth
has receded into a past from which it can only be dug up in bits by the
assiduous relic-hunter; and its smallest fragments begin to be worth
collecting and putting together before the last of those who knew the live
structure are swept away with it" (7). The archaeological metaphor nicely
illustrates Wharton's autobiographical impulse, though she might even
more accurately have called herself a folklorist. Her well-born acquaintances would hardly be considered the *folk* in any class designation; but,
like a folklorist, she painstakingly took down the remnants of a living
tradition, its customs, its "discarded pageants" (40), and many of its
stories, legends, and anecdotes.

According to Nevius, "Edith Wharton had a fatal weakness for the
anecdote, for the situation capable of taking a surprising turn or of lending
itself to an ironic or merely amusing treatment. Her recollections in *A
Backward Glance* are punctuated with anecdotes related to her by Edward
Robinson, Cecil Spring-Rice, Jean Cocteau, and others, all of them bizarre
or ironic" (28). Though Nevius, in this context, is primarily criticizing
Wharton's anecdotal approach to short fiction, he nevertheless isolates a
central pattern in the autobiography, which contains a number of strange
and amusing sketches. One such story, delivered by Cecil Spring-Rice to
Wharton at a yachting party, is about a young man who sits across from a
captivating woman at a dull dinner party. They wander from one delightful
subject to another, until they begin to discuss the supernatural. When the
man asks the woman if she believes in ghosts, she replies, "I am one," and
disappears. After dinner, the hostess apologizes for putting the man next
to an empty chair and explains that she has just received a telegram
announcing the expected guest's death (81–82). This anecdote is informative not so much for its originality as literature but because it evokes a
context of social performance. It is the kind of story that would have been
shared, perhaps at a dull dinner party, among members of Wharton's inner
circle. Like the other anecdotes in *A Backward Glance*, this one recon-

structs a cultural milieu and identifies members of the intellectual elite. In this sense, Wharton's passion for preserving remnants of a vanishing order is consistent with the spiritual autobiography form. Each story becomes another sign of her redemption.

Wharton's "conversion" transformed her life and enabled her to lead a vital intellectual existence, yet, curiously, for someone who so acutely realized the constraints placed upon women, she could find the independence and approval she sought only in a male-dominated community. Biographers and critics alike have noted that Wharton's greatest friendships were with men, that her intellectual qualities were often called masculine, and that she liked and repeated the remark that she was a "self-made man."[7] Wharton actually had close friendships with both men and women, but in *A Backward Glance* she made it clear that her "spiritual kin" were primarily male. She also put gender qualifications upon the stimulating women she mentioned. Vernon Lee, for instance, "was the first highly cultivated and brilliant woman I had ever known" (132), and Matilde Serao's monologues "rose to greater heights than the talk of any other woman I have known" (277). Because Wharton clearly treated the women included in her intellectual community as exceptions, she probably saw herself as one.

Wharton's peculiar adaptation of the spiritual autobiography form reveals the extent to which she was caught in a cultural bind. Aware of the patriarchal bias in life and letters, she nevertheless had no choice but to seek fulfillment almost exclusively in this world's values. Never able to renounce fully the expectations of Old New York, she could conceive of no other group that would have given her the sense of self-worth and intellectual satisfaction for which she longed. If she was a member of an elite group, however, she was an uneasy insider, and she used the spiritual autobiography form to justify in literature what caused her anxiety in life.[8] Wharton herself documented her uneasiness by lamenting that she often felt either speechlessly shy, or "dazzled," to the point of forgetfulness, when in "high company" (170–71). Her rhetorical stance explains why she

---

7. See Percy Lubbock, *Portrait of Edith Wharton*, ii, 28, 54; R.W.B. Lewis, *Edith Wharton*, 327, 475; and Louis Auchincloss, *Edith Wharton*, 65.

8. Though she does not discuss the book's conversion rhetoric, Judith Fryer also finds that *A Backward Glance* allowed Wharton to mend some of the divisions she felt in her life. Fryer's "Edith Wharton's 'Tact of Omission': Harmony and Proportion in *A Backward Glance*" is one of the few critical studies of the autobiography. Fryer revised this article for her book *Felicitous Space*, 143–66.

felt it necessary to omit the painful side of her intellectual development: justifiably anxious about her place in a world dominated by patriarchal values, she may have feared that an admission of uncertainty would have compromised her achievement.

In addition to the many anecdotes she shared, Wharton recounted a series of improbable occurrences—similar to the uncanny spiritual "signs" found in Puritan conversion rhetoric—all of which depict an acceptance of her work by literary and political figures, most of them male. One such event happened shortly after the publication of her first volume of stories, when Wharton asked James Bain, a well-known London bookseller, if there were any interesting new books. Bain, of course, handed her *The Greater Inclination*. In a similar incident, Wharton's anxiety about meeting George Meredith was assuaged when she discovered that the open volume at his elbow was her own *Motor Flight through France*.[9] Wharton remembered, "I read the title, and the blood rushed over me like fire" (252). Her literary reputation caused other remarkable incidents during the war, notably when Jean-Louis Vaudoyer, a poet and novelist, recognized her behind the lines and offered his lodgings after she had despaired of finding a place to sleep. In such cases, Wharton responded with surprise and gratitude, just as she had when her first volume of stories was published.

Wharton's tendency to present incidents that validate, and in a sense reconstitute, her initiation into the world of letters is consistent with her decision to describe her awakening as a publishing event, rather than an inner transformation. In *A Portrait of the Artist as a Young Man*, Stephen Dedalus has an awakening much like Wharton's, but his occurs before he has published, indeed scarcely written, anything. That Wharton needed a visible, tangible—and positively reviewed—artifact to confirm her choice of a vocation illustrates the precarious position women novelists found themselves in during the early years of the twentieth century. Their eyes had to be constantly on a literary establishment that still assumed women writers were "scribblers." Wharton herself deprecated her work and frequently refrained from talking about it, but her autobiography reinforces what her long list of publications already reveals: she was a woman, as Cynthia Griffin Wolff states, "with an iron determination to pursue the

9. Citing a letter Wharton wrote to Walter Berry, Louis Auchincloss shows that the day before she met Meredith, Wharton was extremely despondent about the state of her marriage to Teddy Wharton. This sequence of events is another example how she omitted painful episodes of her life in the autobiography and how she silently associated literary triumphs and personal affliction. See *Edith Wharton*, 99–110.

occupation of writing" (47). Howard Sturgis and other members of her literary circle could afford to be dilettantes, but Wharton knew that as a woman she would be judged according to stricter standards. She believed—and she was probably right—that professional success was a necessary condition of being accepted into the circles she eventually joined. Given the conditions under which she was writing, as well as the people and opinions she admired, it is hardly surprising that she wrote a rhetorically controlled, highly organized conversion narrative, one that some theorists would find to be more consistent with the male autobiographical tradition than with the tradition of women's life-writing.

Of course, Wharton's election to a privileged community is not the only story to be told in *A Backward Glance*; she also described how the Great War destroyed "the world I had grown up in and been formed by" (369–70). Wharton underscored the poignancy of this loss by filling "those last years of peace with every charm and pleasure" and by remembering the intellectual excitement generated by Isadora Duncan, Marcel Proust, and the Russian ballet. Though R.W.B. Lewis claims that the war actually "put no end to her thickening republic of the spirit" (408), in the autobiography Wharton implied that her inner circle was one of its casualties. Referring to Madame de Fitz-James's salon, she wrote, "The war broke up that company of friendly people; death followed on war, and now the whole scene seems as remote as if it had belonged to a past century" (281–82). Even when her friends were able to get together, the war had taken the joy out of their meeting: "Our separate loneliness seemed to merge in one great sense of solitude, of being cut off forever from the old untroubled world we had always known, so that my friends and I felt that our being together was really not much help to any of us" (343). The disintegration of Wharton's inner group is thus meant to symbolize the general fragmentation of Western culture. Her election to an artistic community had been her salvation, but the Great War destroyed the conditions that made that way of life possible. Wharton emphasized this by linking James's death and the war, which "really gave him his death blow." If the world that produced a Henry James ended with the war, then for Wharton it was fitting, almost fortunate, that he died before it was over. Once her inner group dispersed, she resumed an isolated life of reading, traveling, and gardening. In this sense, *A Backward Glance* ends where it began, as she retreats into an inner life similar to the one she had before her awakening. Here her figuration of self deviates from the synecdochical model of the other twentieth-century writers I have discussed, and is grounded on a kind of circular structure similar to the metonymic construction of Melville's protagonist in *Typee.*But if Tommo's attraction to and withdrawal from community appears to be part of a continuing cycle, the possibility of a communal self seems to be permanently closed at the end of *A Backward Glance.*

In the last few pages of the text, Wharton described a cruise she took in the Aegean. Wandering from island to island in "unbroken bliss," her party narrowly missed two earthquakes:

> We had the luck to slip into Santorin and Crete between two earthquakes of considerable violence, one of which occurred only a few weeks before our visit, and the other just afterward. So it was that in Santorin's mysterious harbour we lay close to a new lava-island still visibly edged with subterranean fires, and at Candia, in Crete, beheld in all their plastic perfection the glorious Minoan jars garlanded with seaweed and sea-monsters, the slim Prince Charming of the lilies, and the frivolous young ladies leaning from their box above the arena to watch the young acrobats leap from bull to bull, where, a few weeks after our visit, the Museum floor was strewn with their shattered fragments. (374)

Is this, then, Wharton's life in microcosm? The priceless treasures of the past shattered beyond repair, violently replaced by the barren lava of a new era? Can she only re-collect the fragments of a lost age after withdrawing into the same kind of isolation she had experienced as a child? The autobiography, after all, resonates with archeological imagery. Not quite. She has spent too much time and effort preserving the values she cherished. As Jay Martin suggests, Wharton, like some of her contemporaries, "guaranteed social order by tying it to the individual consciousness" (274). By describing her elect group, its conversation, its customs, its anecdotes, and its humor, Wharton invited readers to become members, if not by imitation, at least by identification. Not unlike the traditional conversion narrative, Wharton's autobiographical project had a purpose: as the spiritual autobiographer hoped to awaken others, Wharton wanted to insure the continuance of a redeemed way of life, if not in existing institutions, then within. In the midst of postwar disillusionment, she brilliantly adapted the spiritual autobiography form, not only to unite her narrative and to demonstrate her relationship to a larger culture, but to transmit the values she had lived.

Jay Martin's approach to modern autobiographical literature applies even more forcibly to *The Woman Within*. Though Glasgow's "original rough draft" lacks the polished organization of *A Backward Glance*, in several places it seems to respond to Wharton's work. Glasgow, in fact, cited *A Backward Glance* in *A Certain Measure*, her collection of critical prefaces, where she envied Wharton's having a literary mentor in Walter Berry. Glasgow never had such an advisor, and she might well have envied Wharton: she often disparaged contemporary authors. Yet, uncharacteristically, she admitted to liking Wharton's novels and may have been inspired by them.[10] Additional evidence of Wharton's influence can be found within the pages of *The Woman Within*, where Glasgow appealed to a "republic of the spirit," a phrase Wharton gave Lawrence Selden in *The House of Mirth*. Interestingly, Wharton never used this term in her autobiography, though it would have accurately described her "spiritual kin." If Glasgow, however, borrowed the phrase and applied it to her own life, she placed it in a context that encapsulates the difference between these two writers. Containing a single citizen, her "republic of the spirit" describes, not a group of exceptional individuals, but the solitary inner life (40–41). While Wharton used conversion rhetoric to validate her (uneasy) place in a community of like-minded people, Glasgow used it to demonstrate her profound isolation.

If critics were disappointed because Wharton left out the unpleasant details of her life in *A Backward Glance*, people who knew Glasgow were dismayed about the suffering she included in *The Woman Within*. They felt her autobiography misled readers about an individual who "always seemed in life so gay and bright and full of sympathy for others" (Auchincloss, *Ellen Glasgow*, 38). Glasgow's biographer, E. Stanly Godbold, believes that the suffering in *The Woman Within* is exaggerated; yet, by any standard, her life was filled with tragedy (208–9). Both her beloved mother and her favorite sister, Cary, died prematurely, and her brother Frank and her brother-in-law, Walter McCormack, committed suicide. She fell in love with a married man who would not divorce his wife, and she agonized over a deafness that grew progressively worse.

In the autobiography, Glasgow invested her suffering with a malevolent ubiquity. Even her first infant memory—of a bodiless face—conveys the sense of doom and separateness that followed her throughout life:

10. For Glasgow's admiration of Wharton's work, see her *Letters*, 257. J. R. Raper indicates that contemporary reviewers believed that Glasgow's *Wheel of Life* was based on Wharton's *House of Mirth*. See *Without Shelter*, 227–28.

> Beyond the top windowpanes, in the midst of a red glow, I see a face without a body staring in at me, a vacant face, round, pallid, grotesque, malevolent. Terror—or was it merely sensation?—stabbed me into consciousness. Terror of the sinking sun? Or terror of the formless, the unknown, the mystery, terror of life, of the world, of nothing or everything? . . . One minute, I was not; the next minute, I was. I felt. I was separate. I could be hurt. (3–4)

Though Glasgow remembered having a few years of relative happiness as a child, she experienced a series of shocks when she was about seven or eight years old that drove her "to unchildlike brooding over my sense of exile in a hostile world, and back again to that half-forgotten presence of the evil face without a body" (25). Even her few moments of happiness were inexorably followed by cataclysm. Her mother died, for example, just as she was "eagerly grasping at the careless youth I had never known" (83). If *A Backward Glance* is a conversion narrative uncharacteristically free of personal affliction, the suffering in *The Woman Within* is typical of the spiritual autobiography form.

Glasgow's own suffering was greatly magnified by her sympathy with other beings, human, animal, and vegetable. In the book's opening chapter, she illustrated her sensitivity to the pain of others by merging her narrative viewpoint with that of a baited dog: "Down the middle of the street, coming toward me through the sun and dust, a large black dog flees in terror. . . . I have seen what it means to be hunted. I run on with the black dog. I am chased into an area over the street. I am beaten with clubs, and caught in a net. I am seized and dragged away to something unseen and frightful" (9). This Whitmanesque fusion permanently awakened "a heartbreaking pity for the abused and inarticulate, for all the helpless victims of life everywhere" (10). Glasgow felt similar emotions when Uncle Henry, an old black man from her neighborhood, was unwillingly carried to the poorhouse. This time, she blurred, not the narrative's point of view, but the distinction between past and present. Her childish helplessness becomes one with her inability to stifle a painful memory: "Nothing that I can do will keep the old man from crying out in his grieving voice that he does not want to be taken. Nothing that I can do will make the world different" (11). In these representative scenes, Glasgow was overwhelmed by her powerlessness to remedy pain. Though she hoped that her sensitivity would decrease as time passed, the pattern of vicarious suffering continued throughout the autobiography and was expanded into a global "*danse macabre*" as she contemplated the horror of World War I (233). Glasgow's awareness of the suffering of others and of her inability to assuage it made her believe she was the victim of a hostile universe, a world she "would not have created" (233). Feeling responsible for horrors she had nothing to do with, she wrote, "My soul is the last unwilling scapegoat of Predestination" (275).

One of the most painful events in Glasgow's early life occurred when her mother left home to visit a brother in Mississippi. Glasgow's father used the occasion to give away her favorite dog, and her oldest sister, Emily, sabotaged the letter of indignation Ellen addressed to her mother:

> In those months of Mother's absence, I know that I broke forever with my childhood. For the first time I was standing alone, without the shelter and the comfort of her love and her sympathy. Her silence, inexplicable and utterly unlike her, seemed to thrust me still farther and farther into loneliness, until at last . . . I began to love, not to fear, loneliness. (71)

This incident alienated Glasgow from her family and caused her to rebel against her father's wish that she attend religious services. Feeling that she had won her liberty, Glasgow became consumed with intellectual curiosity:

> And, then, in the midst of it all, while my mother was still away, I was seized, I was overwhelmed by a consuming desire to find out things for myself, to know the true from the false, the real from the make-believe. The longing was so intense that I flung myself on knowledge as a thirsty man might fling himself into a desert spring. I read everything in our library. . . . [E]ven with . . . my two closest friends, I felt that I had changed beyond understanding and recognition. They lived happy lives on the outside of things, accepting what they were taught, while I was devoured by this hunger to know, to discover some meaning, some underlying reason for the mystery and the pain of the world.
> . . . Something had gone out of me for good, and, in exchange, I had found something that, to me, was more precious. I had found the greatest consolation of my life; but I had found also an unconquerable loneliness. (72–73)

This incident, partly patterned on a religious conversion, is revealing for a number of reasons. For one thing, it signals the beginning of Glasgow's desire to understand the existence of pain and suffering, her search "for some hidden clue to experience, for some truth, or at least for some philosophy, which would help me to adjust my identity to a world I had found hostile and even malign" (89). To Glasgow, the ubiquity and intensity of pain implied that there must be an explanation for it, and she experimented with a variety of intellectual systems and causes: Stoicism, Eastern and Christian mysticism, Fabian socialism, women's suffrage, and organized relief. None of these callings lasted, however, because none offered a remedy or even an explanation for the cruelty that seemed to be inherent in the human psyche. Glasgow's "continuous search for a creed" thus led to a frustrated skepticism that she expressed in a paradoxical language similar to that found in *The Education of Henry Adams*. She states, "Though I was a skeptic in mind, I was in my heart a believer. . . . My mind, however, was faithful to its disbelief" (56, 140–41).

In addition to introducing the book's pattern of intellectual wandering, the temporary absence of Glasgow's mother also reveals her profound ambivalence to loneliness. Throughout *The Woman Within*, Glasgow referred to the pains of her exile, how the worst part of suffering was facing it alone, yet she admitted that she grew to love her estrangement. Like Henry James and the young Edith Wharton, she found solace in an inner world of inquiry and art. In moments of stress, she was eager to return to "that strange, secret, hidden happiness that belonged to myself alone" and to "the world within and my own special act of creation" (54, 151).

Glasgow's skepticism, of course, made her an unlikely spiritual autobiographer. In an essay describing her personal philosophy, she shows the same distrust of conversion seen in William James's *Varieties*: "There is danger in any too sudden conversion of the unthinking mind. . . . I believe, therefore, that faith has its victories, but that skepticism remains the only permanent basis of tolerance" ("Ellen Glasgow," 109–10). But if Glasgow distrusted sudden awakenings, she nevertheless remembered having several, all of which relieved her suffering and marked turning points in her life. With *A Backward Glance*, one senses that Wharton viewed conversion as a convenient frame upon which to hang her life story. In *The Woman Within*, however, conversion is a powerfully felt phenomenon. In an inversion of the spiritual autobiography form much like the one used by Adams, Glasgow grounded the text's conversion discourse on her skepticism.

Though Glasgow flirted with the language of revelation throughout *The*

Woman Within, her first fully developed "conversion" is constructed around
her falling in love with the Gerald B—— of the autobiography. Before they
met, she had reached an emotional crisis typical of conversion rhetoric.
Despairing over her mother's death, feeling that she had wasted her youth,
and embarrassed by her deafness, she discovered that "without warning, a
miracle changed my life":

> The flash came from an empty sky, and my whole life was transfig-
> ured.
>   Like all other romantic episodes, great or small, in my life, this
> began with a sudden illumination. Or, rather, it did not begin at all;
> it was not there, and then it was there. One moment the world had
> appeared in stark outlines, colorless and unlit, and the next mo-
> ment, it was flooded with radiance. . . . And this first love, as
> always, created the illusion of its own immortality.
>   . . . All I felt was a swifter vibration, a quivering joy, as if some
> long imprisoned stream of life were beginning to flow again under
> the open sky.
>   . . . this passionate awakening to life had restored my lost faith in
> myself. Love had proved to me that my personality, or my charm,
> could overcome, not only my deafness, but the morbid terror of
> that affliction, and, especially, of its effect upon others. (153–57)

This awakening, which is similar to the one Wharton records, marks a
dramatic change in Glasgow's personality. She cast off her "half-mourning,"
bought colorful clothes, and began to exercise, winning back "at least
moderate health and nervous equilibrium" (160). Even a friend noticed that
her whole outlook, even her appearance, had improved. If Wharton's
"conversion" was occasioned by the publication of her first short-story
collection, Glasgow's was caused by a romantic relationship: falling in love
had "destroyed and then re-created the entire inner world of my consciousness" (160). But she filled this scene with ambivalence too; the flash she
described came from an "empty sky" and carried only the "illusion" of
permanence. Though the affair with Gerald B—— that followed led to
some transient happiness, she called it an "arrested pause between
dreaming and waking," almost as if she were unsure of the reality of her
transformation. And because Gerald B—— was married, she was unwilling
to discuss her relationship with anyone: it too became part of her "secret
life" (160). Instead of initiating her into a community, her uncharacteristic

conversion only isolated her further and had little to do with a vocation that, she explained (as did James before her), had been hers from birth.

This "romantic" awakening to first love is one of a pair of related experiences, both described in the chapter entitled "Miracle—or Illusion." After their affair had lasted for seven years, Gerald sent a letter to Glasgow, explaining that he was terminally ill. Vacationing in Murren, Switzerland, at the time, Glasgow was struck once again by her inability to attain lasting happiness. Some days later, she climbed into the hills and felt a profound peace. She left two accounts of this mystical vision. In a letter to her friend and fellow novelist, Mary Johnston, written just a year after it occurred, she described a very positive experience, much like an actual religious conversion:

> For a year I was so dead that I couldn't feel even when I was hurt because of some curious emotional anaesthesia, and, like you, I had to fight—fight, a sleepless battle night and day, not for my reason but for my very soul. Then at the end of a year—at Murren last summer I came out triumphant, and for three whole months it was as if I walked on light, not air. I was like one who had come out of a dark prison into the presence of God and saw and knew him, and cared for nothing in the way of pain that had gone before the vision. Of course, dear heart, the exhilaration, the first rapture of the mere rebound to physical or spiritual health cannot be permanent, but, I think, the strength of the victory and the memory of it, are built into the eternal forces of one's spirit. (*Letters*, 55–56)

Though Glasgow hedged a little about the origin of this experience, stating not that God caused it but that she was "like" one who had been touched by God, still her interpretation follows the conventional religious pattern. In the midst of physical and emotional affliction, she felt a rapturous release—apparently caused by a benevolent agent—which appeared to permanently strengthen her spirit.

In *The Woman Within*, however, Glasgow recorded a much different experience:

> I went up on the hillside, and lay down in the grass, where a high wind was blowing. Could I never escape from death? Or was it life that would not cease its hostilities? . . . I tried with all my strength to find absorption in the Power people called God, or in the vast

hollowness of the universe. . . . Then, after long effort, I sank into
an effortless peace. Lying there, in that golden August light, I knew,
or felt, or beheld, a union deeper than knowledge, deeper than
sense, deeper than vision. Light streamed through me, after anguish, and for one instant of awareness, if but for that one instant, I
felt pure ecstasy. In a single blinding flash of illumination, I knew
blessedness. I was part of the spirit that moved in the light and the
wind and the grass. I was—or felt I was—in communion with
reality, with ultimate being. (165–66)

This event, like the experience described in the letter, seems to provide
the peace for which Glasgow had longed, but the language that follows is
filled with uncertainty:

Then the moment sped on; the illumination flashed by me; the wind
raced through the grass; the golden light shone and faded. Ecstasy
born out of agony was as fleeting as the old delusions of mind or of
heart. . . .
    Spirit? Matter? Imagination? Or a fantasy of tortured nerves? I
do not know. But I do know that, for a solitary instant, . . . I saw
that mystic vision, I found communion with the Absolute, or with
Absolute Nothingness; I know, too, that the recognition was lost
again in the very moment in which it was found, and that I never
recovered the miracle or the delusion. (166)

After experiencing her vision, Glasgow wrote that she went through a
period of "death-in-life" that caused "an anaesthesia of the mind and the
heart" (167). This passage is strikingly less positive than the one Glasgow
sent to Mary Johnston. Far from being akin to the regeneration of a
Christian, the autobiography's second conversion is more puzzling than
anything else. Glasgow could not decide if it was a product of her
imagination, a miracle, a communion with the absolute, or a recognition of
nothingness. While her letter to Mary Johnston indicates that her spiritual
deadness came before her awakening, like the depression that typically
precedes conversion, in *The Woman Within* she said it occurred after this
experience.[11] Altering this sequence of events may have helped Glasgow

11. Raper argues that Glasgow's emotional crisis was caused by a strain in her relationship
with Gerald B——, 178.

finalize an affair long over, but it also enabled her to use the second awakening to deconstruct the first. If first love saved her from despair and transformed her life, then the event at Murren, which roughly coincided with Gerald's death, ended that love and dropped her back into misery. Whether miracles or illusions, both experiences provided only temporary relief and left her the same isolated, suffering being she had always been. As she concluded the chapter, she wrote, "My essential problem had not altered since that moment of dumb fear, when I saw the face without a body looming toward me from the sunset" (168). In *The Woman Within*, each conversion functions synecdochically, showing the equivalence of every emotional crisis to Glasgow's initial memory of achieving consciousness. At each critical juncture in the text, the same sense of self is reinvoked and re-enacted.

Glasgow's inscribing her first experience with heterosexual love and the later loss of that love as conversion experiences reveals if nothing else the large emotional stakes she placed on romance. This attachment is perhaps explained by her early loss of a supportive communal network, which, as theorists have noted, is in many cases central to female subjectivity. Having lost her mother at an early age—first through an extended absence and then through death—and subsequently losing other beloved family members, Glasgow must have felt that all her significant relationships had been cut out from under her. Only by conforming to the myth of romantic love could she fill her emotional void. Romance functioned as the single possible source of redemption. Like Wharton, Glasgow was caught in a cultural bind. Lacking a supportive (female) network of interpersonal relations, she felt acutely the pressure of conforming to the expectations of a patriarchal culture that defined women according to the success of their romantic attachments. Even though at the time of writing she saw the absurdity of measuring her self-worth according to those expectations, she could not escape them completely. For her, there was no appealing cultural alternative. Since she was unable to recover or replace her lost female community and since her love affairs all ended in disappointment, it is little wonder that her "conversions" were to alienation.

Glasgow went on to describe two more conversionlike experiences, though neither is as fully developed as the earlier awakenings. The first of these was also centered around a failed romantic attachment. When her fiancé, Henry Anderson, the Harold S—— of the autobiography, was in Rumania during the Great War, Glasgow believed that he had used his position with the Red Cross to advance his reputation and to flirt with the queen. Upon his return to the States, she argued with him for the first time. Later that night, the futility of their relationship merged with the horror of the war, and she underwent an emotional crisis typical of conversion rhetoric:

> With or without reason, the bold mortal sickness of the spirit, black, malignant, unutterably hideous, curved toward me, engulfed me, and scattered through the room, the house, the world, and the universe. Nothing, I felt, was left, not so much as the merest glimmer of faith or of desire. There was no help in religion; there was no help in philosophy; there was no help in human relationships. (237)

After taking an overdose of sleeping pills, however, Glasgow was engulfed in blessedness and dreamed that all the people and animals she had ever loved passed before her through a pastoral landscape in groups of two and three. She acknowledged that either the pills or the "mental anguish of an overwrought mood" caused this vision, but, significantly, her dream parallels the experience at Murren: she emphasized not the peace of awakening but the isolating pain that inevitably followed. Her return to consciousness recalls her initial recognition of the bodiless face: "I could feel pain drumming back into my brain and my nerves. Nausea gripped me, like a black chill, in the pit of my stomach, and the violence was renewing consciousness, identity, utter despair. . . . The dream, for ecstasy was a dream, had vanished forever" (240). Glasgow had a similar experience—again when she was sedated—after a heart attack. Believing she was dying, she felt that death would be a "warm and friendly welcome to the universe, to the Being beyond and above consciousness, or any vestige of self." But like her other moments of heightened awareness, this one signified a reunion with the "Unknown Everything or with Nothing" (290). It too was either a miracle or a delusion.

Glasgow slips into this disjunctive mood in all of the book's conversion scenes and in other important passages as well. For instance, she did not know whether the vacant, bodiless face made her afraid of "nothing or everything." "Terror," she states, "or was it merely sensation?—stabbed me into consciousness" (3–4). Much later, as she described the beginning of her relationship with Anderson, she asked herself, "Was my search for reality succeeding at last? Or was the way leading only into a blind alley?" (226). She similarly could not decide if St. Francis Assisi, whom she greatly admired, had found "his Christ," or whether he found " 'the flight of the alone to the Alone.' " (266). Embedded in the book's conversion discourse, this disjunctive mood is a result of her ambivalence toward suffering. In an unorthodox application of the law of the excluded middle, Glasgow believed that her pain had either a transcendent meaning or none at all.

By applying mutually exclusive terms to important events in her life, Glasgow reveals her inability to discover the cause of unwarranted pain. All she could say, for instance, of her mystical dream was that "it was the revulsion from protracted despair, the sharp relief, the sudden cessation of torture" (238). These words could apply to all her awakenings, which conform to the language and structure of traditional conversion narratives in that they mark crucial turning points in her life and signal a release from extreme affliction, but which are devoid of intellectual or spiritual content. Glasgow was fascinated by modern psychology and had some experience with psychoanalysis; one of her stated motives, in fact, for writing the autobiography was to "shed some beam of light, however faint, into the troubled darkness of human psychology" (161). Like William James, she knew conversion as a psychological reality, but, unlike him, she failed to see its utility. For Glasgow, the process of conversion became an inexplicable experiential pattern that organized her life story but offered little guidance or illumination. Consequently, she was converted to no single worldview, religious, aesthetic, political, or otherwise.

For all of her self-professed skepticism, however, Glasgow did attempt to resolve the tensions manifested by her disjunctive approach to suffering and conversion. Finding it impossible to discover any other metaphysical place to stand upon, she grounded all reality on the thinking self. To her, "the life of the mind is reality," and it alone "contains an antidote to experience" (163, 296). Near the end of the autobiography, she formulated an extremely subjective ethic:

> It is true that I recognized no obligation toward an unknown and invisible Power. I had ceased to believe that ideal goodness, or indeed anything ideal, existed as an abstract Reality in the universe. Yet within myself I found a sense of justice and compassion that I could not betray. . . . The question of whether or not a God ruled the universe had no bearing whatever on my private belief that it was better to be humane than to be cruel. (271–72)

Glasgow's somewhat solipsistic solution to her metaphysical problem, however, only reinforces the isolation at once the cause and the effect—

the agony and the ecstasy—of her uncertainty. On the inside back cover of her edition of Plotinus, she wrote, "For those who lead a solitary life being *converted to themselves* have the hope of salvation in themselves" (her underlining).[12] Redemption, for Glasgow, could only come in isolation. If the author of a traditional conversion narrative becomes socialized, she was antisocialized, a rhetorical position enhanced by the "impenetrable wall" of her deafness (181). "The lonelier the universe became," she wrote, "the more at home I should feel in it. I could hold out hands empty of both faith and knowledge, and say, 'I, too, am a part of you—of what was not, is not, and never shall be' " (177).

Like other postwar writers, Glasgow attempted to resolve life's conflicts by referring to an exclusive inner world, yet, unlike them, she drew little consolation from a modernist conception of art. Though she felt that a life of suffering had made her a better writer, she actually lamented that experience crumbled "in the end to mere literary material" (226). In *A Certain Measure* she went so far as to say that writing fiction is not worth "a penny more or less than the release of mind that it brings" (207). Glasgow stood alone, not only in defiance of cruelty, but also as an artist. She claimed to have been influenced by no one and had "no slightest inclination ever to become a disciple" (142). For her, conversion had little to do with a vocation and only reinforced her role as a perennial outsider, whose very identity was based on exclusion.

Glasgow saw herself as a rebel, always on the side of the weak and the unfortunate, always against the individual, group, or idea in power: "Life in my imagination," she said, "was divided between the stronger and the weaker, the fortunate and the unfortunate. Either by fate or by choice, I had found myself on the side of the weaker" (59). Because Glasgow was born into a world where social structures, public morals, and literary tastes had changed dramatically, she felt that committing to any ideology or value system would be futile. To be *always* on the side of the weak is to be prepared to switch sympathies when the sources of power shift. She states, "By the time an idea has won its way in the world, I have rushed ahead to another" (42). Disliking Christianity because it separated the elect from the damned, Glasgow as a girl chose to side with the unregenerate; as a woman she followed the same pattern, preferring to remain outside of

---

12. See Carrington C. Tutwiler, *A Catalogue of the Library of Ellen Glasgow*, 21–22. Glasgow's library reveals not only her fascination with mystical experience, but also her fondness for spiritual autobiographies. It contained Augustine's *Confessions*, the autobiographies of John Stuart Mill and Harriet Martineau, as well as *The Education of Henry Adams*.

any privileged system: "I was a radical," she says, "when everyone else I knew was conservative, and now I am conservative when most other people appear to be radical" ("Ellen Glasgow," 95; *Woman Within*, 42). In an extreme application of the "paradox of Puritan piety," she suggested that the only way to be saved was to be damned.

The Woman Within thus provided a kind of self-justification for Glasgow because she always found herself among the unfortunate with whom she sided. Her isolation, in this sense, was her most prized possession, the measure of her self-worth as well as her greatest complaint. But this justification, as the ambivalence of the text's conversion discourse makes clear, offered little satisfaction. One wonders why, unlike Wharton, she could not find solace in a community of artists. She knew many literary figures and frequently corresponded with them, but she was never a part of an artistic community. Since Glasgow used conversion rhetoric to show her alienation from all groups, not just those dominated by patriarchal values, the discourse in *The Woman Within* seems less obviously gendered than that of *A Backward Glance*. But Glasgow's intellectual isolation, in part, was caused by her sex: her acquaintance with the male literary establishment was largely negative. When she began reading works of science and philosophy, she was told that she was "too attractive to be strongminded"; when she first sought publication, an agent sexually harassed her; and when she sought the advice of an editor from Macmillan's, he suggested she stop writing "and have some babies" (97, 108). Other members of the literary establishment, if less threatening, were nevertheless paternalistic: "All one needed to make a reputation as a novelist," she wrote, "was to belong to the oldest and the most respectable of the fraternities. . . . But I did not like to be patronized" (110). Given this initiation into the world of professional letters, it is hardly surprising that Glasgow hesitated to join an artistic circle likely to be dominated by males.

Edith Wharton's peculiar adaptation of the conversion narrative in *A Backward Glance* defines her uneasy relationship to a patriarchal literary and intellectual culture. Though she began life locked in a world where sex seemed to be an insurmountable barrier, her literary talent enabled her to be accepted into an artistic community that became her salvation. Unlike the other twentieth-century authors whom I examine in this study, Wharton alone chose not to subvert the socializing function of conversion discourse. But her autobiography nevertheless testifies to the subtle ways that, despite her accomplishments, she remained a marginal figure in her world. Glasgow, who experienced worse discrimination, responded by making marginality the very source of her identity. Defining herself in opposition to the dominant culture, she wrote an exploratory autobiography, less organized and less traditional than the one written by Wharton, but one that is more in keeping with the privatized and estranging notion of conversion presented by the two Jameses and by Henry Adams. That both women achieved their rhetorical goals by adapting conversion discourse illustrates both the flexibility of the spiritual autobiography form and the need for early twentieth-century women writers to defend their choice of vocation in a culture that still believed they were an abnormality.

6

· · ·

THE VARIETIES OF BLACK EXPERIENCE

Zora Neale Hurston's *Dust Tracks on a Road* and the Autobiography of Richard Wright

In 1945, just a few months after *Black Boy* was published, Richard Wright wrote to his boyhood friend Joe Brown, "There is a great novel yet to be written about the Negro in the South; just a simple, straight, easy, great novel, telling how they live and how they die, what they see and how they feel each day. . . . Just a novel telling of the quiet ritual of their lives" (*Letters*, 13). Today, most critics would agree that by the time *Black Boy* appeared, such a novel had already been written, Zora Neale Hurston's *Their Eyes Were Watching God*, yet when Wright reviewed it for *New Masses* seven years earlier, he did not think so. He caustically argued that Hurston used a "minstrel technique" designed to make "the 'white folks' laugh" and that she created characters who "swing like a pendulum eternally in that safe and narrow orbit in which America likes to see the Negro live: between laughter and tears" (22–25).

Not long after Wright's review appeared, Hurston took advantage of an opportunity to respond in kind. If Wright accused Hurston of using racial stereotypes to create a false picture of the South, she charged him with the same offense. In a review that attacked the violence and Communism of *Uncle Tom's Children*, Hurston argued that Wright's hate-filled characters were unrepresentative types. He was the one who falsely presented the South as a "dismal, hopeless section ruled by brutish hatred and nothing else." Applying a Howellsian aesthetic to Wright's stories, she said he would have done better had he "dealt with plots that touched the broader and more fundamental phases of Negro life instead of confining himself to the spectacular" (32).

Significantly, this exchange anticipates some of the most enduring criticism of Wright and Hurston's work. Like many who followed, Wright complained that Hurston subordinated the effects of racial discrimination in an idyllic representation of black folk life, while Hurston suggested that Wright's devastating picture of the South ignored the salvific and nurturing effect of African-American culture. These two critical approaches have especially been brought to bear on their respective autobiographies, Hurston's *Dust Tracks on a Road*, and Wright's *Black Boy* and *American Hunger*. Generally, Hurston's *Dust Tracks* has been called a disturbing failure, a book that announces the demise of her talent and her increasingly conservative approach to race relations. Alice Walker called it the "most unfortunate thing Zora ever wrote" (68); Hurston's biographer Robert Hemenway states that it "sacrifices truth to the politics of racial harmony" (Introduction, xiii). Wright's autobiography, of course, has been widely acclaimed; but many critics have taken exception to his grim presentation of black Southern culture, arguing most notably with his depiction of the African-American family. It was in the context of discussing *Black Boy*, for instance, that George Kent famously called Wright an "exaggerated Westerner."[1]

Despite their artistic incompatibility, however, these two writers were more similar than they appear. Their divergent attitudes toward racial issues sprang from the same cultural problem: how to fashion a unique, "American" sense of worth in a society that systematically demanded that they see themselves as members of an inferior group. Different as they were, both responded to this problem by formulating a radical individualism. To be sure, they grounded their responses on the Western—if not purely American—principles of egalitarianism, pluralism, and pragmatism. Yet their individualism had deep personal roots as well, best illustrated by their early rejection of religious belief. When Wright and Hurston composed their autobiographies, they made this rejection a focus of their life stories. At hand, of course, was a literary form that had dominated autobiographical writing—the conversion narrative. But in rejecting religion, these writers also rejected this conventional form. And since, in many cases, the slave narrative drew upon the conversion pattern, they at once individualistically distanced themselves from both the dominant white and the dominant black

1. See George Kent, *Blackness and the Adventure of Western Culture*, 79–82; Ralph Ellison, "Richard Wright's Blues," 205; and Houston Baker, "Racial Wisdom and Richard Wright's Native Son," 78–79. Baker revises his approach to Wright in *Blues, Ideology, and Afro-American Literature*, 139–57.

autobiographical tradition.[2] If the slave narrative, like the traditional conversion narrative, illustrated the relationship between the self and a community, Hurston and Wright linguistically denied any such association. Authors such as Henry James and Ellen Glasgow subverted the conventions of the spiritual autobiography to emphasize their uniqueness, but they still relied on the expectations of the genre. Wright and Hurston took the secularizing process one step further. By creating the impression that their narratives would be variations on the pattern, and then by renouncing the structural unity generated by it, they signified a rejection of social and literary expectations more complete than those suggested by the other writers I have examined. By the mid-twentieth century, the process of anticonversion had itself become conventional, and Hurston and Wright sought a form that would distance them from established cultural and textual norms. In their life as in their writing, they wrenched themselves, often violently, away from the expectations of others, white or black.

Daughter of a Baptist minister and an experienced anthropologist, Hurston saw African-American religion as a rich source of folk material, and she devoted much of her life to bringing the music, sermons, and visions associated with her Eatonville community to a larger—predominately white—public. She was a careful observer of conversion accounts, and she published a black "morphology of conversion," based on her fieldwork, which appeared in *Negro: An Anthology* in 1934. Hurston later incorporated this morphology in a slightly condensed form in *Dust Tracks*:

> In the conversion the vision is sought. The individual goes forth into waste places and by fasting and prayer induces the vision. . . . the sinner is first made conscious of his guilt. This is followed by a period called "lyin' under conviction" which lasts for three days. After which Jesus [a little white man] converts the supplicant, and the supplicant refuses to believe without proof, and only gives in under threat of eternal damnation. He flees from this to open acknowledgment of God and salvation. First from the outside comes the accusation of sin. Then from within the man comes the consciousness of guilt, and the sufferer seeks relief from Heaven.

---

2. *Black Boy* has been compared to the slave narrative by Robert Stepto in "I Thought I Knew These People," 202–4, and in *From Behind the Veil*, 128–47. Stephen Butterfield makes the same comparison, *Black Autobiography in America*, 156–79, as does Michel Fabre in the Afterword to *American Hunger*, 140–42. *Dust Tracks* has been linked to the slave narrative tradition by Lillie Howard, *Zora Neale Hurston*, 16, 61.

When it is granted, it is at first doubted, but later accepted. We
have a mixture of external and internal struggles. ("Conversions
and Visions," 47)

In its broad outline, Hurston's analysis of African-American conversion
narratives follows the logic of the typical Calvinist account, which has been
a model for much autobiographical writing, yet her morphology contains a
number of black folk variants. First, while conversion traditionally occurred
spontaneously and was frequently accompanied by the acceptance of a
vocation, in Hurston's congregation, conversion could be induced—by
prayer and fasting—and was distinguished from the "call to preach," which
took place unexpectedly: "In conversion, then, we have the cultural pattern
of the person seeking the vision and inducing it by isolation and fasting. In
the call to preach we have the involuntary vision—the call seeking the man"
(47). An Arminian variation of the Calvinist explanation for conversion, this
morphology implies that the "converted" have control over their religious
destinies, while "preachers" do not. Hurston's ministers underwent an
experience much different from that of the laity. Their call, like those of
the Old Testament prophets, separated them from the worshiping community and was unsought and, perhaps, unwanted as well.

Second, if the typical Calvinist often blurred the distinction between
conversion and mystical experience, Hurston's African-American wor-
shipers appear to merge the two. In her morphology, vision almost always
accompanies conversion and in practice is often indistinguishable from it.
"The vision," she states, "is a very definite part of Negro religion. It
almost always accompanies conversion. It always accompanies the call to
preach" (47). With its emphasis on dramatic and ecstatic theophanies,
Hurston's morphology privileges the roles of imagination and performance
in religious life. She made it clear that her congregation responded favorably
to originality and creativity:

Certain conversion visions have become traditional, but all sorts of
variations are interpolated in the general framework of the convention, from the exceedingly frivolous to the most solemn. One may
go to a dismal swamp, the other to the privy house. The imagination
of one may carry him to the last judgement and the rimbones of
nothing, the vision of another may hobble him at washing collard
greens. (47)

The members of Hurston's evangelical congregation thus emphasized the flexibility of conversion discourse. The more imaginative the vision, the more uniquely detailed the conversion account, and the more dramatic its rendition, the better. "These visions are traditional," she states, "I knew them by heart as did the rest of the congregation, but still it was exciting to see how the converts would handle them. Some of them made up new details" (*Dust Tracks*, 272).

Finally, in Hurston's morphology, new believers, at first, were not convinced that they had received grace: "But in each case there is an unwillingness to believe—to accept the great fortune too quickly. So God is asked for proof." The black believers whom Hurston observed not only received such proof, they *demanded* it as condition of their assent to God's word. The newly elect typically asked for three such signs, but having complied twice, God lost patience and threatened to renounce his promise of salvation. Believers then submitted to divine authority, but not before testing it.

If much of the enthusiasm Hurston recorded can be attributed to the Southern Protestant tradition generally, still it is not hard to observe the seeds of an African-American aesthetic in her morphology of conversion: conversion could be induced by individual action, visions were valuable in their own right, and believers were less than reverent toward supreme authority. Hurston's religious community clearly privileged individuality, diversity, and improvisation; and it valued the principles of performance, subversion, and humor in the life of faith. As others have noted, these values—performance, subversion, improvisation, imagination, and humor—were, in part, responses to a racist culture. They were channels of self-affirmation in the midst of cultural degradation, and they are found in African-American art as well as religion.

Hurston's construction of an African-American morphology of conversion is consistent with her role as a professional anthropologist. Like William James, she held that the diverse beliefs of people served universal human needs, saying, for example, "I hold that any religion that satisfies the individual urge is valid for that person" (205). Despite her fascination with the religious practices of her father's congregation, however, she never experienced conversion herself. She remembers "questing and seeking" since she was a child, but she "made the motions and went on," fascinated with, yet emotionally detached from, the fervor so much a part of her Eatonville culture (275). When she talked about her own experience in *Dust Tracks*, she stepped outside her anthropological relativism and disparaged the religious impulse altogether, implying that it was grounded on personal inadequacy:

> So, having looked at the subject from many sides, studied beliefs by word of mouth and then as they fit into great rigid forms, I find I know a great deal about form, but little or nothing about the mysteries I sought as a child. . . . People need religion because the great masses fear life and its consequences. . . . Feeling a weakness in the face of great forces, men seek an alliance with omnipotence to bolster up their feeling of weakness, even though the omnipotence they rely upon is a creature of their own minds. (277–78)

Much like William James, Hurston tested the validity of religious experience by appealing to its utility. But if James in the *Varieties of Religious Experience* found that belief often yielded personal and communal benefits, Hurston claimed that despite the emotional excitement that accompanies conversion, it had little permanent impact on believers. The converted, she wrote, "should have looked and acted differently from other people after experiences like that. But these people looked and acted like everybody else—or so it seemed to me" (267). Though Hurston acknowledged the efficacy of religion for some, she argued that most of the world's conversions have occurred as the result of coercion—psychological or military. She suggested that conversions took place because individuals were not strong enough to resist them. Religious belief was thus a manifestation of instability. "Prayer," she states, "is for those who need it. Prayer seems to me a cry of weakness, and an attempt to avoid, by trickery, the rules of the game as laid down. I do not choose to admit weakness" (278). For her, as for Nietzsche, any appeal to a supernatural authority amounted to an admission that one had failed to take command of one's destiny.

Hurston ended the chapter in *Dust Tracks* on religion by saying, "Somebody else may have my rapturous glance at the archangels," yet, strangely, for all her disparagement of the supernatural, her autobiographical writing is filled with visions and other mystical events. In *Dust Tracks*, as well as in her folklore collections, she frequently commented on the cogency of sympathetic magic, and she remembered having had numerous psychic experiences while being initiated into the mysteries of hoodoo. As this ambivalence toward religious life makes clear, the visionary imagination that Hurston brought from Eatonville often bumped against the hard logic of a rationalistic world, the world of Barnard and anthropological research. [3] She wrote, "You cannot have knowledge and worship at the same time" (93).

This tension between a folk and a scientific worldview drives much of the narrative and is illustrated by her "doubled" story of how her Eatonville neighbor Mrs. Bronson became paralyzed. As a girl, Hurston told her friends that Mr. Pendir, a quiet man from the neighborhood, had turned into an alligator and had attacked Mrs. Bronson while she was fishing. As a result of this explanation, Mr. Pendir was shunned by Hurston's girlhood friends and acquired the reputation of a hoodoo doctor. Even though the town's physician had explained that the woman had suffered a stroke, Hurston remembered, "No matter what the doctor said, I knew the real truth of the matter" (82). When the ostensibly immortal Mr. Pendir died some time later, however, she was forced to confront the rational explanation: "The truth of the matter was, that poor Mr. Pendir was the one man in the village who could not swim a lick. He died a very ordinary death. . . . His life had not agreed with my phantasy at any point" (82–83). Hurston, of course, never believed her "lie," but by asserting the "truth" of both explanations, she underscores the conflict between a folk (visionary) and a rationalistic system of belief. This tension is reinvoked when she remembers being confronted in a hoodoo ceremony with what appeared to be "terrible monsters." She wrote, "It took months for me to doubt it afterwards," as if she recognized a need to consciously suppress her folk sensibility (192).

The twelve visions Hurston remembers having while still a child are marked by the same tension. As presented in *Dust Tracks*, these visions were unexpected and unsought. They occurred after she and her brother had been caught trying to force a hen to take back its recently laid egg. Afraid of being found out, she ran to the porch of a vacant house, where she found and ate a juicy raisin, after which she fell asleep. While dreaming, Hurston saw twelve scenes flash before her, which previewed a life of aimlessness followed by eventual deliverance. In this sequence (which

3. Robert Hemenway illustrates the conflict between Hurston's Eatonville values and those of New York and Barnard in *Zora Neale Hurston: A Literary Biography* as well as in "Zora Neale Hurston and the Eatonville Anthropology." Hemenway's approach to Hurston's biculturalism sheds much light on her career, but he tends to polarize Hurston's professional and folk experience more than is necessary. Evidence of both racism and rationalism can be found even in the early pages of *Dust Tracks*.

bears some resemblance to the storyline of *Paradise Lost*), Hurston flees from punishment, tastes a forbidden fruit, sees a future filled with misery, and receives a promise of final salvation.[4] In one sense these visions are not far removed from the etiological tales and the religious visions characteristic of the folklife of her Eatonville community, yet they are alien too—like "stereopticon slides"—the product of a technological world:

> Like clearcut stereopticon slides, I saw twelve scenes flash before me, each one held until I had seen it well in every detail, and then be replaced by another. There was no continuity as in an average dream. Just disconnected scene after scene with blank spaces in between. I knew that they were all true, a preview of things to come, and my soul writhed in agony and shrunk away. But I knew that there was no shrinking. These things had to be. (57)

These scenes foreshadow the breakup of her family and the despair and wandering that would follow. In the last vision, however, Hurston comes to a "big house," where two women wait and where she believes she would at last "know peace and love and what goes with those things."

Even if these visions predict that Hurston would achieve peace and love in the end, still she confronted the sober realization that her life had suddenly, ineradicably changed:

> So when I left the porch, I left a great deal behind me. I was weighed down with a power I did not want. I had knowledge before its time. I knew my fate. . . . I never told anyone around me about these strange things. It was too different. They would laugh me off as a story-teller. Besides, I had a feeling of difference from my fellow men, and I did not want it to be found out . . . I stood in a world of vanished communion with my kind, which is worse than if it had never been. (57–59)

Immediately after receiving the visions, Hurston felt a sense of both awe and alienation. She had "knowledge before its time" and a "power I did not want." Critics have argued that Hurston's visions introduce a messianic theme into her autobiography and signify her alienation from black culture—a "personal transcendence of racial realities."[5] But they do not

4. I mention the parallel to *Paradise Lost* because Hurston herself describes her fondness for it in *Dust Tracks*, 127.

5. See Hemenway, *Zora Neale Hurston*, 281, and Anne Rayson, "*Dust Tracks on a Road*: Zora Neale Hurston and the Form of Black Autobiography," 41.

sufficiently see the way that, for Hurston, marginality itself could be traditional. Hurston's unexpected and unwanted visions arrive in a manner very much like the "call to preach" described by her African-American morphology of conversion. These visions caused her to stand "apart within," but they still bound her to her folk culture's system of belief. The power she received was the gift of expression; even she connected these unwelcome visions to the alienation of the "story-teller." Upon first reading, then, Hurston's twelve visions appear to occupy a pivotal place in the structure of the narrative; it seems they initiate her into the republic of letters.

Hurston appears to confirm these suspicions in a draft chapter of *Dust Tracks*, where she identified one of the women in the final, peaceful vision as Charlotte Osgood Mason, the New York benefactor who helped launch her career as a professional folklorist and writer:

> It was decreed in the beginning of things that I should meet Mrs. R. Osgood Mason. She had been in the last of my prophetic visions from the first coming of them. I could not know that until I met her. But the moment I walked into the room, I knew that this was the end.
>   . . . Born so widely apart in every way, the key to certain phases of my life had been placed in her hand. I had been sent to her to get it. I owe her and owe her and owe her! Not only for material help, but for spiritual guidance. (309)

Substitute Hurston's "Godmother" for Jesus—the "little white man" who called black sinners—and the twelve visions describe a conventional, though difficult, path toward the literary life. Though Hurston's gratitude toward Mason has been called less than genuine, she wrote to her as if she were a "high priestess," not unlike the conjurers Hurston met as a folklorist.[6] Hurston often addressed Mason in mystical terms, calling her, among other things, "True one." If *Dust Tracks* is read in light of such statements, then it appears to transpose the very conventional rhetoric of conversion onto the story of her unusual rise to professional accomplishment.

Seen in this way, Hurston's twelve visions ostensibly announce the

6. Mary Helen Washington discusses Hurston's "Godmother" and refers to several of Hurston's letters to Mason, in "A Woman Half in Shadow," 127–29.

structure of her autobiography, a structure based on the conversion narrative. She chose, however, not to fulfill those expectations. In the final draft of the autobiography, she excised the passage that identifies Mason as the figure in the final vision. As critics have noticed, she also neglected to fulfill the narrative expectations generated by the other visions, only briefly referring to visions one, two, three, and seven, and failing to mention any of the others. This posture is consistent with the dominant tone of the book: *Dust Tracks* is not ultimately a story of personal redemption. Hurston did not dwell on her literary career, and far from being filled with a sense of her own achievement, she lamented, "I regret all of my books. It is one of the tragedies of life that one cannot have all the wisdom one is ever to possess in the beginning" (212). Her mood was pensive, unsure.

When critics, as most of them do, call Hurston's failure to integrate the twelve visions into the book's structure a literary liability, they evaluate *Dust Tracks* according to the aesthetic standards generated by the conventional spiritual autobiography, a genre dominated by white males.[7] Hurston subverted—indeed conspicuously ignored—these conventions to demonstrate an entirely different aesthetic, one based less on continuity and a logical plot sequence than on individual linguistic moments, which themselves resemble the "disconnected scene after scene with blank spaces in between" that make up her twelve visions. While discussing her relationships with men, Hurston reveals an existential notion of time that underlies this aesthetic:

> No two moments are any more alike than two snowflakes. Like snowflakes, they get that same look from being so plentiful and falling so close together. But examine them closely and see the multiple differences between them. Each moment has its own task and capacity; doesn't melt down like snow and form again. It keeps its character forever. (264)

Here Hurston denies a strong causal connection between the past and present.[8] Like snowflakes, moments of time are distinct and unrepeatable;

---

7. Hemenway is especially critical of Hurston's failure to integrate the twelve visions into *Dust Tracks*. See *Zora Neale Hurston*, 282.

8. Compare Hurston's simile of time as snowflakes to the one proposed by William James in his *Principles of Psychology*: "Let one try . . . to notice or attend to, the *present* moment of time. One of the most baffling experiences occurs. Where is it, this present? It has melted in our grasp, fled ere we could touch it, gone in the instant of becoming" (1:608). James's notion of time as a "stream" is more fluid than Hurston's, whose "snowflakes" do not melt.

the same may be said of the linguistic codes in her texts. Since the twelve visions do not organize the narrative, they become simply twelve of the many examples of folk belief captured in the autobiography. They are a product of her culture's valuing of unconventional and improvised religious visions. Like the other "lies" in the text—whether formulated by Hurston or recorded by her—they are valuable in themselves, and constitute a celebration of the African-American imagination. [9]

In a peculiar sense, then, these visions *do* announce the structure of *Dust Tracks*, just not the expected one. Its structure is one of disconnection, designed to focus on discrete moments—on different variations of what it was to be Zora Neale Hurston, an individualistic, iconoclastic African-American woman (with all the tensions these words imply). For as Barbara Johnson has noted, Hurston's aesthetic was an aesthetic of difference (172). Throughout her life, she emphasized that the greatness of African-American speech lay in its "will to adorn." Black expression, like black music and like the black conversion experience, is based on improvisation, on making the familiar different and therefore new. In her autobiography, as in her folklore collections, she placed her "lies" in a storytelling context because she knew what later folklorists have come to recognize: that each performance captures a distinct, unrepeatable moment. Since each strand of text refers back to this "will to adorn" and celebrates the creativity of African Americans, then her autobiography too is based on the trope of synecdoche. There is a continuity of self that is present in each autobiographical act, much like that found in the memoirs of Henry James.

Hurston may have begun *Dust Tracks* intending to write a spiritual autobiography, but as her handling of the twelve visions reveals (especially her decision to drop any reference to the final vision), she chose to ignore the structure that would have presented her "Godmother" as a false white god. Instead, her subversive act of self-authoring was a declaration of independence. Where autobiographers such as Adams and Glasgow denied the socializing function of the conversion narrative to emphasize their distance from mainstream American values, Hurston renounced even the anticonversion pattern, which would have linked her to a tradition with which she did not want to identify. In the end, she refused to model her autobiographical act on the formulation of anyone.

---

9. Karla Holloway insightfully discusses Hurston's aesthetic throughout *The Character of the Word*, though she does not apply her findings to *Dust Tracks*.

Hurston's subversion of religious and linguistic expectations is consistent with her controversial attitude toward racial discrimination. Various and contradictory as were her public statements on race, they are united by an underlying iconoclasm. To a Northern newspaper reporter, she allegedly announced that blacks had more equality under Jim Crow than they did in the North. To a Southern American Legion periodical, she wrote that she opposed the Supreme Court's desegregation decision because it insulted black teachers and schools. When Howard students refused to sing spirituals for the white president of their university, on the grounds that such an act recalled the days of slavery, she urged them to do so because of the beauty and cultural value of the music. In each case, Hurston, rightly or wrongly, was more interested in shocking her audience than in making absolute political judgments, though her statements typically, if idiosyncratically, stressed black achievement.

This iconoclasm is made clear throughout the autobiography as well. When her mother died, she attempted to commit the "sacrilege" of thwarting her community's death rituals. As a schoolgirl, she was "rated as sassy" because she "just had to talk back at established authority" (87–88). Working as a child domestic, she similarly "did not know how to be humble" (117), and in one of the book's manuscript chapters she admits "I do not have much of a herd instinct" (345). These passages too reveal how her sense of self was synecdochical: each textual act was based on resistance to cultural imperatives—from whatever source. To have allowed herself to be so "written" from without was to submit to a kind of slavery:

> What is the principle of slavery? Only the literal buying and selling of human flesh on the block? That was only an outside symbol. Real slavery is couched in the desire and the efforts of any man or community to live and advance their interests at the expense of the lives and interests of others. All of the outward signs come out of that. (283)

In calling the "buying and selling of human flesh" an "outside symbol" Hurston reveals her extremely subjective ethic. For her, as for William James, freedom was an internal act of will. Her greatest fear was to lose that freedom by being forced to "convert" to an externally imposed cultural, intellectual, or linguistic system. Her identity depended on her maintaining a psychological consistency in the face of all challenges to it.

As a writer, Hurston was fanatically opposed to voicing—in a received discourse—the evils of racism, because she believed that to do so was to conform to a stereotype created by whites. To the newspaper reporter mentioned above (whom she accused of misquotation) she wrote:[10]

> It looks as if a Negro shall not be permitted to depart from a standard pattern. As I said, the nation is too sentimental about us to know us. It has a cut-and-dried formula for us which must not be violated. Either there is no interest in knowing us, or a determination not to destroy the pattern made and provided. We are even supposed to use certain sentences at all times, and if we are too stubborn to do so, we must be made to conform to type.

Hurston was thus caught in a potentially destructive bind. As essays like "Crazy for This Democracy" make clear, she was outraged by the inequitable application of American democratic principles; yet, at the same time, she felt that when blacks denounced discrimination they conformed to a stereotype. This perception, in addition to her antipathy to Communism, explains her feelings toward Richard Wright. To her, black protest literature was a confession of weakness, the stereotypical product of a racist society. Her only recourse was a radical individualism and a plea for racial justice only in the most broad, international terms.

Though critics have found Hurston's thought, particularly as presented in *Dust Tracks*, to be self-conscious and simplistic, her philosophy is more unified and more complex than she has been given credit for. Her commitment to "destroy the pattern made and provided," even if it meant appearing to side with racists, was the product of an individualism so radical that, like Franz Boas, she sought to deconstruct the notion of racial difference itself, going so far as to suggest that the "Negro doesn't really exist" (304):

> Light came to me when I realized that I did not have to consider any racial group as a whole. God made them duck by duck and that was the only way I could see them. I learned that skins were no measure of what was inside people. So none of the Race clichés meant anything any more. I began to laugh at both white and black who claimed special blessings on the basis of race. (235)

10. Hemenway quotes from this letter in his introduction to *Dust Tracks*, xviii–xxx.

Because "personal benefits run counter to race lines" and "self-interest rides over all sorts of lines"—biological, economic, and national—Hurston argued that "the fate of each and every group is bound up with the others," and thus found little meaning in broad statements about racial difference (218, 164, 327). Her attitude toward racism thus recalls her feelings about religion: she admitted its reality but believed that describing society in received "racial" terms offered limited benefits, cognitive or otherwise. To Hurston, using the "conventional" terms of racial protest was similar to finding solace in religious belief: it was "the last refuge of the weak." Her response was to deliver the unexpected.

As her approach to religion, art, and race makes clear, Hurston resolved the tension between her Eatonville values and those of modern society by formulating a kind of pragmatism. Wishing to deny neither the realities of psychic phenomena and racism—both of which she had experienced—nor her conviction of the inutility of such concepts, she applied to her life a radical empiricism much like that of William James. Truth, for Hurston, was primarily determined by self-interest and its ability to do work (or help one get work) in the world. Her pragmatic philosophy enabled her to come to terms with her biculturalism, but it necessarily led to an exaggerated individualism and relativism. "Nothing that God ever made," she explains, "is the same thing to more than one person. That is natural. There is no single face in nature, because every eye that looks upon it, sees it from its own angle" (61). Such an approach, of course, made it difficult for her to posit broad solutions to racial problems. "The solace of easy generalization was taken from me," she states, "but I received the richer gift of individualism" (323).

At the root of Hurston's philosophy, however, lies a paradox, the same paradox between individuality and universality embedded in the structure of the traditional conversion narrative. Noticing this paradox, critics have found that her celebration of African-American culture (which is centered in the early portions of *Dust Tracks*) is inconsistent with her references to "universal" values, such as those found later in the text. For example, Hemenway writes, "Zora seems to be both an advocate for the universal, demonstrating that this black woman does not look at the world in racial terms," and at the same time "the celebrant of a unique ethnic upbringing in an all-black village" (*Hurston*, 276). Hurston, however, rested easily over this paradox, because it was the same paradox that informs American political thought: universal equality is possible only when the values and ambitions of individuals are respected. Her celebration of black culture was based on this democratic principle. She praised not a racial consciousness but the individualizing creativity of black artists. In this sense, the black artist, because she or he is fully conscious of the value of difference, becomes not a "special case" but a universal model for aesthetic expression.

Though Hurston's individualism appears to owe much to the pragmatic method of William James, biographers and critics have not discovered any direct influence. Such evidence is available for Richard Wright, however, who read and admired James throughout his life.[11] Wright, in fact, cited James several times in his work, particularly in his introduction to *Black Metropolis*, where he states:

> The philosophies of William James and John Dewey, and all the pragmatists in between, are but intellectual labors to allay the anxieties of modern man, adjurations to the white man of the West to accept uncertainty as a way of life, to live within the vivid, present moment and let the meaning of that moment suffice as a rationale for life and death. (xxiii)

According to Wright, however, modern Americans continue to act irrationally; their consciousness "spills disdainfully over the banks of pragmatism," and they "hoist up the old slogans of liberty, love, justice, and happiness; and no authority, civil or religious, has yet found a way to divest their minds completely of a belief and trust in these magic signs" (xxiii). This tension, between a pragmatism that Wright clearly admired and the persistence of what he called a feudal belief system, parallels the tension between scientific rationalism and mysticism in *Dust Tracks*. Both Hurston and Wright acknowledged the empirical reality of religious visions, but if Hurston admitted that religious beliefs were useful for some—though not for her—Wright aggressively denied their utility for anyone. "Mystical visions of life," he states, "freeze millions in static degradation, no matter how emotionally satisfying such degradation seems to those who wallow in it" (*White Man Listen!* 48–49).

Wright distrusted religion for the same pragmatic reasons that Hurston did: those who had it often behaved worse than those who didn't. For him,

11. See Robert Bone, *Richard Wright*, 27, and Constance Webb, *Richard Wright: A Biography*, 130.

Masses. Though he had left the meeting wondering how the members *"really* regarded Negroes," he became convinced of their sincerity after a night of absorbed reading. "The revolutionary words leaped from the printed page," he states, "and struck me with tremendous force": "Here at last in the realm of revolutionary expression was where Negro experience could find a home, a functioning value and role. Out of the magazines I read came a passionate call for the experiences of the disinherited, and there were none of the same lispings of the missionary in it" (63). Though these scenes preserve Wright's distaste for mysticism, they nevertheless follow the broad outlines of a religious conversion and appear to announce the "redemption" toward which the narrative had been moving. Wright acquired a new set of beliefs and the "passionate call" to express them. Becoming a Communist, he claimed, not only enabled him to make lasting friends for the first time in his life, it also provided an environment that nurtured his artistic ambition.

Wright's awakening, however, like Hurston's twelve visions, proves to be "false" to our narrative expectations. He goes on to subvert the conventions of the spiritual autobiography as he describes the trial of Ross, a fellow party member and onetime friend. Feeling that he was being silently implicated for his own political wavering, Wright, as he witnessed the trial, observed that its mechanics were patterned on the process of conversion. Before formal charges were brought against Ross, party members rose to describe their mission, with increasing specificity, from a global to a local perspective. Wright explains:

> An absolute had first to be established in the minds of the comrades so that they could measure the success or failure of their deeds by it. . . .
>
> This presentation had lasted for more than three hours, but it had enthroned a new sense of reality in the hearts of those present, a sense of man on earth. With the exception of the church and its myths and legends, there was no agency in the world so capable of making men feel the earth and the people upon it as the Communist party. (121–22)

Struck by the inexorable logic of his comrades, Ross confessed his guilt without defending himself. Wright continues:

> Ross had not been doped; he had been awakened. . . . This, to me, was a spectacle of glory; and yet, because it had condemned me,

because it was blind and ignorant, I felt that it was a spectacle of horror. The blindness of their limited lives—lives truncated and impoverished by the oppression they had suffered long before they had ever heard of Communism—made them think that I was with their enemies. (124–25)

Though Wright admired the psychological efficiency of the Communists' rhetoric, especially its absence of mysticism, he was unmoved by the spectacle. He believed that he was "looking at the future of mankind," but he also knew that he was looking at himself, at the political acculturation he had undergone several years earlier. Despite his lifelong attraction toward suppressing the self and joining a like-minded community, he was finally horrified by a commitment that would limit his vision and destroy an identity he had spent his life creating—an identity built partly upon his desire for the literary life. The party did not make sufficient allowance for his need to be a creative writer, who—Wright felt—must work in isolation.[14] The kind of commitment the party required thus made his submission to the admirable goals of Communism impossible.

This sequence of conversion and backsliding in *American Hunger*, however, is more than simply a single climactic instance of narrative irresolution; it is merely the most obvious example of a larger pattern in the autobiography that underlies the synecdochical character of the work. Wright similarly flirts with conversion discourse throughout *Black Boy* as well. A particularly visible instance would be his dramatic discovery and later rediscovery of literature. The first of these events occurred on his grandmother's porch, after he had asked Ella, a young boarder living at the house, to tell him about the book she was reading. As she whispered to him the story of *Bluebeard and His Seven Wives*, "reality changed, the look of things altered, and the world became peopled with magical presences." "Enchanted and enthralled," Wright had found the "gateway to a forbidden and enchanting land": "As her words fell upon my new ears, I endowed them with a reality that welled up somewhere within me. She told how Bluebeard had duped and married seven wives, how he had loved and slain them, how he had hanged them up by their hair in a dark closet. The tale made the world around me be, throb, live" (34–36). Although this awakening does not define a relationship to a specific community, and in that

14. Fabre outlines Wright's growing alienation from the Communist party in *The Unfinished Quest*, 228–31.

sense it is much less like a typical conversion than was his temporary acceptance of Communism, still it contains a sense of rapture at odds with Wright's documented antipathy for mysticism.

This scene, of course, nicely complements his dramatic exposure to Mencken's *Book of Prefaces*, which is situated at the opposite end of *Black Boy* and which led to his discovery of realistic and naturalistic fiction:

> I was jarred and shocked by the style, the clear, clean, sweeping sentences. . . .
>
> I concluded the book with the conviction that I had somehow overlooked something terribly important in life. I had once tried to write, had once reveled in feeling, . . . but the impulse to dream had been slowly beaten out of me by experience. Now it surged up again and I hungered for books, new ways of looking and seeing. (217–18)

Though the first of these passages evokes a sense of magic absent from the second, both describe a passionate awakening to the power of books, which opened avenues of perception that had been closed by a narrow Southern environment. Though there seems to be a great distance between the sensation of *Bluebeard* and the more "serious" literature Mencken introduced him to, both shared the theme of violence: his early reading is significant for its description of crime and its horrors; and Mencken and the writers he recommended, for their using "words as a weapon."

Reading was a violent, imaginative response to a threatening culture, and it widened Wright's world; but it also allowed him to forget it. Being converted while reading a text has been a convention from Augustine to the present, but Wright subverts this one too—by clearly indicating that reading led to no permanent sense of value: "It was not a matter of believing or disbelieving what I read, but of feeling something new, of being affected by something that made the look of the world different. . . . Reading was like a drug, a dope. The novels created moods in which I lived for days" (218–19). Written by those from a world "as alien to me as the moon," books, at best, were "vicarious cultural transfusions" that allowed him to stay alive in a "negatively vital way" (226–27). For Wright, reading was an ecstatic process of submission, a losing of his identity in an imaginary world created by whites. His distrust of mysticism thus governs these two conversionlike events: reading was a rejection of a racist culture, not a positive growth, but a means of escaping oppression.

If literature offered "vague glimpses" of life's possibilities, then the alien northern land from which it sprang was no less vague. Wright linguistically linked the experience of reading with his conception of the North, which "symbolized to me all that I had not felt and seen; it had no relation whatever to what actually existed. Yet by imagining a place where everything was possible, I kept hope alive in me" (147). Like much of the fiction he read, the North existed primarily in his imagination and was fashioned out of negation. His flight there, like his voracious reading, was an escape from oppression, "a kind of self-defense," rather than the attainment of a tangible goal. "The substance of my hope," he states, "was formless and devoid of any real sense of direction, for in my southern living I had seen no looming landmark by which I could, in a positive sense, guide my daily actions" (226). Critics who have complained of an unjustified optimism in the conclusion to *Black Boy* have failed to understand the irony that Wright builds throughout the text.[15] The end of the book is written from the perspective of a boy's optimistic—yet deluded—flight, not as many have suggested, from the perspective of Wright's literary success. A still young Richard boards a northbound train following a "hazy notion" that life could provide some "redeeming meaning." Far from being inappropriate, Wright's visionary language is a fitting prelude for the disillusionment he goes on to describe in *American Hunger*.

If Wright's autobiography, like Hurston's, flirts with conversion discourse only in the end to deny its value as an epistemological model, then all of the work's mystical language can be interpreted in light of his faked religious conversion. This event, like Hurston's twelve visions, brings into focus Wright's radical individualism. As a boy, he was constantly pressured to convert, first to his grandmother's Seventh-Day Adventism, and later to his mother's Methodism. Wright never gave in to the fanaticism of his grandmother, but he did join his mother's congregation during a church revival. After asking all the professed Christians to stand, the minister began to work on the few sinners who remained in their pews, Wright among them. Embarrassed and disgusted, he succumbed to the tactics of his mother, his friends, and the minister:

15. Critics who find the ending of *Black Boy* to be inconsistent with the rest of the book are Michel Fabre, Afterword, 141; John Reilly, "The Self-creation of the Intellectual," 216; and Janice Thaddeus, "The Metamorphosis of Richard Wright's *Black Boy*."

> We young men had been trapped by the community, the tribe in which we lived and of which we were a part. The tribe, for its own safety, was asking us to be at one with it. Our mothers were kneeling in public and praying for us to give the sign of allegiance. . . .
>
> It was no longer a question of my believing in God; . . . it was a simple, urgent matter of public pride. . . . If I refused, it meant that I did not love my mother, and no man in that tight little black community had ever been crazy enough to let himself be placed in such a position. My mother pulled my arm and I walked with her to the preacher and shook his hand. . . . I walked home limp as a rag; I had not felt anything except sullen anger and a crushing sense of shame. (134–35)

In this single, unpleasant episode, Wright undercuts the conversion experience more directly and more emphatically than any of the writers I have examined. Even as a boy, he acutely realized the consequences of conversion: to be converted was to conform to certain social and cultural expectations, to become part of the "tribe"—a word Wright uses pejoratively. Where Hurston linked conversion and coercion, Wright fused the two: conversion was coercion, "the attempt of one individual or group to rule another in the name of God."

Because conversion traditionally entailed a complete surrender of the self, Wright used it as a metaphor for the process of submission he thought was necessary for survival in a racist culture. Christianity's otherworldliness encouraged blacks to accept their social condition and discouraged any form of rebellion. It also fostered a disturbingly familiar ethic: if black Southern Christians believed, as did Wright's grandmother, that "success spelled the reward of righteousness and that failure was the wages of sin" (120), then a sense of defeat was likely for poverty-stricken blacks. To Wright, Christianity discouraged the self-assertion necessary for social change; and he recognized it as a form of racism, just as he presented racism as a kind of religion. Conversion blessed the status quo, and for that reason Wright associated it with fixity, even death. He makes this clear by using conversion discourse to celebrate his *escape* from his grandmother's pressure: he remembers "that I could breath again, live again, that I had been released from a prison" only after she had permanently placed him among the reprobate.

The sense of shame that lies at the heart of Wright's faked conversion recalls other incidents in the autobiography, when he was forced to act "in conformity with what others expected of me even though, by the very nature and form of my life, I did not and could not share their spirit" (33). Wright feels the same shame—an emotion akin to the Christian sense of sin—on numerous occasions: when he grudgingly shakes the hands of other children at the orphanage, when he stands before his father to ask for money, when he realizes that the black principal of his school was a "bought man," when he unwillingly fights Harrison, and when he quits his job at the optical company as the result of racial harassment.

Wright's reaction to religion thus illuminates his overall response to a culture that sought to deny his full humanity. His greatest fear—much like Hurston's—was to be reduced to a stereotype, to lose his identity by forced submission. "It was inconceivable to me," he states, "that one should surrender to what seemed wrong, and most of the people I had met seemed wrong" (144). His constant defiance of authority figures, whether open or covert, was motivated by this fear, and much of the conflict in *Black Boy* results from his almost instinctive revolt against racial conditioning. Wright threatens his "Uncle Tom" with a razor, for example, because he was "going to teach me to act as I had seen the backward black boys act on the plantations, was going to teach me to grin, hang my head, and mumble apologetically when I was spoken to" (138).

Despite its attractiveness, submission in its various forms was impossible for Wright because his very identity was built upon rejection. To him, racism was inextricable from even the most benign aspects of American culture. His only recourse was escape; and reading, dreaming of the North, and even embracing Communism were the means by which he did so. These responses, however, were acts of self-defense rather than acts of self-actualization. His whole sense of self-esteem was a result of rebellion; he had been "conditioned in feeling *against* something daily" (178). Elsewhere, he states, "Life had trapped me in a realm of emotional rejection; I had not embraced insurgency through open choice" (226). Wright's solution to the problems posed by racism, like Hurston's, was potentially self-destructive. If his personality was built on a rejection of racial suffering, then in a sense he needed it to give his life meaning. His awareness of this paradox is nicely illustrated by the cryptic comment, "The meaning of living came only when one was struggling to wring a meaning out of meaningless suffering" (88). In a racist environment, meaning itself becomes problematic. One's self-worth depends on the forces bent on suffocating it.

In its entirety, Wright's autobiography systematically examines various possibilities of redemption: religion, flight, bourgeois materialism, literary modernism, and Communism. Yet despite his recognition of the urge to submit—to lose the self in a community of people or a system of belief—he chose to define himself in opposition to such entities. Even more so than Hurston, Wright did not want to identify with any group, however admirable. In *Pagan Spain*, he wrote, "I have no religion in the formal sense of the word. . . . I have no race except that which is forced upon me. I have no country except that to which I'm obliged to belong. I have no traditions. I'm free" (17). Elsewhere he wrote, "Color is not my country . . . I am opposed to all racial definitions."[16] Wright's radical deconstruction of racial difference, of course, recalls that of Hurston; different as they were, they responded to racism in strikingly similar ways.

If writers such as William and Henry James, Henry Adams, and Ellen Glasgow variously subverted the socializing function of the traditional conversion narrative, they nevertheless found it a useful cognitive model. Hurston and Wright aggressively denied the utility of such a model, and this explains why they parted company with the authors I have examined in previous chapters. Though these two African Americans appear to occupy opposite ends of the black literary spectrum, both responded to American racism by advocating an extreme individualism. By today's standards, their solution to the conflicts between the self and the community, between mysticism and rationality, and between the West and the Third World may seem less than ideal, but their narrative acts were Promethean: they were affirmations of the value of individual black voices. Their necessary task was to destroy expectations, social, political, and literary—to free black expression from the dogmatism of the larger culture. Their achievement was a more fully independent African-American tradition.

If Hurston and Wright's subversion of the spiritual autobiography tradition and the extreme individualism that subversion entailed distance them from the other twentieth-century writers I have examined, their use of conversion discourse is different in degree and not kind. The notion of self inscribed by all of these modern Americans is built upon a desire for continuity and stability. Achieving this stability required that individuals resist those pressures they believed were culturally imposed. The secular

16. This passage is cited in Dan McCall's *Example of Richard Wright*, 145.

selves of the nineteenth-century, as I described them in the second chapter, were preoccupied by reform: by reforming the self and then applying that reform to the world at large. This link between the self and the world drew upon the socializing process embedded in conversion discourse. Even those writers such as DeQuincey and Melville, who subverted this socializing impulse, still documented "corrected" selves and alerted readers to the dangers they had experienced. There were cultural threats to be sure—mainly conceived as institutional and cognitive threats to freedom. But a changeable self and its logical extension, a changeable world, offered comfort to those who felt the weight of such hazards.

The figures I have discussed in Chapters 3 through 6 distrusted this notion of a "reformed self" because they realized more acutely than writers of previous generations that psychological change comes not from within but from without—not as in the Christian tradition from the external imposition of grace, but from cultural forces that sought conformity to existing values and power structures. Afraid of being swept away by such pressures, these writers defined themselves by their very resistance to them. Their desire was to present selves stronger than the cultural forces that threatened their identity. It is ironic indeed that they chose the rhetoric of conversion—a discourse that had carried a tremendous cultural weight. But this discourse had potentially always sanctioned countercultural behavior, and so they revised it to encode—not a metaphorical change or a metonymic division—but a synecdochical continuity of self that placed them apart from the worlds that surrounded them. From the standpoint of poststructuralism, perhaps, their belief that they could resist culture and the language that constitutes it seems naive. Yet their radical revision of conversion discourse and of the poetics of selfhood signals a freedom also, a freedom encoded in the power and persuasiveness of their autobiographical writing.

AFTERWORD

Conversion and Cultural Poetics

This process of breaking through the confines of one's organized self—the ego—and of getting in touch with the excluded and disassociated part of oneself, the unconscious, . . . is closely related to the religious experience of breaking down individuation and feeling one with the All. (96)

—Erich Fromm, *Psychoanalysis and Religion*

For conversion to be effective, the subject may first have to have his emotions worked upon until he reaches an abnormal condition of anger, fear, or exaltation. If this condition is maintained or intensified by one means or another, hysteria may supervene, whereupon the subject can become more open to suggestions which in normal circumstances he would have summarily rejected. . . . Or a sudden complete inhibitory collapse may bring about a suppression of previously held beliefs and behavior patterns. The same phenomena will be noted in many of the more successful modern psychiatric treatments, discovered independently of one another. (42)

—William Sargent, *Battle for the Mind*

The withdrawal into the self, and the emptying of the self
that it may be filled with God; the need for quietness and
passivity; the disappearance of the sense of personal
identity; the sudden intense and total satisfaction; the
awareness that this experience is different in *kind* from
any other, and the consequent difficulty in communicating
it—all these have been described again and again, from
ancient India to modern America, and in much the same
terms. In my view it is recognizably the same psychological experience everywhere, however different the glosses
that have been put upon it, however incompatible the
theologies which it has been held to confirm. (86)
   —E. R. Dodds, *Pagan and Christian in an Age of Anxiety*

Stripped of its supernatural components, it is simply a
moment of fundamental human growth, of overwhelming
feeling and understanding when an individual pushes
through to those higher levels of consciousness that
distinguish us as human beings. For the prophet, the
genius, and the average citizen alike, life moves forward
in such sudden leaps, peak moments, and turning points.
(38)
             —Flo Conway and Jim Siegelman, *Snapping*

I began this study with a series of quotations having to do with conversion,
and I end it in the same way, perhaps because I am aware of having failed
to answer a fundamental question. I hope I have illustrated the pervasiveness of conversion rhetoric in Anglo-American culture, the manifold ways
autobiographers have used it, how particular adoptions of it inscribe
relationships between individuals and larger communities, and how American autobiographers in the early twentieth century radically altered conversion discourse by using it to express their estrangement from mainstream
culture rather than an identification with it. But even if I have accomplished
these things, I am conscious that I have not explained what conversion is,
what causes it, or where it comes from.

   The passages that stand at the head of this chapter attempt to do this,
and in so doing they lead at once back to William James's *Varieties of
Religious Experience* and into contemporary literary theory. For James,

conversion in its multitudinous forms was a transhistorical psychological process—not a metaphor for cognitive change but a mechanism by which cognitive change takes place. Psychologists, sociologists, and cultural historians have followed James in describing conversion as a "natural" means by which people and societies experience the world. Implicit in James's psychological approach is the idea that personality transformation takes place in a nonverbal or a subverbal realm. For James and for many of his followers, conversion is a phenomenon embedded in the structure of the human mind.

James's psychological approach raises a question about the entire tradition of the conversion narrative that also underlies this book. Is the process of conversion somehow independent of the texts that describe it? This question brings to mind a larger question raised by Paul de Man on the nature of autobiography as a whole:

> We assume that life *produces* the autobiography as an act produces its consequences, but can we not suggest, with equal justice, that the autobiographical project may itself produce and determine the life and that whatever the writer *does* is in fact governed by the technical demands of self-portraiture and thus determined, in all its aspects, by the resources of his medium? (69)

Substituting "conversion narrative" for "autobiography" here, one could restate the question: Does conversion produce the self that writes about it or is that self produced by the trope of conversion? Or, which came first, conversion or the text? De Man argues that the answer to this question is not reducible to an either/or assertion, but he nevertheless suggests that the tropes of self-writing (conversion presumably among them) are inescapable: "The study of autobiography is caught in this double motion, the necessity to escape from the tropology of the subject and the equally inevitable reinscription of this necessity within a specular model of cognition" (72).

When applied to conversion discourse, the "double motion" described by de Man recalls the "double" definition of conversion supplied by Geoffrey Galt Harpham that I mentioned in the introduction. For Harpham, there are two kinds of conversion, the first corresponding to an "epistemological certainty" of self-knowledge and the second amounting to the actualizing of "this certainty in a narrative of the self" (42). These two types of conversion are realized simultaneously in autobiographical writing as authors "read" their lives as conforming to the "culturally validated" textual model of conversion.

Harpham's synchronic model of conversion is more placid than de Man's "double motion," where the oscillation between textual models and the necessity to escape them is a constant tug-of-war. Both authors, however, concede the dual pressures of linguistic conformity as well as the presence of (seemingly) independent cognitive activity. In neither case are the authors able to escape completely from a "psychological" explanation for conversion. This is particularly true of Harpham's definition, since his theory is partly determined by the conscious awareness of an "epistemological certainty," a psychological change that is somehow synchronic with the use of conversion discourse.[1]

Clearly, Harpham's model of conversion improves upon the theories of James and his followers, who do not sufficiently acknowledge the linguistic and cultural underpinnings of conversion discourse. But it also illustrates the difficulty of completely exorcising James's psychological approach. If James at the turn of the century left open the possibility that conversion is caused by a supernatural agency, autobiographical theorists appear to leave open the possibility that conversion has a psychological (or physiological) basis that structures language, rather than vice versa.

Following de Man's lead, I can agree that conversion can not be fully explained as either a psychological change or a linguistic structure but that it results from an interrelationship between biology and the world of language, operating on the yet to be defined borders between linguistic processes and nerve endings. One of the distinguishing characteristics of the trope of conversion is that its structure appears to be encoded well before it is applied to the self. It is not so much the acquisition of a linguistic code as it is the activation of one previously acquired. For this reason, it is rarely experienced as a linguistic "event" and typically appears to spring from a source outside the conscious, language-forming self. Because the acquisition of conversion discourse almost always precedes its use as a means of self-interpretation, James's analysis of conversion as a subconscious (or subverbal) event will continue to have cogency.

1. Harpham's approach to conversion appears to work fairly well for the traditional conversion narrative, or—to borrow again from Hayden White's "tropics of discourse"—for the "metaphorical" conversion narrative, where the self inscribes a radical change in orientation and conforms unanxiously to a received model. But his approach works less well with the "synecdochical" conversion narrative, where the author employs conversion discourse to encode the continuity of self and his or her resistance to cultural norms.

Even if finally we must see conversion as one instance of our living in a "prison house of language," we are still left with the question of why some people experience it and others don't. If the trope of conversion "writes" the text of a person's life, then it is a selective author, much like the Calvinistic God who arbitrarily chooses those whom He will save. We could certainly begin to explain why some experience conversion and others don't by suggesting that the degree to which people perceive personal change in the terms of conversion discourse depends upon the extent to which they are immersed in a linguistic community that privileges it. But then how do we understand someone like Richard Wright, who was immersed in such a culture, yet who resisted it with an almost fanatical intensity? We might then theorize that conversion for such a person can only be resisted, never escaped. One can reject a discourse, only after being "written" by it. But then how do we explain Ellen Glasgow, who, like Wright, appeared to resist conversion consciously, yet who still experienced it, even after she had rejected the metaphysical system that made it tenable?

Perhaps twentieth-century autobiographers such as Wright, Glasgow, and other authors of "synecdochical" narratives resist the socializing function of conversion discourse because their written lives are determined by their immersion in another linguistic community: an extremely rationalistic community whose highly redundant discourse of "individuality" appears to deconstruct itself. Perhaps their inscribed estrangement from American culture is as predictable as a Puritan's conformity to the older autobiographical form of the church relation. Such an explanation works well for the autobiographical writings of the two Jameses, Henry Adams, Ellen Glasgow, Zora Neale Hurston, and Richard Wright, but it does not account for the autobiography of Edith Wharton, whose immersion in the same intellectual culture resulted in her relatively uncritical acceptance of conversion discourse. It seems that each time we attempt to construct a cultural model of conversion, we are confronted as much by exceptions as by confirmations.

Perhaps one can best explain the various and unpredictable adoptions of conversion discourse in the twentieth century by saying that discursive lives are best understood as being the product of the multiculturalism of capitalistic society. Instead of seeing any discourse as being determinative, new historicists such as Louis Montrose cogently situate individuals in a matrix of "interactive social practices," the multiplicity of which not only produces them but also allows them the "capacity for agency" (21). These approaches appear to be best able to explain the diverse and often unpredictable adoptions of conversion discourse in twentieth-century America, particularly by writers on the margin, those very likely to feel acutely the conflicting tugs of bi- and multiculturalism.

Since the new-historicist project appears to carve out a place (however small) for human subjectivity, we must fall back on psychology if we wish to explain why a particular discourse prevailed in a particular person. We might theorize that certain personality types are more inclined toward mystical experience than others. Glasgow certainly was; Wright certainly was not. We might further suggest the characteristics of those predisposed toward having conversion experiences: perhaps those who have been culturally deprived, or those who lacked nurturing in their formative years, or those who lived in high-stress environments, or those who have failed to attain autonomy. Such speculation, however, seems haphazard at best. Certainly, cultural poetics gives us a language that enables us to chart the various social practices that account for the multiple uses of conversion discourse, but I am aware that I still have not adequately defined what conversion is or why one person experiences it and another does not. I have also failed to explain why the discourse shifted dramatically in the early years in the twentieth century. To describe the cultural redefinition of conversion discourse in terms of radical individualism is one thing; to uncover the roots of such a change is another.

What I am suggesting is that presently neither literary theory nor contemporary psychology gives us an adequate framework for understanding conversion and that much work remains to be done on this phenomenon, which continues to structure many aspects of American life. Even if frustrated by linguistic and psychological explanations, literary critics (myself included) would probably hesitate to fall back on a theological or supernatural explanation for conversion, but there are many who continue to believe that to be the most plausible interpretation—including some of our colleagues in theology departments. Among other things, the theological explanation is attractive because it is most consistent with the puzzling nature of conversion. And it is with the continuance of this puzzle that I will end.

WORKS CITED

Abrams, M. H. *Natural Supernaturalism: Tradition and Revolution in Romantic Literature*. New York: W. W. Norton, 1971.

Adams, Henry. *The Education of Henry Adams*. New York: Random House, 1931.

———. *Letters of Henry Adams (1892–1918)*. Ed. Worthington Chauncey Ford. Boston: Houghton Mifflin, 1938.

Adams, Timothy Dow. *Telling Lies in Modern American Autobiography*. Chapel Hill: University of North Carolina Press, 1990.

Ahlstrom, Sydney E. *A Religious History of the American People*. New Haven, Conn.: Yale University Press, 1972

Allen, Gay Wilson. *William James: A Biography*. New York: Viking, 1967.

Anderson, Bernhard W. *Understanding the Old Testament*. 3d ed. Englewood Cliffs, N.J.: Prentice-Hall, 1975.

Anderson, Quentin. *The American Henry James*. New Brunswick, N.J.: Rutgers University Press, 1957.

Andrews, William L. *To Tell a Free Story: The First Century of Afro-American Autobiography, 1760–1865*. Urbana: University of Illinois Press, 1986.

———, ed. *Sisters of the Spirit: Three Black Women's Autobiographies of the Nineteenth Century*. Bloomington: Indiana University Press, 1986.

Apuleius, Lucius. *The Golden Ass*. Trans. Robert Graves. New York: Farrar, Straus & Giroux, 1951.

Ashbridge, Elizabeth. *Some Account of the Fore-Part of the Life of Elizabeth Ashbridge*. In *The Norton Anthology of American Literature*, ed. Nina Baym et al., 3d ed., 1:524–45. New York: Norton, 1989.

Auchincloss, Louis. *Edith Wharton: A Woman in Her Time*. New York: Viking Press, 1971.

———. *Ellen Glasgow*. Minneapolis: University of Minnesota Press, 1964.

———. Introduction to *A Backward Glance*, by Edith Wharton. New York: Scribner's, 1934.

Augustine, St. *The Confessions*. Trans. R. S. Pine-Coffin. New York: Penguin, 1961.

Baker, Houston A., Jr. *Blues, Ideology, and Afro-American Literature: A Vernacular Theory*. Chicago: University of Chicago Press, 1984.

———. *The Journey Back: Issues in Black Literature and Criticism*. Chicago: University of Chicago Press, 1980.

————. "Racial Wisdom and Richard Wright's Native Son." In *Long Black Song*, 122–41. Charlottesville: University Press of Virginia, 1972. Reprinted in *Critical Essays on Richard Wright*, ed. Yoshinobu Hakutani, 66–81. Boston: G. K. Hall, 1982.

Banner, Lois W. *Elizabeth Cady Stanton: A Radical for Woman's Rights*. Boston: Little, Brown, 1980.

Baxter, Annette K. "What Is Not Said Illuminates What Is So Gracefully Said." Review of *A Backward Glance*, by Edith Wharton. *New York Times Book Review*, 9 August 1964, 4.

Baym, Max I. "William James and Henry Adams." *New England Quarterly* 10 (1937): 717–42.

Bell, Millicent. "Henry James and the Fiction of Autobiography." *Southern Review* 18 (1983): 463–79.

Benstock, Shari. "Authorizing the Autobiographical." In *The Private Self: Theory and Practice of Women's Autobiographical Writings*, ed. Shari Benstock, 10–33. Chapel Hill: University of North Carolina Press, 1988.

Bercovitch, Sacvan. *The Puritan Origins of the American Self*. New Haven, Conn.: Yale University Press, 1975.

Blackmur, R. P. *Henry Adams*. Ed. Veronica A. Makowsky. New York: Harcourt Brace Jovanovich, 1980.

Bloom, Lynn Z., and Orlee Holder. "Anaïs Nin's *Diary* in Context." In *Women's Autobiography: Essays in Criticism*, ed. Estelle Jelinek, 206–20. Bloomington: Indiana University Press, 1980.

Bone, Robert A. *Richard Wright*. Minneapolis: University of Minnesota Press, 1969.

Bonner, Gerald. *St. Augustine of Hippo: Life and Controversies*. Philadelphia: Westminster Press, 1963.

Bradstreet, Anne. *The Works of Anne Bradstreet*. Ed. Jeanine Hensley. Cambridge, Mass.: Harvard University Press, 1967.

Braswell, Mary Flowers. *The Medieval Sinner: Characterization and Confession in the Literature of the English Middle Ages*. Rutherford, N.J.: Fairleigh Dickinson University Press, 1983.

Brauer, Jerald C. "Conversion: From Puritanism to Revivalism." *Journal of Religion* 58 (1978): 227–43.

Brée, Germaine. Foreword to *Life/Lines: Theorizing Women's Autobiography*, ed. Bella Brodzki and Celeste Schenck. Ithaca, N.Y.: Cornell University Press, 1988.

Brodzki, Bella, and Celeste Schenck. Introduction to *Life/Lines: Theorizing Women's Autobiography*, ed. Bella Brodzki and Celeste Schenck. Ithaca, N.Y.: Cornell University Press, 1988.

Brown, John. *An help for the ignorant. An essay toward an easy explication of the Westminster Confession of Faith and Catechisms*. Edinburgh, Eng., 1758.

Brown, Peter. *Augustine of Hippo: A Biography*. Berkeley and Los Angeles: University of California Press, 1967.

Buckley, Jerome Hamilton. *The Turning Key: Autobiography and the Subjective Impulse Since 1800*. Cambridge, Mass.: Harvard University Press, 1984.

————. *The Victorian Temper: A Study in Literary Culture*. Cambridge, Mass.: Harvard University Press, 1951.

Buell, Lawrence. "Autobiography in the American Renaissance." In *American Autobiography: Retrospect and Prospect*, ed. Paul John Eakin, 47–69. Madison: University of Wisconsin Press, 1991.

———. *New England Literary Culture: From Revolution Through Renaissance*. New York: Cambridge University Press, 1986.

Bunyan, John. *Grace Abounding to the Chief of Sinners*. Ed. Roger Sharrock. London: Oxford University Press, 1962.

Butterfield, Stephen. *Black Autobiography in America*. Amherst: University of Massachusetts Press, 1974.

Caldwell, Patricia. *The Puritan Conversion Narrative: The Beginnings of American Expression*. New York: Cambridge University Press, 1983.

Carlyle, Thomas. *Sartor Resartus: The Life and Opinions of Herr Teufelsdröckh*. London: Chapman and Hall, 1896. Reprint. New York: AMS Press, 1969.

Cohen, Charles Lloyd. *God's Caress: The Psychology of Puritan Religious Experience*. New York: Oxford University Press, 1986.

Conn, Peter. *The Divided Mind: Ideology and Imagination in America, 1898–1917*. Cambridge, Eng.: Cambridge University Press, 1983.

Conway, Flo, and Jim Siegelman. *Snapping: America's Epidemic of Sudden Personality Change*. New York: Dell, 1979.

Cooley, Thomas. *Educated Lives: The Rise of Modern Autobiography in America*. Columbus: Ohio State University Press, 1976.

Couser, G. Thomas. *Altered Egos: Authority in American Autobiography*. New York: Oxford University Press, 1989.

———. *American Autobiography: The Prophetic Mode*. Amherst: University of Massachusetts Press, 1979.

Cox, James M. "Autobiography and America." *The Virginia Quarterly Review* 47 (1971): 252–77.

———. "The Memoirs of Henry James: Self-Interest as Autobiography." In *Studies in Autobiography*, ed. James Olney, 3–23. New York: Oxford University Press, 1988.

Delany, Paul. *British Autobiography in the Seventeenth Century*. New York: Columbia University Press, 1969.

DeLaura, David J. "The Allegory of Life: The Autobiographical Impulse in Victorian Prose." In *Approaches to Victorian Autobiography*, ed. George P. Landow, 333–54. Athens: Ohio University Press, 1979.

de Man, Paul. "Autobiography as De-Facement." In *The Rhetoric of Romanticism*, 67–82. New York: Columbia University Press, 1984.

DeQuincey, Thomas. *Confessions of an English Opium Eater*. New York: Viking, 1971.

Dodd, Philip. "Criticism and the Autobiographical Tradition." In *Modern Selves: Essays of Modern British and American Autobiography*, 1–13. Totowa, N.J.: Frank Cass, 1986.

Dodds, E. R. *Pagan and Christian in an Age of Anxiety*. London: W. W. Norton, 1965.

Douglass, Frederick. *Narrative of the Life of Frederick Douglass, an American Slave*. Ed. Houston A. Baker., Jr. New York: Penguin, 1982.

Dupee, F. W. *Henry James*. 1951. Reprint. Westport, Conn.: Greenwood Press, 1973.

Dusinberre, William. *Henry Adams: The Myth of Failure*. Charlottesville: University Press of Virginia, 1980.

Eakin, Paul John. *Fictions in Autobiography: Studies in the Art of Self-Invention.* Princeton, N.J.: Princeton University Press, 1985.

Edel, Leon. *The Life of Henry James: The Master, 1901–1916.* Philadelphia: J. B. Lippincott, 1972.

———. *The Life of Henry James, The Untried Years, 1843–1870.* Philadelphia: J. B. Lippincott, 1953.

Edkins, Carol. "Quest for Community: Spiritual Autobiographies of Eighteenth-Century Quaker and Puritan Women in America." In *Woman's Autobiography: Essays in Criticism,* ed. Estelle C. Jelinek, 39–52. Bloomington: Indiana University Press, 1980.

Edwards, Jonathan. *Personal Narrative.* In *Jonathan Edwards: Representative Selections,* ed. Clarence H. Faust and Thomas H. Johnson, 57–72. New York: American Book, 1935.

Ellison, Ralph. "Richard Wright's Blues." *Antioch Review* 5 (1945): 198–204. Reprinted in *Critical Essays on Richard Wright,* ed. Yoshinobu Hakutani, 201–12. Boston: G. K. Hall, 1982.

Emerson, Ralph Waldo. *Selections from Ralph Waldo Emerson.* Ed. Stephen E. Whicher. Boston: Houghton Mifflin, 1957.

Equiano, Olaudah. *The Life of Olaudah Equiano, or Gustavus Vassa, the African. Written by Himself.* In *Great Slave Narratives,* ed. Arna Bontemps, 1–192. Boston: Beacon Press, 1969.

Fabre, Michel. Afterword to *American Hunger,* by Richard Wright. New York: Harper & Row, 1977.

———. "Richard Wright's First Hundred Books." *CLA Journal* 16 (1973): 458–74.

———. *The Unfinished Quest of Richard Wright.* Trans. Isabel Barzun. New York: William Morrow & Co., 1973.

Feinstein, Howard M. *Becoming William James.* Ithaca, N.Y.: Cornell University Press, 1984.

Finney, Charles G. *Charles G. Finney: An Autobiography.* Old Tappen, N.J.: Fleming H. Revell, 1908.

Fleishman, Avrom. *Figures of Autobiography: The Language of Self-Writing in Victorian and Modern England.* Berkeley and Los Angeles: University of California Press, 1983.

Fliegelman, Jay. *Prodigals and Pilgrims: The American Revolution Against Patriarchal Authority, 1750–1800.* Cambridge, Eng.: Cambridge University Press, 1982.

Foster, Frances Smith. *Witnessing Slavery: The Development of Ante-Bellum Slave Narratives.* Westport, Conn.: Greenwood Press, 1979.

Fredriksen, Paula. "Conversion Narratives, Orthodox Traditions, and the Retrospective Self." *Journal of Theological Studies* 37 (1986): 3–34.

Friedman, Susan Stanford. "Women's Autobiographical Selves: Theory and Practice." In *The Private Self: Theory and Practice of Women's Autobiographical Writings,* ed. Shari Benstock, 34–62. Chapel Hill: University of North Carolina Press, 1988.

Fromm, Erich. *Psychoanalysis and Religion.* New Haven, Conn.: Yale University Press, 1950.

Fryer, Judith. "Edith Wharton's 'Tact of Omission': Harmony and Proportion in *A Backward Glance.*" *Biography* 6 (1983): 148–69.

———. *Felicitous Space: The Imaginative Structures of Edith Wharton and Willa Cather.* Chapel Hill: University of North Carolina Press, 1986.

Gates, Henry Louis, Jr. "Frederick Douglass and the Language of the Self." In *Figures in Black: Words, Signs, and the "Racial" Self*, 98–124. New York: Oxford University Press, 1987.

Glasgow, Ellen. *A Certain Measure: An Interpretation of Prose Fiction.* New York: Harcourt, Brace, 1943.

———. "Ellen Glasgow." In *I Believe: The Personal Philosophies of Certain Eminent Men and Women of Our Time*, ed. Clifton Fadiman, 93–110. New York: Simon and Schuster.

———. *Letters of Ellen Glasgow.* Ed. Blair Rouse. New York: Harcourt, Brace, 1958.

———. *The Woman Within.* New York: Harcourt, Brace, 1954.

Godbold, E. Stanly, Jr. *Ellen Glasgow and the Woman Within.* Baton Rouge: Louisiana State University Press, 1972.

Goen, C. C., ed. Introduction to *The Great Awakening*, by Jonathan Edwards. New Haven, Conn.: Yale University Press, 1972.

Goldman, Emma. *Living My Life.* Garden City, 1934. Reprint. New York: AMS Press, 1970.

Griffith, Elisabeth. *In Her Own Right: The Life of Elizabeth Cady Stanton.* New York: Oxford University Press, 1984.

Gunn, Giles. Introduction to *Henry James, Senior: A Collection of His Writings*, ed. Giles Gunn. Chicago: American Library, 1974.

Gura, Philip F. *A Glimpse of Sion's Glory: Puritan Radicalism in New England, 1620–1660.* Middletown, Conn.: Wesleyan University Press, 1984.

Habegger, Alfred. *Henry James and the "Women Business."* New York: Cambridge University Press, 1989.

Haller, William. *The Rise of Puritanism.* 1938. Reprint. New York: Harper & Row, 1957.

Harpham, Geoffrey Galt. "Conversion and the Language of Autobiography." In *Studies in Autobiography*, ed. James Olney, 42–50. New York: Oxford University Press, 1988.

Harran, Marilyn J. *Luther on Conversion: The Early Years.* Ithaca, N.Y.: Cornell University Press, 1983.

Hartman, Geoffrey. "Romanticism and 'Anti-Self-consciousness.' " In *Romanticism and Consciousness*, ed. Harold Bloom, 46–56. New York: Norton, 1970.

Heilbrun, Carolyn G. "Non-autobiographies of 'Privileged' Women: England and America." In *Life/Lines: Theorizing Women's Autobiography*, ed. Bella Brodzki and Celeste Schenck, 62–76. Ithaca, N.Y.: Cornell University Press, 1989.

Helsinger, Howard. "Credence and Credibility: The Concern for Honesty in Victorian Autobiography." In *Approaches to Victorian Autobiography*, ed. George P. Landow, 39–63. Athens: Ohio University Press, 1979.

Hemenway, Robert. Introduction to *Dust Tracks on a Road*, by Zora Neale Hurston. Urbana: University of Illinois Press, 1984.

———. *Zora Neale Hurston: A Literary Biography.* Urbana: University of Illinois Press, 1977.

———. "Zora Neale Hurston and the Eatonville Anthropology." In *The Harlem*

Renaissance Remembered, ed. Arna Bontemps, 190–214. New York: Dodd, Mead, 1972.

Hill, Christopher. *The World Turned Upside Down: Radical Ideas During the English Revolution.* New York: Viking, 1972.

Hochfield, George. *Henry Adams: An Introduction and Interpretation.* New York: Barnes & Noble, 1962.

Hocks, Richard. *Henry James and Pragmatistic Thought: A Study in the Relationship between the Philosophy of William James and the Literary Art of Henry James.* Chapel Hill: University of North Carolina Press, 1974.

Holloway, Karla F. C. *The Character of the Word: The Texts of Zora Neale Hurston.* Westport, Conn.: Greenwood Press, 1987.

Holly, Carol. "A Drama of Intention in Henry James's *Autobiography.*" *Modern Language Studies* 13 (1983): 22–31.

———. "Henry James's Autobiographical Fragment: 'The Turning Point of My Life.'" *Harvard Library Bulletin* 31 (1983): 40–51.

Howard, Lillie P. *Zora Neale Hurston.* Boston: Twayne, 1980.

Hunter, J. Paul. *The Reluctant Pilgrim: Defoe's Emblematic Method and Quest for Form in "Robinson Crusoe."* Baltimore: Johns Hopkins University Press, 1966.

Hurston, Zora Neale. "Conversions and Visions." In *Negro: An Anthology,* ed. Nancy Cunard, 47–49. New York: Frederick Ungar, 1934.

———. *Dust Tracks on a Road.* Ed. Robert Hemenway. Urbana: University of Illinois Press, 1984.

———. "Stories of Conflict." Review of *Uncle Tom's Children,* by Richard Wright. *Saturday Review,* April 1938, 32.

Ikeler, A. Abbott. *Puritan Temper and Transcendental Faith: Carlyle's Literary Vision.* Cleveland: Ohio State University Press, 1972.

James, Henry. *Henry James: Autobiography.* Ed. Frederick W. Dupee. New York: Criterion Books, 1956.

———. *Henry James Letters: 1895–1916.* Ed. Leon Edel. Vol. 4. Cambridge, Mass.: Harvard University Press, 1984.

———. *The Letters of Henry James.* 2 vols. Ed. Percy Lubbock. New York: Scribners, 1920.

James, Henry, Sr. *Henry James, Senior: A Collection of His Writings.* Ed. Giles Gunn. Chicago: American Library, 1974.

James, William. *The Letters of William James.* 2 vols. Ed. Henry James. Boston: Atlantic Monthly, 1920. Reprint. New York: Kraus, 1969.

———. *Pragmatism: A New Name for Some Old Ways of Thinking & the Meaning of Truth: A Sequel to Pragmatism.* Ed. Frederick Burkhardt et al. Cambridge, Mass.: Harvard University Press, 1978.

———. *The Principles of Psychology.* 2 vols. London: Macmillan, 1907.

———. *The Varieties of Religious Experience.* Ed. Frederick Burkhardt et al. Cambridge, Mass.: Harvard University Press, 1985.

Jay, Paul. *Being in the Text: Self-representation from Wordsworth to Roland Barthes.* Ithaca, N.Y.: Cornell University Press, 1984.

Jelinek, Estelle C. "Introduction: Women's Autobiography and the Male Tradition." In *Women's Autobiography: Essays in Criticism,* ed. Estelle Jelinek, 1–20. Bloomington: Indiana University Press, 1980.

Johnson, Barbara. "Metaphor, Metonymy, and Voice in *Their Eyes Were Watching God.*" In *Zora Neale Hurston: Modern Critical Views*, ed. Harold Bloom, 157–74. New York: Chelsea House, 1987.

Juhasz, Suzanne. "Towards a Theory of Form in Feminist Autobiography: Kate Millett's *Flying* and *Sita*; Maxine Hong Kingston's *The Woman Warrior.*" In *Women's Autobiography: Essays in Criticism*, ed. Estelle Jelinek, 221–37. Bloomington: Indiana University Press, 1980.

Keckley, Elizabeth. *Behind the Scenes: Or Thirty Years a Slave and Four Years in the White House.* New York: Oxford University Press, 1988.

Kent, George. *Blackness and the Adventure of Western Culture.* Chicago: Third World Press, 1972.

King, John Owen. *The Iron of Melancholy: Structures of Spiritual Conversion in America from the Puritan Conscience to Victorian Neurosis.* Middletown, Conn.: Wesleyan University Press, 1983.

Kirby, David. "Henry James: Art and Autobiography." *Dalhousie Review* 52 (1972): 637–44.

Koretz, Gene H. "Augustine's *Confessions* and *The Education of Henry Adams.*" *Comparative Literature* 12 (1960): 193–206.

Kuklick, Bruce. *The Rise of American Philosophy: Cambridge Massachusetts 1860–1930.* New Haven, Conn.: Yale University Press, 1977.

Lane, Lunsford. *The Narrative of Lunsford Lane.* Boston: J. E. Torrey, 1842.

Levenson, J. C. *The Mind and Art of Henry Adams.* Cambridge, Mass.: Houghton Mifflin, 1957.

Levinson, Henry Samuel. *The Religious Investigations of William James.* Chapel Hill: University of North Carolina Press, 1981.

Lewis, R.W.B. *The American Adam: Innocence, Tragedy, and Tradition in the Nineteenth Century.* Chicago: University of Chicago Press, 1955.

———. *Edith Wharton: A Biography.* New York: Harper & Row, 1977.

———. "The Histrionic Vision of Henry James." *Jahrbuch für Amerikastudien* 4 (1959): 39–51.

Lubbock, Percy. *Portrait of Edith Wharton.* New York: D. Appleton-Century, 1947.

Lyon, Melvin. *Symbol and Idea in Henry Adams.* Lincoln: University of Nebraska Press, 1970.

MacKethan, Lucinda H. "From Fugitive Slave to Man of Letters: The Conversion of Frederick Douglass." *The Journal of Narrative Technique* 16 (1986): 55–71.

Mackey, James, P. *Jesus the Man and the Myth: A Contemporary Christology.* New York: Paulist Press, 1979.

Marcus, Jane. "Invincible Mediocrity: The Private Selves of Public Women." In *The Private Self: Theory and Practice of Women's Autobiographical Writings*, ed. Shari Benstock, 114–45. Chapel Hill: University of North Carolina Press, 1988.

Martin, Jay. *Harvests of Change: American Literature, 1865–1914.* Englewood Cliffs, N.J.: Prentice Hall, 1967.

Martineau, Harriet. *Harriet Martineau's Autobiography.* 2 vols. Ed. Maria Weston Chapman. Boston: James R. Osgood, 1877.

Marty, Martin. *Righteous Empire: The Protestant Experience in America.* New York: Dial, 1970.

Martz, Louis Lohr. *The Poetry of Meditation: A Study in English Religious Literature of the Seventeenth Century*. New Haven, Conn.: Yale University Press, 1954.

Mason, Mary G. "The Other Voice: Autobiographies of Women Writers." In *Life/Lines: Theorizing Women's Autobiography*, ed. Bella Brodzki and Celeste Schenck, 19–44. Ithaca, N.Y.: Cornell University Press, 1988.

Matthiessen, F. O. *Henry James: The Major Phase*. New York: Oxford University Press, 1963.

———. *The James Family*. New York: Alfred A. Knopf, 1947.

McCall, Dan. *The Example of Richard Wright*. New York: Harcourt, Brace & World, 1969.

McGiffert, Michael. Introduction to *God's Plot: The Paradoxes of Puritan Piety, Being the Autobiography and Journal of Thomas Shepard*. Amherst: University of Massachusetts Press, 1972.

McGuire, Anne. "Conversion and Gnosis in the *Gospel of Truth*." *Novum Testamentum* 28 (1986): 338–55.

McKay, Nellie Y. "Nineteenth-Century Black Women's Spiritual Autobiographies: Religious Faith and Self-Empowerment." In *Interpreting Women's Lives: Feminist Theory and Personal Narratives*, ed. Joy Webster Barbre et al., 139–54. Bloomington: Indiana University Press, 1989.

McLoughlin, William G. *Revivals, Awakenings, and Reform: An Essay on Religion and Social Change in America, 1607–1977*. Chicago: University of Chicago Press, 1978.

Melville, Herman. *Typee: A Peep at Polynesian Life*. Ed. Harrison Hayford, Hershel Parker, G. Thomas Tanselle. Evanston: Northwestern University Press, 1968.

Mill, John Stuart. *Autobiography of John Stuart Mill*. New York: Columbia University Press, 1924.

Miller, Perry. *The New England Mind: The Seventeenth Century*. Cambridge, Mass.: Harvard University Press, 1939.

Miller, Ross. "Autobiography as Fact and Fiction: Franklin, Adams, Malcolm X." *Centennial Review* 16 (1972): 221–32.

Minter, David L. *The Interpreted Design as a Structural Principle in American Prose*. New Haven, Conn.: Yale University Press, 1969.

Misch, Georg. *A History of Autobiography in Antiquity*. Trans. E. W. Dickes. London: Routledge and Kegan Paul, 1950.

Montrose, Louis A. "Professing the Renaissance: The Poetics and Politics of Culture." In *The New Historicism*, ed. H. Aram Veeser, 15–36. New York: Routledge, 1989.

Moore, Carlisle. "*Sartor Resartus* and the Problem of Carlyle's 'Conversion.' " *PMLA* 70 (1955): 662–81.

Morgan, Edmund. *Visible Saints: The History of a Puritan Idea*. New York: New York University Press, 1963.

Morris, John N. *Versions of the Self: Studies in English Autobiography from John Bunyan to John Stuart Mill*. New York: Basic Books, 1966.

Myers, Gerald E. *William James: His Life and Thought*. New Haven, Conn.: Yale University Press, 1986.

Myers, Mitzi. "Harriet Martineau's *Autobiography*: The Making of a Female Philosopher." In *Women's Autobiography: Essays in Criticism*, ed. Estelle Jelinek, 53–70. Bloomington: Indiana University Press, 1980.

Nevius, Blake. *Edith Wharton: A Study of Her Fiction*. Berkeley and Los Angeles: University of California Press, 1953.

New English Bible with the Apocrypha. London: Oxford University Press, Cambridge University Press, 1970.

Nichols, Charles H. *Many Thousand Gone: The Ex-Slaves' Account of Their Bondage and Freedom*. Leiden, Neth.: E. J. Brill, 1963.

Nock, A. D. *Conversion: The Old and the New in Religion from Alexander the Great to Augustine of Hippo*. Oxford: Clarendon Press, 1933.

Nussbaum, Felicity A. "Eighteenth-Century Women's Autobiographical Commonplaces." In *The Private Self: Theory and Practice of Women's Autobiographical Writings*, ed. Shari Benstock, 147–71. Chapel Hill: University of North Carolina Press, 1988.

Olney, James. " 'I was born': Slave Narratives, Their Status as Autobiography and as Literature." In *The Slave's Narrative: Texts and Contexts*, 148–75. New York: Oxford University Press, 1985.

Paine, Thomas. *The Age of Reason*. New York: Putnam, 1896.

Pascal, Roy. *Design and Truth in Autobiography*. Cambridge, Mass.: Harvard University Press, 1960.

Pease, Jane H., and William H. Pease. *They Who Would Be Free: Blacks' Search for Freedom, 1830–1861*. New York: Atheneum, 1974.

Pennington, James W. C. *The Fugitive Blacksmith; or Events in the History of James W. C. Pennington, Pastor of a Presbyterian Church, New York, Formerly a Slave in the State of Maryland*. In *Great Slave Narratives*, ed. Arna Bontemps, 193–267. Boston: Beacon Press, 1969.

Perkins, William. *The Works of William Perkins*. 3 vols. London: I. Legatt, 1608–31.

Perry, Ralph Barton. *The Thought and Character of William James*. Briefer Edition. Cambridge, Mass.: Harvard University Press, 1948.

Peterson, Linda H. *Victorian Autobiography: The Tradition of Self-Interpretation*. New Haven, Conn.: Yale University Press, 1986.

Phillips, Kathy J. "Conversion to Text, Initiation to Symbolism in Mann's *Der Tod in Venedig* and James' *The Ambassadors*." *Canadian Review of Comparative Literature* 4 (1979): 376–88.

Quarles, Benjamin. *Black Abolitionists*. New York: Oxford University Press, 1969.

Raper, Julius Rowan. *Without Shelter: The Early Career of Ellen Glasgow*. Baton Rouge: Louisiana State University Press, 1971.

Rayson, Ann L. "*Dust Tracks on a Road*: Zora Neale Hurston and the Form of Black Autobiography." *Negro American Literature Forum* 7 (1973): 39–45.

Reed, Walter L. "The Pattern of Conversion in *Sartor Resartus*." *ELH* 38 (1971): 411–31.

Reilly, John M. "The Self-Creation of the Intellectual: *American Hunger* and *Black Power*." In *Critical Essays on Richard Wright*, ed. Yoshinobu Hakutani, 213–27. Boston: G. K. Hall, 1972.

Reilly, Robert. "Henry James and the Morality of Fiction." *American Literature* 39 (1967): 1–30.

Rosenzweig, Saul. "The Ghost of Henry James: Revised with a Postscript." In *Modern Criticism: Theory and Practice*, ed. Walter Sutton and Richard Foster, 401–16. Indianapolis, Ind.: Odyssey Press, 1963.

Rousseau, Jean-Jacques. *Confessions of Jean-Jacques Rousseau.* Trans. J. M. Cohen. New York: Penguin Books, 1953.

Ryan, Mary P. *Cradle of the Middle Class: The Family in Oneida County, New York, 1790–1865.* Cambridge, Eng.: Cambridge University Press, 1981.

Samuels, Ernest. *Henry Adams: The Major Phase.* Cambridge, Mass.: Harvard University Press, 1964.

———. *Henry Adams: The Middle Years.* Cambridge, Mass.: Harvard University Press, 1965.

———. *The Young Henry Adams.* Cambridge, Mass.: Harvard University Press, 1948.

Sargant, William. *Battle for the Mind: A Physiology of Conversion and Brain Washing.* New York: Doubleday, 1957.

Sayre, Robert F. *The Examined Self: Benjamin Franklin, Henry Adams, Henry James.* Princeton, N.J.: Princeton University Press, 1964.

Schneider, Daniel J. *The Crystal Cage: Adventures of the Imagination in the Fiction of Henry James.* Lawrence: Regents Press of Kansas, 1978.

Sharrock, Roger. *John Bunyan.* London: Hutchinson's University Press, 1954.

Shea, Daniel B., Jr. *Spiritual Autobiography in Early America.* Princeton, N.J.: Princeton University Press, 1968.

Shine, Hill. *Carlyle's Early Reading to 1834.* Lexington: University of Kentucky Libraries, 1953.

Showalter, Elaine. "Introduction: The Feminist Critical Revolution." In *The New Feminist Criticism: Essays on Women, Literature, and Theory*, ed. Elaine Showalter, 3–18. New York: Random House, 1985.

Shumaker, Wayne. *English Autobiography: Its Emergence, Materials, and Form.* Berkeley and Los Angeles: University of California Press, 1954.

Sizer, Sandra. *Gospel Hymns and Social Religion: The Rhetoric of Nineteenth-Century Revivalism.* Philadelphia: Temple University Press, 1979.

Smith, David E. "Publication of John Bunyan's Works in America." *Bulletin of the New York Public Library* 66 (1962): 630–52.

Smith, Sidonie. *A Poetics of Women's Autobiography: Marginality and the Fictions of Self-representation.* Bloomington: Indiana University Press, 1987.

———. *Where I'm Bound: Patterns of Slavery and Freedom in Black American Autobiography.* Westport, Conn.: Greenwood Press, 1974.

Spacks, Patricia Meyer. "Female Rhetorics." In *The Private Self: Theory and Practice of Women's Autobiographical Writings*, ed. Shari Benstock, 177–91. Chapel Hill: University of North Carolina Press, 1988.

———. *Imagining a Self: Autobiography and Novel in Eighteenth-Century England.* Cambridge, Mass.: Harvard University Press, 1976.

Spengemann, William C. *The Forms of Autobiography: Episodes in the History of a Literary Genre.* New Haven, Conn.: Yale University Press, 1980.

Stanton, Domna C. "Autogynography: Is the Subject Different?" In *The Female Autograph: Theory and Practice of Autobiography from the Tenth to the Twentieth Century*, ed. Domna C. Stanton, 3–20. Chicago: University of Chicago Press, 1987.

Stanton, Elizabeth Cady. *Eighty Years and More: Reminiscences, 1815–1897*. New York: Schocken, 1971.

Stanton, Elizabeth Cady, Susan B. Anthony, Matilda Joslyn Gage, and Ida Husted Harper. *The History of Woman Suffrage*. 6 vols. New York: Fowler & Wells, 1881–86. Reprint. New York: Source Books, 1970.

Starbuck, E. D. *The Psychology of Religion: An Empirical Study of the Growth of Religious Consciousness*. New York: Charles Scribner's Sons, 1903.

Starobinski, Jean. "The Style of Autobiography." In *Autobiography: Essays Theoretical and Critical*, ed. James Olney, 73–83. Princeton, N.J.: Princeton University Press, 1980.

Starr, G. A. *Defoe and Spiritual Autobiography*. Princeton, N.J.: Princeton University Press, 1965.

Steele, Jeffrey. *The Representation of the Self in the American Renaissance*. Chapel Hill: University of North Carolina Press, 1987.

Stepto, Robert B. *From Behind the Veil: A Study of Afro-American Narrative*. Urbana: University of Illinois Press, 1979.

———. "I Thought I Knew These People: Richard Wright and the Afro-American Literary Tradition." In *Chant of Saints: A Gathering of Afro-American Literature, Art, and Scholarship*, ed. Michael S. Harper and Robert B. Stepto, 195–211. Urbana: University of Illinois Press, 1979.

Strout, Cushing. "Henry James's Dream of the Louvre and Psychological Interpretation." *Psychohistory Review* 8 (1979): 47–52.

———. "The Pluralistic Identity of William James: A Psycho-historical Reading of *The Varieties of Religious Experience*." *American Quarterly* 23 (1971): 135–52.

———. "William James and the Twice-Born Sick Soul." *Daedalus* 97 (1968): 1062–82.

Tanner, Tony. "Henry Adams and Henry James." *Tri-Quarterly* 11 (1968): 91–108.

Tennyson, G. B. *Sartor Called Resartus: The Genesis, Structure, and Style of Thomas Carlyle's First Major Work*. Princeton, N.J.: Princeton University Press, 1966.

Thaddeus, Janice. "The Metamorphosis of Richard Wright's *Black Boy*." *American Literature* 57 (1985): 199–214.

Thompson, John. *The Life of John Thompson, a Fugitive Slave*. 1856. Reprint. Westport, Conn.: Negro Universities Press, 1968.

Thoreau, Henry David. *Walden*. Ed. J. Lyndon Shanley. Princeton, N.J.: Princeton University Press, 1971.

Tintner, Adeline R. "Autobiography as Fiction: The Usurping Consciousness as Hero of James's Memoirs." *Twentieth Century Literature* 23 (1977): 239–60.

Tompkins, Jane P. "The Redemption of Time in *Notes of a Son and Brother*." *Texas Studies in Language and Literature* 14 (1973): 681–90.

Tutwiler, Carrington C., Jr. *A Catalogue of the Library of Ellen Glasgow*. Charlottesville: Bibliographical Society of the University of Virginia, 1969.

Vance, Eugene. "Augustine's *Confessions* and the Grammar of Selfhood." *Genre* 6 (1973): 1–28.

Wagner, Vern. *The Suspension of Henry Adams: A Study of Manner and Matter*. Detroit: Wayne State University Press, 1969.

Walker, Alice. "A Cautionary Tale and a Partisan Review." In *Zora Neale Hurston: Modern Critical Views*, ed. Harold Bloom, 63–70. New York: Chelsea House, 1987.

Walsh, William. "A Sense of Identity in a World of Circumstance: The Autobiography of Henry James." In *A Human Idiom: Literature and Humanity*, 52–73. London: Chatto & Windus, 1964.

Walzer, Michael. *The Revolution of the Saints: A Study of the Evolution of Radical Politics*. Cambridge, Mass.: Harvard University Press, 1965.

Washington, Booker T. *Up from Slavery*. 1900. Reprint. Williamstown, Mass.: Corner House, 1971.

Washington, Mary Helen. "A Woman Half in Shadow." In *Zora Neale Hurston: Modern Critical Views*, ed. Harold Bloom, 123–38. New York: Chelsea House, 1987.

Webb, Constance. *Richard Wright: A Biography*. New York: G. P. Putnam's Sons, 1968.

Weber, Max. *The Protestant Ethic and the Spirit of Capitalism*. Trans. Talcott Parsons. New York: Scribners, 1958.

Weintraub, Carl Joachim. *The Value of the Individual: Self and Circumstance in Autobiography*. Chicago: University of Chicago Press, 1978.

Wharton, Edith. *A Backward Glance*. New York: Scribner's, 1934.

White, Hayden. *Tropics of Discourse: Essays in Cultural Criticism*. Baltimore: Johns Hopkins University Press, 1985.

Wigglesworth, Michael. *The Diary of Michael Wigglesworth 1653–1657*. Ed. Edmund S. Morgan. Gloucester, Mass.: Peter Smith, 1965.

Williams, Huntington. *Rousseau and Romantic Autobiography*. London: Oxford University Press, 1983.

Winters, Yvor. "Henry Adams or the Creation of Confusion." In *Defense of Reason*, 374–430. Denver, Colo.: Alan Swallow, 1947.

Wolff, Cynthia Griffin. *A Feast of Words: The Triumph of Edith Wharton*. New York: Oxford University Press, 1977.

Wordsworth, William. *The Fourteen-Book Prelude*. Ed. W.J.B. Owen. Ithaca, N.Y.: Cornell University Press, 1985.

Wright, Richard. *American Hunger*. New York: Harper & Row, 1977.

———. "Between Laughter and Tears." Review of *Their Eyes Were Watching God* by Zora Neale Hurston and *These Low Grounds* by Waters E. Turpin. *New Masses* 25 (5 October 1937): 22–25.

———. *Black Boy: A Record of Childhood and Youth*. New York: Harper & Brothers, 1945.

———. "How Bigger Was Born." In *Native Son*, vii–xxxiv. New York: Harper & Row, 1940.

———. Introduction to *Black Metropolis*, by Horace R. Cayton and St. Clair Drake. New York: Harcourt, Brace, 1945.

———. *Letters to Joe C. Brown*. Ed. Thomas Knipp. Kent, Ohio: Kent State University Libraries, 1968.

———. *Pagan Spain*. New York: Harper, 1956.

———. *White Man, Listen!* New York: Doubleday, 1957.

Ziff, Larzer. *Puritanism in America: New Culture in a New World*. New York: Viking, 1973.

INDEX